···FOR DUMMIES

COMPUTER
BOOK SERIES
FROM IDG

Desktop Publishing & D...
For Dummies...

D0515380

The desktop publishing and design process

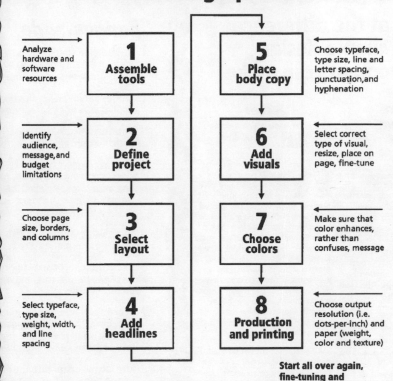

Analyze hardware and software resources

1 Assemble tools

Identify audience, message, and budget limitations

2 Define project

Choose page size, borders, and columns

3 Select layout

Select typeface, type size, weight, width, and line spacing

4 Add headlines

5 Place body copy

Choose typeface, type size, line and letter spacing, punctuation, and hyphenation

6 Add visuals

Select correct type of visual, resize, place on page, fine-tune

7 Choose colors

Make sure that color enhances, rather than confuses, message

8 Production and printing

Choose output resolution (i.e. dots-per-inch) and paper (weight, color and texture)

Start all over again, fine-tuning and reviewing each step

Eight rules you should never forget!

This is your mother speaking. Keep your room clean, never leave the house with dirty underwear, and follow these eight rules:

1. Never reduce type size in order to squeeze something in.
2. Never reduce line spacing in order to fit something in.
3. Eliminate the habit of adding two spaces after periods.
4. Avoid underlining.
5. Never set headlines entirely in uppercase type.
6. Don't press Enter/Return twice at the end of each paragraph.
7. Don't forget to hyphenate.
8. Avoid typewriter punctuation.

Desktop Publishing & Design For Dummies®

Cheat Sheet

Look at the difference 10 simple design improvements can make!

Before

This column needs help!

Effective desktop publishing publication design and production is based on your willingness to pay lots of disciplined attention to detail. It's the little things that count. Even outstandingly beautiful publication layouts can be sabotaged by failure to pay attention to detail. No matter how masterful the publication designer's intent, if the type is too large or too small, or the lines of type are too closely spaced, or hyphenation is inadvertantly omitted, the page will be difficult to read and readers will pass it by.

Likewise, text will not be read if paragraph spacing is off or--worse yet--the wrong punctuation characters are used! Master the details in order to master the page!

After

Notice the dramatic improvement that takes place when you pay attention to details!

EFFECTIVE DESKTOP PUBLISHING publication design and production is based on your willingness to pay lots of disciplined attention to detail. It's the little things that count. Even outstandingly beautiful publication layouts can be sabotaged by failure to pay attention to detail. No matter how masterful the publication designer's intent, if the type is too large or too small, or the lines of type are too closely spaced, or hyphenation is inadvertently omitted, the page will be difficult to read and readers will pass it by.

Likewise, text will not be read if paragraph spacing is off or—worse yet—the wrong punctuation characters are used! Master the details in order to master the page!

Changes made...

1. Default line spacing was replaced by a measurement more suitable for the typeface, type size, and column width.

2. The larger initial cap now looks deliberate instead of accidental.

3. The bottom of the initial cap now aligns with the third line of the paragraph.

4. The text was wrapped as closely as possible to the initial cap, and the first line of text is set in small caps to form a transition between the initial cap and the text that follows.

5. By splitting words over two lines, word spacing was made more consistent.

6. Letter spacing appears more natural because normal tracking was turned on.

7. Word spacing was fine-tuned by reducing the amount of possible variation between closely spaced words and widely spaced words.

8. The large horizontal band of white space between the two paragraphs, created by pressing the Enter/Return key twice after each paragraph, was replaced by the minimal amount of space necessary to indicate a new paragraph.

9. The first-line indent was eliminated.

10. The two hyphens introducing the parenthetical expression were replaced by the typographically correct em dash.

...For Dummies: #1 Computer Book Series for Beginners

About Desktop Publishing & Design For Dummies...

"Desktop Publishing & Design For Dummies provides a new and easy-to-understand perspective on creating better-looking print communications with any desktop publishing or word processing program."

> David Field
> Director, Desktop Publishing Group
> Boston Computer Society

"Roger not only shows you the how and what of desktop publishing and design, but also the why and when."

> Dan Gookin
> Author
> *DOS For Dummies*

"You'll be amazed at how this book will lead you by the hand from the ABCs of what you need to know about design to the XYZs of working with printers and getting the whole job done. It will take you step-by-step through every phase of desktop publishing and turn you into a real pro — despite how little you may know to start with."

> Frank Grazian
> Executive Editor
> *Communication Briefings*

"Desktop Publishing & Design For Dummies provides the reader with all the basics for successful design in a simple, step-by-step manner. This book teaches you more than how to design — it tells you why the design will work!"

> Jill Robbins Israel
> Editor-In-Chief
> *Technique Magazine*

"Contains what you need to make effective design decisions, including the authority to back them up."

> Ronnie Lipton
> Editor
> *InHouse Graphics*

"Parker's new book will help jumpstart the skills of any newcomer to desktop design."

> Jake Widman
> Editor
> *Publish Magazine*

DESKTOP PUBLISHING & DESIGN FOR DUMMIES®

DESKTOP PUBLISHING & DESIGN FOR DUMMIES®

by Roger C. Parker

IDG Books Worldwide, Inc.
An International Data Group Company

Foster City, CA ♦ Chicago, IL ♦ Indianapolis, IN ♦ New York, NY

Desktop Publishing & Design For Dummies®

Published by
IDG Books Worldwide, Inc.
An International Data Group Company
919 E. Hillsdale Blvd.
Suite 400
Foster City, CA 94404
www.idgbooks.com (IDG Books Worldwide Web site)
www.dummies.com (Dummies Press Web site)

Library of Congress Catalog Card No.: 94-72817

ISBN: 1-56884-234-1

Printed in the United States of America

10 9 8 7 6

1E/SX/QY/ZY/IN

Distributed in the United States by IDG Books Worldwide, Inc.

Distributed by Macmillan Canada for Canada; by Transworld Publishers Limited in the United Kingdom; by IDG Norge Books for Norway; by IDG Sweden Books for Sweden; by Woodslane Pty. Ltd. for Australia; by Woodslane Enterprises Ltd. for New Zealand; by Longman Singapore Publishers Ltd. for Singapore, Malaysia, Thailand, and Indonesia; by Simron Pty. Ltd. for South Africa; by Toppan Company Ltd. for Japan; by Distribuidora Cuspide for Argentina; by Livraria Cultura for Brazil; by Ediciencia S.A. for Ecuador; by Addison-Wesley Publishing Company for Korea; by Ediciones ZETA S.C.R. Ltda. for Peru; by WS Computer Publishing Corporation, Inc., for the Philippines; by Unalis Corporation for Taiwan; by Contemporanea de Ediciones for Venezuela; by Computer Book & Magazine Store for Puerto Rico; by Express Computer Distributors for the Caribbean and West Indies. Authorized Sales Agent: Anthony Rudkin Associates for the Middle East and North Africa.

For general information on IDG Books Worldwide's books in the U.S., please call our Consumer Customer Service department at 800-762-2974. For reseller information, including discounts and premium sales, please call our Reseller Customer Service department at 800-434-3422.

For information on where to purchase IDG Books Worldwide's books outside the U.S., please contact our International Sales department at 650-655-3200 or fax 650-655-3297.

For information on foreign language translations, please contact our Foreign & Subsidiary Rights department at 650-655-3021 or fax 650-655-3281.

For sales inquiries and special prices for bulk quantities, please contact our Sales department at 650-655-3200 or write to the address above.

For information on using IDG Books Worldwide's books in the classroom or for ordering examination copies, please contact our Educational Sales department at 800-434-2086 or fax 317-596-5499.

For press review copies, author interviews, or other publicity information, please contact our Public Relations department at 650-655-3000 or fax 650-655-3299.

For authorization to photocopy items for corporate, personal, or educational use, please contact Copyright Clearance Center, 222 Rosewood Drive, Danvers, MA 01923, or fax 978-750-4470.

 is a trademark under exclusive license to IDG Books Worldwide, Inc., from International Data Group, Inc.

About the Author

According to the *National Association of Desktop Publishers Journal,* **Roger C. Parker** is the "leading guru" of desktop publishing design. In addition to frequently contributing to a variety of publications, including *Graphic Solutions, Publish, Technique,* and *x-height,* Roger has written numerous books on desktop publishing design and conducted design seminars and workshops throughout the United States and Australia.

More than 750,000 desktop publishers around the world own books by Roger C. Parker. During the past few years, Roger has been the Keynote Speaker and lead presenter at PageMaker conferences conducted throughout the United States.

Roger became interested in design issues almost twenty years ago, while writing a monthly advertising and marketing column for a leading electronics publication. His columns in leading consumer electronics and computer retail trade publications frequently included before and after analysis of newspaper ads and newsletters.

The year PageMaker 1.0 appeared, Roger immediately approached the Aldus Corporation with an idea for a short, simple book on desktop publishing design. *The Aldus Guide to Basic Design* resulted and led to *Looking Good in Print: A Guide to Basic Design for Desktop Publishing* (Ventana).

Roger's other books for IDG Books Worldwide include *Harvard Graphics 2.0 For Windows For Dummies, Microsoft Office 4.0 For Windows For Dummies, WordPerfect 6.0 (DOS) SECRETS, WordPerfect 6.0 for Windows Power Techniques, Freelance Graphics 2.1 For Dummies, Freelance Graphics 96 For Windows 95 For Dummies,* and *Microsoft Office For Windows 95 For Dummies.*

ABOUT IDG BOOKS WORLDWIDE

Welcome to the world of IDG Books Worldwide.

IDG Books Worldwide, Inc., is a subsidiary of International Data Group, the world's largest publisher of computer-related information and the leading global provider of information services on information technology. IDG was founded more than 25 years ago and now employs more than 8,500 people worldwide. IDG publishes more than 275 computer publications in over 75 countries (see listing below). More than 90 million people read one or more IDG publications each month.

Launched in 1990, IDG Books Worldwide is today the #1 publisher of best-selling computer books in the United States. We are proud to have received eight awards from the Computer Press Association in recognition of editorial excellence and three from *Computer Currents'* First Annual Readers' Choice Awards. Our best-selling *...For Dummies*® series has more than 50 million copies in print with translations in 38 languages. IDG Books Worldwide, through a joint venture with IDG's Hi-Tech Beijing, became the first U.S. publisher to publish a computer book in the People's Republic of China. In record time, IDG Books Worldwide has become the first choice for millions of readers around the world who want to learn how to better manage their businesses.

Our mission is simple: Every one of our books is designed to bring extra value and skill-building instructions to the reader. Our books are written by experts who understand and care about our readers. The knowledge base of our editorial staff comes from years of experience in publishing, education, and journalism — experience we use to produce books for the '90s. In short, we care about books, so we attract the best people. We devote special attention to details such as audience, interior design, use of icons, and illustrations. And because we use an efficient process of authoring, editing, and desktop publishing our books electronically, we can spend more time ensuring superior content and spend less time on the technicalities of making books.

You can count on our commitment to deliver high-quality books at competitive prices on topics you want to read about. At IDG Books Worldwide, we continue in the IDG tradition of delivering quality for more than 25 years. You'll find no better book on a subject than one from IDG Books Worldwide.

John Kilcullen
CEO
IDG Books Worldwide, Inc.

Steven Berkowitz
President and Publisher
IDG Books Worldwide, Inc.

Eighth Annual Computer Press Awards ≥1992

Ninth Annual Computer Press Awards ≥1993

Tenth Annual Computer Press Awards ≥1994

Eleventh Annual Computer Press Awards ≥1995

IDG Books Worldwide, Inc., is a subsidiary of International Data Group, the world's largest publisher of computer-related information and the leading global provider of information services on information technology. International Data Group publishes over 275 computer publications in over 75 countries. More than 90 million people read one or more International Data Group publications each month. International Data Group's publications include: **ARGENTINA:** Buyer's Guide, Computerworld Argentina, PC World Argentina; **AUSTRALIA:** Australian Macworld, Australian PC World, Australian Reseller News, Computerworld, IT Casebook, Network World, Publish, Webmaster; **AUSTRIA:** Computerwelt Osterreich, Networks Austria, PC Tip Austria; **BANGLADESH:** PC World Bangladesh; **BELARUS:** PC World Belarus; **BELGIUM:** Data News; **BRAZIL:** Annuário de Informática, Computerworld, Connections, Macworld, PC Player, PC World, Publish, Reseller News, Supergamepower; **BULGARIA:** Computerworld Bulgaria, Network World Bulgaria, PC & MacWorld Bulgaria; **CANADA:** CIO Canada, Client/Server World, ComputerWorld Canada, InfoWorld Canada, NetworkWorld Canada, WebWorld; **CHILE:** Computerworld Chile, PC World Chile; **COLOMBIA:** Computerworld Colombia, PC World Colombia; **COSTA RICA:** PC World Centro America; **THE CZECH AND SLOVAK REPUBLICS:** Computerworld Czechoslovakia, Macworld Czech Republic, PC World Czechoslovakia; **DENMARK:** Communications World Danmark, Computerworld Danmark, Macworld Danmark, PC World Danmark, Techworld Denmark; **DOMINICAN REPUBLIC:** PC World Republica Dominicana; **ECUADOR:** PC World Ecuador; **EGYPT:** Computerworld Middle East, PC World Middle East; **EL SALVADOR:** PC World Centro America; **FINLAND:** MikroPC, Tietoverkko, Tietoviikko; **FRANCE:** Distributique, Hebdo, Info PC, Le Monde Informatique, Macworld, Reseaux & Telecoms, WebMaster France; **GERMANY:** Computer Partner, Computerwoche, Computerwoche Extra, Computerwoche FOCUS, Global Online, Macwelt, PC Welt; **GREECE:** Amiga Computing, GamePro Greece, Multimedia World; **GUATEMALA:** PC World Centro America; **HONDURAS:** PC World Centro America; **HONG KONG:** Computerworld Hong Kong, PC World Hong Kong, Publish in Asia; **HUNGARY:** ABCD CD-ROM, Computerworld Szamitastechnika, Internetto online Magazine, PC World Hungary, PC-X Magazin Hungary; **ICELAND:** Tolvuheimur PC World Island; **INDIA:** Information Communications World, Information Systems Computerworld, PC World India, Publish in Asia; **INDONESIA:** InfoKomputer PC World, Komputek Computerworld, Publish in Asia; **IRELAND:** ComputerScope, PC Live!; **ISRAEL:** Macworld Israel, People & Computers/Computerworld; **ITALY:** Computerworld Italia, Macworld Italia, Networking Italia, PC World Italia; **JAPAN:** DTP World, Macworld Japan, Nikkei Personal Computing, OS/2 World Japan, SunWorld Japan, Windows NT World, Windows World Japan; **KENYA:** PC World East African; **KOREA:** Hi-Tech Information, Macworld Korea, PC World Korea; **MACEDONIA:** PC World Macedonia; **MALAYSIA:** Computerworld Malaysia, PC World Malaysia, Publish in Asia; **MALTA:** PC World Malta; **MEXICO:** Computerworld Mexico, PC World Mexico; **MYANMAR:** PC World Myanmar; **NETHERLANDS:** Computer! Totaal, LAN Internetworking Magazine, LAN World Buyers Guide, Macworld Netherlands, Net, WebWereld; **NEW ZEALAND:** Absolute Beginners Guide and Plain & Simple Series, Computer Buyer, Computer Industry Directory, Computerworld New Zealand, MTB, Network World, PC World New Zealand; **NICARAGUA:** PC World Centro America; **NORWAY:** Computerworld Norge, CW Rapport, Datamagasinet, Financial Rapport, Kursguide Norge, Macworld Norge, Multimediaworld Norge, PC World Ekspress Norge, PC World Nettverk, PC World Norge, PC World ProduktGuide Norge; **PAKISTAN:** Computerworld Pakistan; **PANAMA:** PC World Panama; **PEOPLE'S REPUBLIC OF CHINA:** China Computer Users, China Computerworld, China InfoWorld, China Telecom World Weekly, Computer & Communication, Electronic Design China, Electronics Today, Electronics Weekly, Game Software, PC World China, Popular Computer Week, Software Weekly, Software World, Telecom World; **PERU:** Computerworld Peru, PC World Profesional Peru, PC World SoHo Peru; **PHILIPPINES:** Click!, Computerworld Philippines, PC World Philippines, Publish in Asia; **POLAND:** Computerworld Poland, Computerworld Special Report Poland, Cyber, Macworld Poland, Networld Poland, PC World Komputer; **PORTUGAL:** Cerebro/PC World, Computerworld/Correio Informático, Dealer World Portugal, Mac*In/PC*In Portugal, Multimedia World; **PUERTO RICO:** PC World Puerto Rico; **ROMANIA:** Computerworld Romania, PC World Romania, Telecom Romania; **RUSSIA:** Computerworld Russia, Mir PK, Publish, Seti; **SINGAPORE:** Computerworld Singapore, PC World Singapore, Publish in Asia; **SLOVENIA:** Monitor; **SOUTH AFRICA:** Computing SA, Network World SA, Software World SA; **SPAIN:** Communicaciones World España, Computerworld España, Dealer World España, Macworld España, PC World España; **SRI LANKA:** Infolink PC World; **SWEDEN:** CAP&Design, Computer Sweden, Corporate Computing Sweden, Internetworld Sweden, it.branschen, Macworld Sweden, MaxiData Sweden, MikroDatorn, Nätverk & Kommunikation, PC World Sweden, PCaktiv, Windows World Sweden; **SWITZERLAND:** Computerworld Schweiz, Macworld Schweiz, PCtip; **TAIWAN:** Computerworld Taiwan, Macworld Taiwan, NEW ViSiON/Publish, PC World Taiwan, Windows World Taiwan; **THAILAND:** Publish in Asia, Thai Computerworld; **TURKEY:** Computerworld Turkiye, Macworld Turkiye, Network World Turkiye, PC World Turkiye; **UKRAINE:** Computerworld Kiev, Multimedia World Ukraine, PC World Ukraine; **UNITED KINGDOM:** Acorn User UK, Amiga Action UK, Amiga Computing UK, Apple Talk UK, Computing, Macworld, Parents and Computers UK, PC Advisor, PC Home, PSX Pro, The WEB; **UNITED STATES:** Cable in the Classroom, CIO Magazine, Computerworld, DOS World, Federal Computer Week, GamePro Magazine, InfoWorld, I-Way, Macworld, Network World, PC Games, PC World, Publish, Video Event, THE WEB Magazine, and WebMaster; online webzines: JavaWorld, NetscapeWorld, and SunWorld Online; **URUGUAY:** InfoWorld Uruguay; **VENEZUELA:** Computerworld Venezuela, PC World Venezuela; and **VIETNAM:** PC World Vietnam. 5/7/98

Dedication

To my wife and children, for their support and understanding.

Author's Acknowledgments

Books are team efforts. During the past few years, many have contributed to the development of my design skills. Among the most important contributors are the participants in my desktop publishing design seminars and workshops who forced me to examine my preconceptions and clarify important issues. Others who have contributed include Howard Penn Hudson and Paul Swift of the Newsletter Clearing House in Rhinebeck, New York, who, by providing me with hundreds of newsletter samples, have allowed me to analyze what works, and what doesn't, in newsletter design. (Their contribution also helped fuel my wood stove, warming my home as well as providing intellectual stimulus during the past cold winter.)

Special thanks are extended to Bill Davis, Vice President of Monotype Typography in Chicago, for his advice, encouragement, and assistance obtaining the typefaces necessary to experiment with the nuances of choosing the right type. Similar thanks are extended to Adrianne Moore at Aldus, Sonya Schaefer at Adobe, Stefin Wennik at Bitstream, and Henry Mitiewicz at URW.

I'd also like to express thanks for the continuing encouragement of others such as Roy Paul Nelson, Professor of Advertising at the University of Oregon, Frank Romano, Hermann Zapf Professor of Typography at the University of Rochester and writers like Jan White (*Editing by Design*), Alex White (*Type in Use*), Richard Bolles (*What Color Is Your Parachute?*), Bob Bly (*Copywriter's Handbook*) and William Zinsser (*On Writing Well*). Thanks also for the continuing support of Ronnie Lipton, editor of *In-House Graphics*. All have taught, inspired, and encouraged.

As far as books are concerned, authors provide only the raw material. It takes a strong editorial team to mold the raw material into a coherent whole. Thanks are extended to Senior Editor Tracy Barr and Project Editor Colleen Rainsberger who helped bring order out of chaos. Thanks are also extended to the early enthusiasm offered by Janna Custer, Acquisitions Editor; Mary Bednarek, Managing Editor; and Diane Steele, Senior Editor. The continuing enthusiasm and support of Bill Gladstone and Lavender Ginsberg are also gratefully acknowledged.

As always, thanks are extended to my family for their patience and forbearance during the writing of this book, and especially Ryan who kept me company during the long nights at the office.

Publisher's Acknowledgments

We're proud of this book; please register your comments through our IDG Books Worldwide Online Registration Form located at: http://my2cents.dummies.com.

Some of the people who helped bring this book to market include the following:

Acquisitions, Development, and Editorial

Senior Project Editor: Colleen Rainsberger

Acquisitions Editor: Tammy Goldfeld

Copy Editors: Kristin A. Cocks, Bill Helling, Suzanne Packer, Jeffrey Waggoner, Jennifer Ehrlich

Technical Reviewer: James Alley

Editorial Managers: Kristin A. Cocks, Mary C. Corder

Production

Layout and Graphics: Cameron Booker, Linda M. Boyer, Elizabeth Cárdenas-Nelson, Chris Collins, Maridee V. Ennis, Angela F. Hunckler, Barry Jorden, Todd Klemme, Drew R. Moore, Mark Owens, Laura Puranen, Carla Radzikinas, Gina Scott, Deirdre Smith

Proofreaders: Alys Caviness-Brosius, Christine Meloy Beck, Joel K. Draper, Rachel Garvey, Dwight Ramsey,

Indexers: Sharon Hilgenberg, Sherry Massey

General and Administrative

IDG Books Worldwide, Inc.: John Kilcullen, CEO; Steven Berkowitz, President and Publisher

IDG Books Technology Publishing: Brenda McLaughlin, Senior Vice President and Group Publisher

Dummies Technology Press and Dummies Editorial: Diane Graves Steele, Vice President and Associate Publisher; Mary Bednarek, Director of Acquisitions and Product Development; Kristin A. Cocks, Editorial Director

Dummies Trade Press: Kathleen A. Welton, Vice President and Publisher; Kevin Thornton, Acquisitions Manager

IDG Books Production for Dummies Press: Michael R. Britton, Vice President of Production and Creative Services; Beth Jenkins Roberts, Production Director; Cindy L. Phipps, Manager of Project Coordination, Production Proofreading, and Indexing; Kathie S. Schutte, Supervisor of Page Layout; Shelley Lea, Supervisor of Graphics and Design; Debbie J. Gates, Production Systems Specialist; Robert Springer, Supervisor of Proofreading; Debbie Stailey, Special Projects Coordinator; Tony Augsburger, Supervisor of Reprints and Bluelines;

Dummies Packaging and Book Design: Robin Seaman, Creative Director; Jocelyn Kelaita, Product Packaging Coordinator; Kavish + Kavish, Cover Design

♦

The publisher would like to give special thanks to Patrick J. McGovern, without whom this book would not have been possible.

♦

Contents at a Glance

Special Supplement:
Newsletters For Dummies

Cartoons at a Glance

By Rich Tennant

page 153

page 238

page 136

page 35

page 209

page 181

page 52

page 196

page 101

page 5

Fax: 978-546-7747 • E-mail: the5wave@tiac.net

Table of Contents

Introduction

You have been involved in the world of design all your life. You're involved with design every time you go to a book or music store and choose one book, magazine, or compact disc over another. You're also involved with design every time you choose to read one magazine or newspaper advertisement instead of another, or decide to immediately read one piece of mail and put the rest aside until "later."

You're involved with design every time you send a letter or a fax. Your choice of typeface and type size reflect design decisions — or a lack of design decisions. Other design decisions you make include your choice of margins, the number of spaces following periods, and the way you indicate new paragraphs and the presence or absence of hyphens. If you use one of your word processor's built-in document templates, your choice of template is a design decision.

An understanding of design offers important career advantages. It gives you the power to add impact to your words. It presells the importance of your words and makes it easy for readers to understand your message. Design helps you get better results from the money you spend to distribute your message.

Who Should Read This Book...

Desktop Publishing & Design For Dummies is for you if you are

- An administrative assistant or executive secretary interested in improving your firm's image by preparing better-looking correspondence

- An entrepreneur or manager interested in higher returns from your newspaper and magazine advertising

- A consultant preparing a capabilities brochure describing your expertise and services offered

- A corporate executive who wants upper-level management to pay more attention to your memos, proposals, and reports

- A marketing communications manager or newsletter editor looking for fresh ideas and a training manual for those who work with you

- A mid-life career changer interested in preparing a more effective résumé

> ✔ A newcomer to design and want to know how much hardware, software, and knowledge you need to produce the documents you're responsible for (or want to be responsible for)
>
> ✔ An established desktop publisher who wants to upgrade your design skills
>
> ✔ A client or supervisor who buys design from freelancers, graphic designers, or advertising agencies

What This Book Is All About

I had three goals in mind when I wrote *Desktop Publishing & Design For Dummies.* The first is to demystify design. The second is to help you determine how much of a designer you need to be in order to achieve your income and satisfaction goals. The third is to help you help you choose the right hardware and software.

Design is usually considered a creative endeavor limited to those with "talents and abilities far beyond those of mortal man" (with apologies to Superman and 1990's gender-sensitive political correctness). But design involves two far more manageable concepts: *marketing* and *details.* Design is marketing to the extent that your goal is to make your message as attractive to your market (your readers) as possible. Design is details to the extent that effective design is achieved by breaking projects into their component parts.

In addition to understanding design concepts, you have to determine how much of a designer you need to be to achieve satisfaction and success. How much do you need to know? Do you really need to know how to electronically retouch a photograph if your only goal is to produce a flyer for a yard sale? What should you do yourself, and what should you delegate to others? To address these issues, I've included several self-evaluation worksheets.

This book also explores hardware and software issues. Desktop publishing is — and always has been — technology-based. You can't separate the process from the tools! Desktop publishing encompasses a mind-numbing plethora of hardware and software, ranging from $59.95 page layout programs to $999.95 page layout programs — not to mention Windows-based word processors, as well as photo-manipulation software programs, graphic accelerators, and large, high-resolution monitors (that is, computer screens) costing several thousands of dollars. How much do you need to buy? Which is best for you? Knowing what's available will help you choose the appropriate equipment or seek out those who have access to it.

How to Read This Book

You can approach *Desktop Publishing & Design For Dummies* in two ways. One is to read it from cover to cover (hopefully, from front cover to back cover — this isn't the *New Yorker*, you know). When you read the chapters, concentrate on the running text and read any sidebars that appeal to you.

Another approach is to go directly to those sections that deal with problem areas in your design. If you're experiencing difficulty working with text or visuals, for example, go directly to the chapters dealing with those areas. Likewise, if you've just been handed responsibility for the company newsletter, turn directly to the *Newsletter For Dummies* bonus insert.

Keep *Desktop Publishing & Design For Dummies* next to your computer as a source of ideas and inspiration. When you find yourself hung up on a design problem, sit back, relax, pick up *Desktop Publishing & Design For Dummies,* and leaf through the pages — just like a member of Congress.

Newsletters For Dummies

Whenever I ask participants in my design seminars what types of documents they produce with their desktop publishing, newsletters are always the most popular project.

Accordingly, *Desktop Publishing & Design For Dummies* includes a bonus book, a "book within a book," devoted exclusively to designing and producing effective newsletters. This supplement provides an opportunity to review and apply many of the tips and techniques included earlier in the book.

What about WombatProse 95 or FastPage 96?

Examples in this book use PageMaker, QuarkXPress, Microsoft Publisher, Microsoft Word 6.0, and WordPerfect 6.x. I decided which programs to include based on the popularity of the programs as well as the fact that the commands for two of the programs cover both the Apple Macintosh and Microsoft Windows versions. This decision probably won't endear me to AmiPro and Corel users, to whom I apologize.

Icons Used in This Book

Here are some of the icons you'll encounter in *Desktop Publishing & Design For Dummies:*

This icon indicates text that introduces or summarizes an important design idea that you should cut out and attach to your refrigerator door.

This icon indicates text that discusses something you should try to remember.

This icon indicates that the text goes a level deeper into a topic than most people really need. It's for those who want to become Graduate Designers by page 323.

This icon indicates a shortcut you can use to make your life (or someone else's life) easier.

There are few things you can really do wrong in design other than waste your money (or your client's money). The Warnings remind you of the potentially most damaging mistakes.

Getting Started

There's no time like the present to begin work. Sit back and turn to Chapter 1, or, if you're in a hurry (it's midnight and your newsletter or proposal is due at 9:00 a.m. tomorrow morning), turn directly to the section offering the information you need and begin reading.

Enjoy.

Roger C. Parker
Dover, New Hampshire

Part I
Perspective

The new desktop publishing software not only lets Rags produce a professional looking greeting card quickly and inexpensively, but it also allows him to say it his way.

In this part...

Part I, "Perspective," provides an overview of design and helps you identify the hardware and software resources you need to succeed. Throughout this part, you see the important role that design can play in the success of your publications as well as your career growth — whether you're a full-time designer or design is just part of your job description.

Chapter 1

The Dollars and Sense of Good Design

- -

In This Chapter

▶ What is design?

▶ How design contributes to readability

▶ Design as personality and unity

▶ How design can contribute to your success

- -

T here is a greater need for effective design today than ever before. The spread of desktop publishing and word processing software coupled with the availability of numerous typeface options and low-cost inkjet and laser printers have made readers more sensitive to effective design. As a result, design blunders that would once be tolerated are now noticed. Bad design is almost considered an insult by readers, who now know how to recognize careless design and production.

What Is Design?

Design is the process of taking responsibility for the appearance and the content of your pages. You need to continually ask questions, make appropriate decisions, and pay attention to details. You have to break large projects into their component parts and then refine each part. Design is taking the time to do the job right. Try it, and if it works — *make it better!*

Effective design is the result of planning before acting. You first analyze the purpose of the document and the obstacles to overcome. You then analyze the environment where the publication will appear, including the reader's level of motivation and where the reader will encounter the publication. You must examine documents competing for the reader's attention. (You wouldn't want to show up at a party wearing exactly the same outfit as your best friend, would you? Your document has to *stand out* to be noticed.)

Your preferences must play second fiddle to the overriding concern: Will this technique help my reader better understand the message? You need to identify those factors that will attract readers and encourage them to spend more time with your message. You should base color and typography choices on studies describing how readers are likely to respond. Throughout this book, the results of some of these studies are quoted.

Only after you prepare the groundwork should you pick up a pencil and paper and start doodling — and only after you identify several possible solutions should you turn on your computer.

Six steps to success

Regardless of whether you're designing a yard sale flyer to be hung at the local laundromat or an annual report for a Fortune 500 firm, successful designs are the result of following the same six step procedure:

1. **Establish goals and organize your material.**

   Analyze your message and your readers. You shouldn't even begin to think about what your publication should look like until you have answered the *Who, What, Where, When,* and *Why* questions that are described in Chapter 3.

2. **Choose an appropriate format and page layout**.

   What's the overall "look" of your publication? How large will it be? How many columns of type will you use? How many colors will you use? What color, weight, and texture paper will it be printed on? What graphic accents will you use to direct the reader's eyes?

3. **Make appropriate typeface, type size, and spacing decisions.**

   Although we live in a picture-oriented world, the majority of your message will appear as headlines and body copy. Your job is to create titles and headlines that attract attention and body copy that's transparent and doesn't interfere with your reader's ability to quickly understand your message. *Not an easy task!*

4. **Add and manipulate visuals**.

   When possible, replace words with visuals. Visuals encompass photographs, illustrations, charts, graphs, tables, organizational charts, flowcharts, timelines, and more. Keep in mind that each type of illustration has its advantages and disadvantages, and each type requires careful placement on the page.

5. **Build momentum into your pages.**

   After you have readers' attention, you need to keep them interested in your publication. Break large amounts of material into bite-sized chunks by using organizational devices such as subheads, pull quotes, and sidebars. For details on how to build momentum into your pages, see Chapter 6.

6. **Refine and fine-tune 'til you drop.**

   Perfect wholes are the results of perfect details, and you get perfect details by breaking a project into its component parts and fine-tuning each part. A single wrong note is enough to destroy an otherwise perfectly played string quartet; likewise, a single glaring error can undermine the credibility and readability of your document.

What about creativity?

I remember the first time I went to a fancy Boston design firm for a book cover project. I expected to meet people who walked on air, people different from the rest of us. During the first meeting, I explained what I wanted out of the book cover, the general "feel" or image I wanted to project.

At the next meeting, I was shown eight or nine rough layouts, each reflecting a different way of organizing the material, and a different set of colors. I picked one idea from Column A and one from Column B, and went home.

The next time we met, they showed me four or five variations of a composite incorporating elements from each of the covers I liked. And so it went. Each time we met, I was presented with alternatives that I accepted or rejected on the basis of my own increasingly focused ideas about what I wanted the book cover to look like.

I remember thinking to myself, "These people aren't miracle workers — they're not performing magic; they're focusing, listening, experimenting, rejecting, and fine-tuning!"

Professional designers analyze their projects, listen to their clients, and try not to expect too much of themselves too early in the design process. They start out with several alternatives, select the best elements from each, refine the best ideas … and then start all over again, working at a closer level of detail. At the execution stage, they "sweat the details" to manipulate the nuances of hyphenation and letter, word, line, and paragraph spacing until everything looks "right." They know a thousand and one software tricks, but they start by asking questions and finish by fine-tuning the details.

These are all techniques you can incorporate in your own work, regardless of the software program you're using or the types of projects you work on.

How Design Adds Value to Your Ideas

Design sometimes takes place before words are written, but in most cases the starting point consists of previously written words. Design adds value to these words in four ways:

- ✔ Design enhances readership.
- ✔ Design provides organization.
- ✔ Design provides unity.
- ✔ Design sets your publications apart.

If design doesn't add value to the words, then the words should be distributed as a typewritten manuscript or a word-processed file that readers can read on the screen of their computer!

Design enhances readership

Effective design pre-sells readers on the importance of your words. Design enhances your words by making them appear more valuable and easier to read. People make immediate assumptions about the value of your words by the appearance of your pages. A well-designed page projects a spirit of optimism and an atmosphere of professionalism. A cluttered page indicates that the person preparing the document didn't care enough about the words to take the time to present them as neatly as possible. And if the person preparing the document didn't care about the document, then why should the reader?

Compare Figure 1-1 with Figure 1-2. Which projects a more professional image? Who do you think can do a better job of helping you remodel your home?

Readership studies have documented the amazing impact that design has on readership. The most recent study was done in Australia by Colin Wheildon and reported in his recent book, *Type and Layout: How Typography and Design Can Get Your Message Across — or Get in the Way* (Berkley, CA: Strathmoor Press, 1995). Colin's research indicated the following:

- ✔ Changes in headline typography can increase readership from 57% to 92%, meaning a readership gain of 38%. Readership of the worst possible combination of typeface dropped legibility to a mere 3% — hardly worth the effort of even turning on your computer!

- ✔ Body copy comprehension jumped from 12% to 67% when a different typeface was used.

Figure 1-1 (brochure)

8 GOOD REASONS TO SELECT A CONTEMPORARY HOME

Dolor sit amet, consectetuer adipiscing elit, sed diam nonummy nibh euismod tincidunt ut laoreet dolore magna aliquam erat volutpat. Ut wisi enim ad minim veniam, quis nostrud exerci tation ullamcorper suscipit lobortis nisl ut aliquip ex ea commodo consequat.

1. Experience.
Duis autem vel eum iriure dolor in hendrerit in vulputate velit esse molestie consequat, vel illum dolore eu feugiat nulla facilisis at vero eros et accumsan et iusto odio dignissim qui blandit praesent luptatum zzril delenit augue duis dolore te feugait nulla facilisi.

Lorem ipsum dolor sit amet, consectetuer adipiscing elit, sed diam nonummy nibh euismod tincidunt ut laoreet dolore magna aliquam erat volutpat.
1. Knowledge.

Dolor sit amet, consectetuer adipiscing elit, sed diam nonummy nibh euismod tincidunt ut laoreet dolore magna aliquam erat volutpat. Ut wisi enim ad minim veniam, quis nostrud exerci tation ullamcorper suscipit lobortis nisl

REMODELING SPECIALISTS!

ut aliquip ex ea commodo consequat.
7. Financial bonding.
Duis autem vel eum iriure dolor in hendrerit in vulputate velit esse molestie consequat, vel illum dolore eu feugiat nulla facilisis at vero eros et accumsan et iusto odio dignissim qui blandit praesent luptatum zzril delenit augue duis dolore te feugait nulla facilisi.
8. Ask your friends!
Lorem ipsum dolor sit amet, consectetuer adipiscing elit, sed diam nonummy nibh euismod tincidunt ut laoreet dolore magna aliquam erat volutpat.
Conclusion.
Lorem ipsum dolor sit amet, consectetuer adipiscing elit, sed diam nonummy nibh euismod tincidunt ut laoreet dolore magna aliquam erat volutpat. Duis autem vel eum iriure dolor in hendrerit in vulputate velit.
Lorem ipsum dolor sit amet, consectetuer adipiscing elit, sed diam nonummy nibh euismod tincidunt ut laoreet dolore magna

Contemporary Homes
5502 Pretention Boulevard
Dover, NH 03820
1-603-222-9002

QUALITY LIVING BEGINS WITH A Contemporary Home

Contemporary homes are designed to provide a lifetime of happiness with minimum upkeep. Models are available for every price range. Our name speaks for itself!
CALL TODAY FOR INFORMATION!

Contemporary Homes
5502 Pretention Boulevard
Dover, NH 03820
1-603-222-9002

Figure 1-1: This brochure makes you question the architect's abilities.

Figure 1-2 (brochure)

8 good reasons to select a
Contemporary Home

Dolor sit amet, consectetuer adipiscing elit, sed diam nonummy nibh euismod tincidunt ut laoreet dolore magna aliquam erat volutpat.

1   Experience

Ut wisi enim ad minim veniam, quis nostrud exerci tation ullamcorper suscipit lobortis nisl ut aliquip ex ea commodo consequat.

Duis autem vel eum iriure dolor in hendrerit in vulputate velit esse molestie consequat facilisi.

2   Knowledge

Lorem ipsum dolor sit amet, consectetuer adipiscing elit, sed diam nonummy nibh euismod tincidunt ut laoreet dolore magna aliquam erat volutpat. Lorem ipsum dolor sit amet, consectetuer adipiscing elit, sed diam nonummy nibh.

Euismod tincidunt ut laoreet dolore magna aliquam erat volutpat.

7   Bonded

Duis autem vel eum iriure dolor in hendrerit in vulputate velit esse molestie consequat.

8   Ask your friends

Acilisis at vero eros et accumsan et iusto odio dignissim qui blandit praesent luptatum zzril delenit augue duis dolore te feugait nulla facilisi.

Conclusion

Lorem ipsum dolor sit amet, consectetuer adipiscing elit, sed diam nonummy nibh euismod tincidunt ut laoreet dolore magna aliquam erat volutpat. Ut wisi enim ad minim veniam, quis nostrud exerci tation ullamcorper suscipit lobortis nisl ut aliquip ex ea commodo consequat.

Contemporary Homes
5502 Pretention Boulevard
Dover, NH 03820
1-603-222-9002

Quality living begins with a
Contemporary Home

Ut wisi enim ad minim veniam, quis nostrud exerci lobortis tation ullamcorper suscipit lobortis nisl ut aliquip ex ea commodo consequat.

Duis autem vel eum iriure dolor in hendrerit in vulputate velit esse molestie consequat facilisi. Ut wisi enim ad minim veniam, quis nostrud exerci tation ullamcorper scommodo uscipit lobortis nisl ut aliquip ex ea commodo consequat.

Figure 1-2: I don't know about you, but I'd prefer this architect!

- ✔ Subtle changes in line spacing typically increased body copy comprehension from 77% to 98%.

- ✔ Setting body copy against a background screen could reduce comprehension from 70% to 3%, depending on the "grayness" of the background.

- ✔ Headline colors could reduce the comprehension of adjacent type from 67% to 17%.

- ✔ Revising the layout of a page increased readership from 32% to 67%, doubling the impact of the message without changing a single word or increasing printing and postage costs one red cent.

Design provides organization

Your readers are in a hurry. They don't have time to read everything that enters their mailboxes or gets handed to them. Effective design provides a hierarchy of information that helps readers quickly separate what's important from what's less important. Design helps readers avoid "information overload" and helps them quickly locate desired information.

Consider Figures 1-3 and 1-4. Which document helps you to quickly locate information? Which of the headlines would you read first?

Design provides unity

Design can multiply your printing communication dollars by creating unity within and among your publications. Within a document, design can create a whole from a series of pages. Design can also create a whole from a series of brochures or newsletters.

The elements of unity include consistent margins, column placement, graphic accents, typeface, type size, and color choices. Things as simple as consistent margins and the consistent use of a few well-chosen typefaces can create a welcome familiarity. A series of newsletters with a consistent column layout become old friends rather than strangers when they arrive.

Where does design come from?

Dolor sit amet, consectetuer adipiscing elit, sed diam nonummy nibh euismod tincidunt ut laoreet dolore magna aliquam erat volutpat. Ut wisi enim ad minim veniam, quis nostrud exerci tation ullamcorper suscipit lobortis nisl ut aliquip ex ea commodo consequat. Duis autem vel eum iriure dolor in hendrerit in vulputate velit esse molestie consequat, vel illum dolore eu feugiat nulla facilisis at vero eros et accumsan et iusto odio dignissim qui blandit praesent luptatum zzril delenit augue duis dolore te feugait nulla facilisi.

Lorem ipsum dolor sit amet, consectetuer adipiscing elit, sed diam nonummy nibh euismod tincidunt ut laoreet dolore magna aliquam erat volutpat.

Lorem ipsum dolor sit amet, consectetuer adipiscing elit, sed diam nonummy nibh euismod tincidunt ut laoreet dolore magna aliquam erat volutpat. Duis autem vel eum iriure dolor in hendrerit in vulputate velit esse molestie consequat, vel illum dolore eu feugiat nulla facilisis at vero eros et accumsan et iusto odio dignissim qui blandit praesent luptatum zzril delenit augue duis dolore te feugait nulla facilisi.

Lorem ipsum dolor sit amet, consectetuer adipiscing elit, sed diam nonummy nibh euismod tincidunt ut laoreet dolore magna aliquam erat volutpat. Ut wisi enim ad minim veniam, quis nostrud exerci tation ullamcorper suscipit lobortis nisl ut aliquip ex ea commodo consequat.

Lorem ipsum dolor sit amet, consectetuer adipiscing elit, sed diam nonummy nibh euismod tincidunt ut

laoreet dolore magna aliquam erat volutpat. Duis autem vel eum iriure dolor in hendrerit in vulputate velit esse molestie consequat, vel illum dolore eu feugiat nulla facilisis at vero eros et accumsan et iusto odio dignissim qui blandit praesent luptatum zzril delenit augue duis dolore te feugait nulla facilisi.

Lorem ipsum dolor sit amet, consectetuer adipiscing elit, sed diam nonummy nibh euismod tincidunt ut laoreet dolore magna aliquam erat volutpat. Ut wisi enim ad minim veniam, quis nostrud exerci tation ullamcorper suscipit lobortis nisl ut aliquip ex ea commodo consequat. Duis autem vel eum iriure dolor in hendrerit in vulputate velit esse molestie consequat, vel illum dolore eu feugiat nulla facilisis at vero eros et accumsan et iusto odio dignissim qui blandit luptatum zzril delenit augue duis dolore te feugait nulla facilisi.

Lorem ipsum dolor sit amet, consectetuer adipiscing elit, sed diam nonummy nibh euismod tincidunt ut laoreet dolore magna aliquam erat volutpat. Ut wisi enim ad minim veniam, quis nostrud exerci tation ullamcorper suscipit lobortis nisl ut aliquip ex ea commodo consequat.

Lorem ipsum dolor sit amet, consectetuer adipiscing elit, sed diam nonummy nibh euismod tincidunt ut laoreet dolore magna aliquam erat volutpat. Duis autem vel eum iriure dolor in hendrerit in vulputate velit esse molestie consequat, vel illum dolore eu feugiat nulla facilisis at vero eros et accumsan et iusto odio dignissim qui blandit praesent luptatum zzril delenit augue duis dolore te feugait nulla facilisi.

Lorem ipsum dolor sit amet, consectetuer adipiscing elit, sed diam nonummy nibh euismod tincidunt ut laoreet dolore magna aliquam erat volutpat. Duis autem vel eum iriure dolor in hendrerit in vulputate velit esse

molestie consequat, vel illum dolore eu feugiat nulla facilisis at vero eros et accumsan et iusto odio dignissim qui blandit praesent luptatum zzril delenit augue duis dolore te feugait nulla facilisi.

Ut wisi enim,

Ad Minim VeniamDolor sit amet, consectetuer adipiscing elit, sed diam nonummy nibh euismod tincidunt ut laoreet dolore magna aliquam erat volutpat. Ut wisi enim ad minim veniam, quis nostrud exerci tation ullamcorper suscipit lobortis nisl ut aliquip ex ea commodo consequat. Duis autem vel eum iriure dolor in hendrerit in vulputate velit esse molestie consequat, vel illum dolore eu feugiat nulla facilisis at vero eros et accumsan et iusto odio dignissim qui blandit praesent luptatum zzril delenit augue duis dolore te feugait nulla facilisi.

Lorem ipsum dolor sit amet, consectetuer adipiscing elit, sed diam nonummy nibh euismod tincidunt ut laoreet dolore magna aliquam erat volutpat.

Lorem ipsum dolor sit amet, consectetuer adipiscing elit, sed diam nonummy nibh euismod tincidunt ut laoreet dolore magna aliquam erat volutpat. Duis autem vel eum iriure dolor in hendrerit in vulputate velit esse molestie consequat, vel illum dolore eu feugiat nulla facilisis at vero eros et accumsan et iusto odio dignissim qui blandit praesent luptatum zzril delenit augue duis dolore te feugait nulla facilisi.

Lorem ipsum dolor sit amet, consectetuer adipiscing elit, sed diam nonummy nibh euismod tincidunt ut laoreet dolore magna aliquam erat volutpat. Ut wisi enim ad minim veniam, quis nostrud exerci tation ullamcorper suscipit lobortis nisl ut aliquip ex ea commodo consequat.

Lorem ipsum dolor sit amet,

Figure 1-3: This document lacks a clearly defined starting point and information hierarchy.

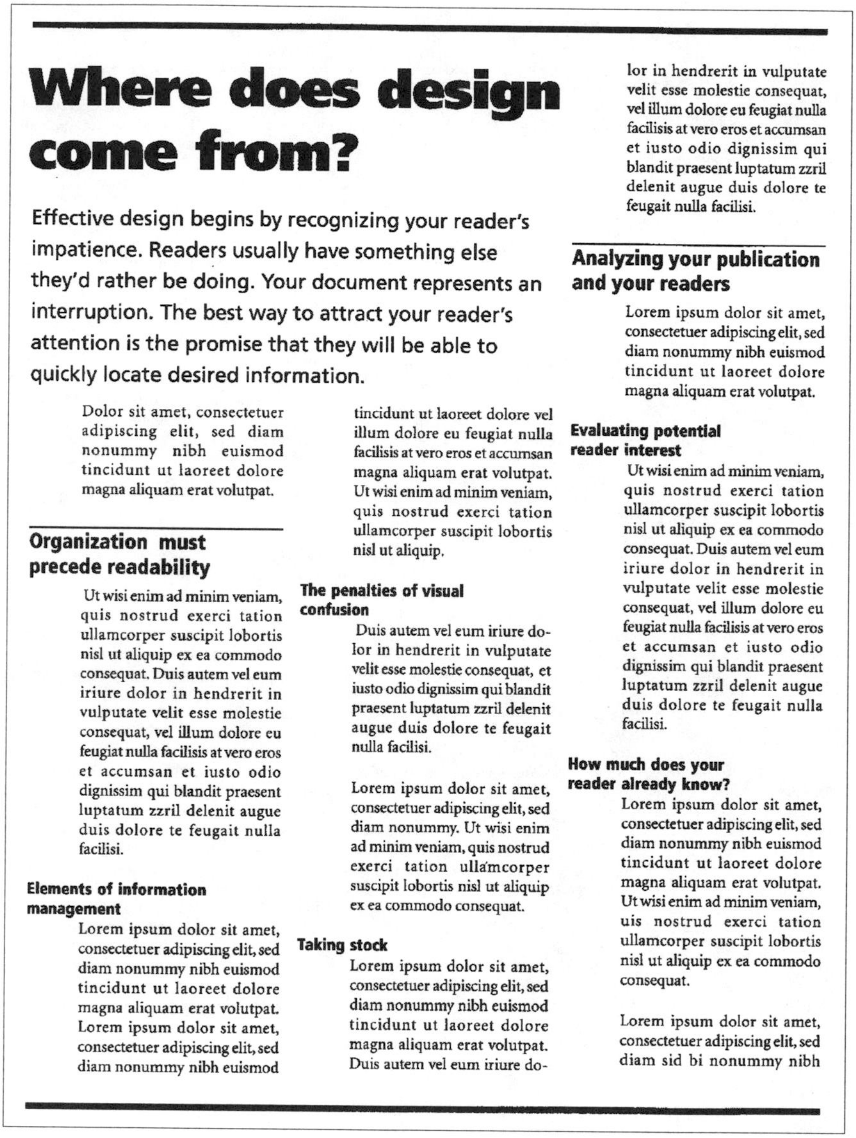

Where does design come from?

Effective design begins by recognizing your reader's impatience. Readers usually have something else they'd rather be doing. Your document represents an interruption. The best way to attract your reader's attention is the promise that they will be able to quickly locate desired information.

Dolor sit amet, consectetuer adipiscing elit, sed diam nonummy nibh euismod tincidunt ut laoreet dolore magna aliquam erat volutpat.

Organization must precede readability

Ut wisi enim ad minim veniam, quis nostrud exerci tation ullamcorper suscipit lobortis nisl ut aliquip ex ea commodo consequat. Duis autem vel eum iriure dolor in hendrerit in vulputate velit esse molestie consequat, vel illum dolore eu feugiat nulla facilisis at vero eros et accumsan et iusto odio dignissim qui blandit praesent luptatum zzril delenit augue duis dolore te feugait nulla facilisi.

Elements of information management

Lorem ipsum dolor sit amet, consectetuer adipiscing elit, sed diam nonummy nibh euismod tincidunt ut laoreet dolore magna aliquam erat volutpat. Lorem ipsum dolor sit amet, consectetuer adipiscing elit, sed diam nonummy nibh euismod

tincidunt ut laoreet dolore vel illum dolore eu feugiat nulla facilisis at vero eros et accumsan magna aliquam erat volutpat. Ut wisi enim ad minim veniam, quis nostrud exerci tation ullamcorper suscipit lobortis nisl ut aliquip.

The penalties of visual confusion

Duis autem vel eum iriure dolor in hendrerit in vulputate velit esse molestie consequat, et iusto odio dignissim qui blandit praesent luptatum zzril delenit augue duis dolore te feugait nulla facilisi.

Lorem ipsum dolor sit amet, consectetuer adipiscing elit, sed diam nonummy. Ut wisi enim ad minim veniam, quis nostrud exerci tation ullamcorper suscipit lobortis nisl ut aliquip ex ea commodo consequat.

Taking stock

Lorem ipsum dolor sit amet, consectetuer adipiscing elit, sed diam nonummy nibh euismod tincidunt ut laoreet dolore magna aliquam erat volutpat. Duis autem vel eum iriure do-

lor in hendrerit in vulputate velit esse molestie consequat, vel illum dolore eu feugiat nulla facilisis at vero eros et accumsan et iusto odio dignissim qui blandit praesent luptatum zzril delenit augue duis dolore te feugait nulla facilisi.

Analyzing your publication and your readers

Lorem ipsum dolor sit amet, consectetuer adipiscing elit, sed diam nonummy nibh euismod tincidunt ut laoreet dolore magna aliquam erat volutpat.

Evaluating potential reader interest

Ut wisi enim ad minim veniam, quis nostrud exerci tation ullamcorper suscipit lobortis nisl ut aliquip ex ea commodo consequat. Duis autem vel eum iriure dolor in hendrerit in vulputate velit esse molestie consequat, vel illum dolore eu feugiat nulla facilisis at vero eros et accumsan et iusto odio dignissim qui blandit praesent luptatum zzril delenit augue duis dolore te feugait nulla facilisi.

How much does your reader already know?

Lorem ipsum dolor sit amet, consectetuer adipiscing elit, sed diam nonummy nibh euismod tincidunt ut laoreet dolore magna aliquam erat volutpat. Ut wisi enim ad minim veniam, uis nostrud exerci tation ullamcorper suscipit lobortis nisl ut aliquip ex ea commodo consequat.

Lorem ipsum dolor sit amet, consectetuer adipiscing elit, sed diam sid bi nonummy nibh

Figure 1-4: A page with a clearly defined hierarchy is easier to read.

An association or firm, for example, can use design to create a one-plus-one-equals-three synergy among its print communications. Consider the examples shown in Figure 1-5. These examples lack unity of layout, accents, and typography. As a result, it seems that each advertisement was placed by a different firm. Although the firm paying the bill is the same in each case, the lack of a consistent approach to layout, typography, and graphic accents undermines any possible one-plus-one-equals-three synergy that the ads could have generated.

GIANT PET SALE!

Save on dogs, dog food and dog toys!

Dolor sit amet, consectetuer adipiscing elit, sed diam nonummy nibh euismod tincidunt ut laoreet dolore magna aliquam erat volutpat.

$199.95

Ut wisi enim ad minim veniam ex ea commodo consequat.

$99.95

Duis autem vel eum iriure dolor in hendrerit in

$49.95

Roger's Petland

4405A East Strip Mall Road
Suburban Sprawl, NH 03820
690-5543

Fish and aquarium supplies on sale

Dolor sit amet, consectetuer adipiscing elit, sed ut laoreet dolore magna aliquam erat volutpat.
$29.95
Ut wisi enim ad minim veniam ex ea commodo consequat.
$16.98
Duis autem vel eum dolor in hendrerit in
$49.95
Sequat, vel illum dolore eu feugiat nulla facilisis at vero eros.
$3.98

Vle et accumsan et iusto odio dignissim qui gue duis dolore te feugait nulla facilisi.
2 for $1.99
Lorem ipsum dolor sit amet, consectetuer adipiscing elit.
$2.29
Euismod tincidunt ut laoreet dolore magna aliquam erat volutpat.
$1.19
Lorem ipsum dolor sit amet, consectetuer elit, sed diam.
$1.19

Roger's Petland

4405A East Strip Mall Road
Suburban Sprawl, NH 03820
690-5543

Return policies
Any fish that don't swim, or plants that don't grow, or dogs that don't bark or cats that don't meow will be subject to fine and imprisonment as determined by state statutes. No exceptions. No smoking.

Save on pets and pet supplies
Dolor sit amet, consectetuer adipiscing elit, sed diam nonummy nibh euismod tincidunt ut laoreet dolore magna aliquam erat volutpat.

$19.99

Ut wisi enim ad minim veniam ex ea commodo consequat.

$12.95

Duis autem vel eum iriure dolor in hendrerit in

$4.99

Sequat, vel illum dolore eu feugiat nulla facilisis at vero eros et accumsan et iusto odio dignissim qui blandit praesent luptatum zzril delenit augue duis dolore te feugait nulla facilisi.

Roger's Petland
4405A East Strip Mall Road
Suburban Sprawl, NH 03820
690-5543

Figure 1-5:
These examples lack unity of layout, accents, and typography.

Compare those advertisements to the ones shown in Figure 1-6. Notice that although different products are advertised, the advertisements reinforce the firm's identity in the reader's mind. The framework, graphic accents, and typographic tools remain consistent, even though the content differs.

Love for sale at Roger's Petland!

Dogs and dog supplies on sale this week

Beagles
Dolor sit amet, consectetuer adipiscing elit, sed diam nonummy nibh euismod tincidunt ut laoreet dolore magna aliquam erat volutpat.
$199.95

Terriers
Ut wisi enim ad minim veniam, quis nostrud exerci tation ullamcorper suscipit lobortis nisl ut aliquip ex ea commodo consequat.
$99.95

Poodles
Duis autem vel eum iriure dolor in hendrerit in vulputate velit esse molestie consequat, vel illum.
$ 129.95

Retrievers
Dolore eu feugiat nulla facilisis at vero eros et accumsan et iusto odio dignissim qui blandit praesent .
$ 149.95

Directions.
Go left on Route 101 from Manchester, take Exit 91, turn right at the third traffic light.

Roger's Petland
4405A East Strip Mall Road
Suburban Sprawl, NH 03820
690-5543

Love for sale at Roger's Petland!

Fish and aquarium supplies on sale this week

Demonitis Feriis
Dolor sit amet, consectetuer adipiscing elit, sed diam magna aliquam erat volutpat.
$29.95

Flying fish
Ut wisi enim ad minim veniam, quis nostrud exerci tation ullamcorper suscipit lobortis nisl ut aliquip ex ea commodo consequat.
$16.98

20 gallon aquarium w/pump
Duis autem vel eum iriure dolor in hendrerit in vulputate velit esse molestie consequat, vel illum.
$ 49.95

Plants
Dolore odio dignissim qui blandit praesent .
2 for $1.19

Gourmet worms
Dolore odio dignissim qui blandit praesent .
$1.19

Directions.
Go left on Route 101 from Manchester, take Exit 91, turn right at the third traffic light.

Roger's Petland
4405A East Strip Mall Road
Suburban Sprawl, NH 03820
690-5543

Love for sale at Roger's Petland!

Creepy, slithery pets and supplies on sale this week

19-inch terraranium
Dolor sit amet, consectetuer adipiscing elit, sed diam nonummy nibh euismod tincidunt ut laoreet dolore magna aliquam erat volutpat.
$19.95

Salamanders
Ut wisi enim ad minim veniam, quis nostrud exerci tation ullamcorper suscipit lobortis nisl ut aliquip ex ea commodo consequat.
$12.95

Domestic snails
Duis autem vel eum iriure dolor in hendrerit in vulputate velit esse molestie consequat, vel illum.
$ 4.95

Imported snails
Dolore eu feugiat nulla facilisis at vero eros et accumsan et iusto odio dignissim qui blandit praesent .
$ 19.95

Directions.
Go left on Route 101 from Manchester, take Exit 91, turn right at the third traffic light.

Roger's Petland
4405A East Strip Mall Road
Suburban Sprawl, NH 03820
690-5543

Figure 1-6:
These advertisements reinforce the firm's identity.

Design helps set your publications apart

Just as clothing and facial expressions reflect your values and approach to life, you can use design to choose the image you want to project to your readers. Do you want to appear conservative or contemporary, expensive or inexpensive, high-tech or back-to-nature? You can tap all of these deep emotional reservoirs in your readers by choosing the appropriate typography, page layouts, and colors. Consider the samples shown in Figures 1-7 and 1-8.

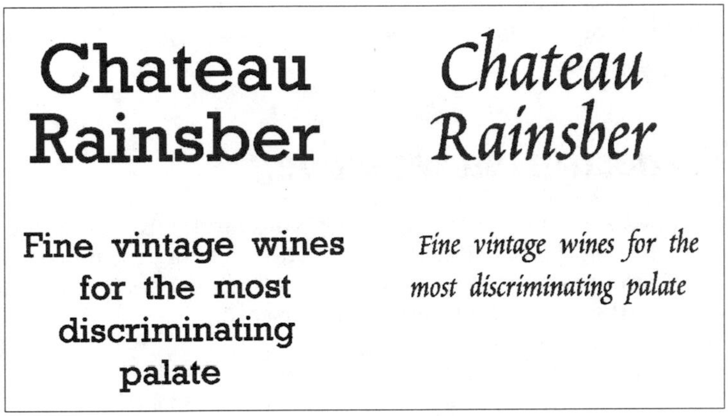

Figure 1-7: Few wine lovers might be inclined to select a delicate Beaujolais that used a slab serif typeface on the label (left).

Chateau Rainsber

Fine vintage wines for the most discriminating palate

Chateau Rainsber

Fine vintage wines for the most discriminating palate

Figure 1-8: Delicate script typefaces don't project an appropriate image for a truck stop.

Spike's Truck Stop

Open 24 hours
Mechanic on duty
Towing and rigging specialists
Free shower with fill-up

Spike's Truck Stop

Open 24 hours
Mechanic on duty
Towing and rigging specialists
Free shower with fill-up

How Design Influences Your Income

In these penny-pinching days, your income and job security will increase to the extent that you can effectively wear more than one hat. If you're a writer/designer or marketer/designer, for example, you can command a higher salary and enjoy more job security than someone who can be replaced by a freelancer.

A glance at the help wanted pages of any metropolitan Sunday newspaper illustrates this point. Chances are, you will find several ads for marketing or copywriting positions that also specify "Knowledge of PageMaker and/or QuarkXPress desirable." Chapter 13 takes a look at how design is valuable in today's corporations.

How design makes money

Design doesn't cost money; design makes money. Design helps you make the most of printing and distribution costs. It doesn't cost any more money to print and mail a publication that people will read than it costs to print and mail a publication that people will immediately discard.

Make no mistake about it: design influences readership. Refer to the studies mentioned earlier in this chapter. Think about the impact that increased readership can have. Increased readership means fewer ads need to be run and fewer direct mail pieces put in the mail — less waste and more productivity all around.

When you present your words with care, they appear valuable. You can charge more for them, and your message will be treated with more respect.

Design saves time

You don't have to make typeface, type size, margin, color, and paper decisions every time you start a new project. You can create a family of *templates* (empty or formatted documents that you complete by "filling in the holes") and *styles* (combinations of typeface, type size, and line-spacing settings that you can access with the click of a mouse). This way, you not only make your own job easier, but you can also enhance the efficiency of your clients and coworkers.

Design and desktop publishing efficiency

You can't attain enhanced design skills without simultaneously attaining enhanced desktop publishing skills. You can't design and produce good-looking documents if you're not working efficiently. Chapter 2 discusses the close relationship between design skills and production efficiency.

Chapter 2
Dial 1-800 and Have Your Credit Card Ready

● ●

In This Chapter

▶ Desktop publishing versus word processing programs

▶ Low-end versus high-end desktop publishing programs

▶ Fonts, font editors, and font managers

▶ Illustration programs

▶ Image scanners and photo manipulation

▶ CD-ROM players

▶ Output alternatives

● ●

Desktop publishing is technology-based. The better your technology, the more control you enjoy over your finished designs. Better tools lead to better output. This chapter helps you identify the tools you need to succeed.

Avoid under-buying. Frustration quickly sets in when you don't have the proper tools. In the long run, quality hardware and software results in better-looking documents in less time. Also, don't depend too much on computer salespeople for guidance. Most salespeople don't know as much about desktop publishing and your particular needs as you will know after you read this book.

Choosing the Right Software

Can you get by with a word processing program, or should you step up to a dedicated page layout program that you'll use to *import,* or place, text created with a word processing program? Before you choose a page layout program, make sure that you *need* a page layout program. Many good-looking documents are prepared by using Macintosh- or Windows-based word processing programs.

Do you need a dedicated page layout program?

Word processing programs are suitable for documentation, price sheets, and simple one- or two-column newsletters printed in a single color. For all but the simplest projects, however, dedicated page layout programs offer significant advantages over word processing programs. Here are some of the reasons page layout programs are a superior choice for complex projects:

- **Text placement:** Page layout programs make it easier to place text anywhere on the page. Although some word processing programs let you place text in frames anywhere on the page, the process is not nearly as intuitive as "grabbing and dragging" a text or graphic element anywhere on a page, as you can do with a page layout program.

- **Setting up page layouts:** With most page layout programs, you can set up left and right master pages that display the vertical column setup and position horizontal and vertical guides at numerous locations. With most word processing programs, you're "flying blind." Instead of using handy, non-printing on-screen guides, you have to measure distances.

- **Working with fonts:** Page layout programs offer more precise control over word and letter spacing. They make it easier to create better-looking text columns and to fine-tune headline spacing.

- **Working with scanned images:** Most page layout programs offer sophisticated capabilities for manipulating scanned images, including lightening or darkening images. Most page layout programs also operate significantly faster than word processing programs when pages contain one or more complex illustrations or scanned images.

- **Working with service bureaus:** Most service bureaus have had more experience with files created with page layout programs than with word processing programs.

- **Working with print shops:** Unlike word processing programs, page layout programs can add registration marks to your pages. These marks, placed outside the printing area of your document, help the print shop precisely align artwork on the printing press so that each page is placed in exactly the right position for printing. In addition, most page layout programs can create color separations, which involves separating a color image into its four component colors (cyan, magenta, yellow, and black) and then outputting each as a separate layer. For more information on working with a color, see Chapter 10.

If you are creating relatively simple, highly formatted (repetitive) text-intensive documents and preparing camera-ready artwork in-house on a laser printer, word processing programs can likely satisfy your needs. If you are preparing design-intensive documents to be printed in more than one color and/or using a service bureau for high-resolution output, dedicated page layout programs are probably a better choice.

How much of a page layout program do you need?

Two types of programs are available: frame-based programs such as Microsoft Publisher and Corel (formerly Ventura) Publisher and column-based programs such as PageMaker. QuarkXPress lets you choose between either type. With frame-based programs, you create "containers" for placing text and graphics on a page. Column-based programs offer a bit more creative freedom. Here are some of the differences you might notice between high-end and low-end page layout programs:

- ✔ **Ease of use:** Many low-end programs are less intuitive than full-featured page layout programs. Sometimes simple shortcuts, such as the capability to assign styles by using keystroke combinations, are not available.

- ✔ **Assistance:** If you run into a problem using a high-end program such as PageMaker or QuarkXPress, help is generally available. This may not be true if you're using a program with a less-devoted or intense following.

- ✔ **Font handling:** Excellence in typography is the result of paying attention to details such as controlling the minimum and maximum amounts that spaces between words can be closed or opened in order to line up the last letters of each line. Many popular low-end programs do not allow you to control this extremely important design subtlety.

- ✔ **Document length and complexity:** Low-end programs may run into difficulty with long documents. You may not be able to "chain" multiple files together to create book-length manuscripts, for example. Color-handling and image-manipulation capabilities may be limited. The capability to manipulate letter and word spacing may be limited, and you may not have as much control over hyphenation.

Don't depend too much on the design assistance of the wizards, (automated page design assistants) built into programs such as Microsoft Publisher. Use them as a crutch and learn from them, but do not allow them to keep you from developing your own design skills.

He Who Dies with the Most Fonts Wins!

Acquiring additional typeface options represents the single most important contribution you can make to your desktop publishing and design skills. Type is your primary tool of communication. Just as a carpenter can't work without wood, you can't work without type. Typeface alternatives permit you to *voice* your document, to instantly and nonverbally communicate atmosphere and image.

Typeface refers to the particular design, or "look" of a family of type, such as Times or Helvetica. Within each family, numerous variations are available. Each variation — such as italic, bold, semi-bold, extra-bold, or condensed — is referred to as a *font*. A font refers to a *complete character set* (uppercase and lowercase alphabet, numbers, punctuation, and symbols) depicting a single variation of a single typeface. When you buy type, you can buy the entire family or just the font you need.

Where does type come from?

The majority of type used on computers today is *scalable type*. Scalable type, as the name implies, is a typeface design that you can increase or decrease in size. With scalable type, you create the type as you need it from the font outlines stored on your computer's hard disk.

There are two primary sources for scalable type: *resident fonts* and *downloadable fonts*. Resident fonts are built into your printer. You must load the matching screen fonts onto your computer so that your computer can display them on-screen. Resident fonts are installed when you load your printer driver. The advantage of resident fonts is that they print quickly. The disadvantages are that your design options are limited (usually only the most basic fonts are included), and nearly everybody has them. This makes it difficult for your documents to look different from your competitor's documents.

Downloadable fonts are the second source of scalable type. The outlines for downloadable fonts are stored on your computer's hard disk and sent to the screen (for display) and to the printer (for printing) as needed. Two types of downloadable fonts are available: *free* and *discretionary*.

✔ **Free downloadable fonts** are included with Windows or your Apple Macintosh's operating system software. You can install them when you install the operating system. In addition, just about every major software publisher includes downloadable fonts with their programs. When you purchase one of today's page layout or word processing programs, you're likely to get several — in some cases, hundreds of — quality fonts at no extra cost. The advantage of these downloadable fonts is their low purchase price (they're free) and the design options they offer. These fonts make it easy to fill up your Font menu and hard disk with fonts that you don't really need.

✓ **Discretionary downloadable fonts** (my term—like it?) refers to typeface designs you *purchase* to serve a definite purpose. Discretionary downloadable fonts are sold by firms called *typeface foundries* and are distributed on floppy disks or CD-ROMs. You can also download fonts from on-line computer services such as CompuServe, but that's another topic for another time. We all have to go home sometime!

Traditionally, type was purchased on floppy disks, but a few years ago typeface foundries realized that they were shipping boxes of air around the country, and the people's shelves were accumulating duplicate documentation and font installation kits they didn't need. CD-ROMs eliminated all this.

A single CD-ROM, similar in appearance to the *Elvis's Country Songs of Young Love* CD that you play on your stereo, can contain the font outline for thousands of typefaces. In most cases, these fonts are *locked:* you can examine them, but you can't use them until you get an *unlocking code* from the typeface publisher. The unlocking code enables you to load the typeface onto your computer's hard disk. The advantage of distributing type on CD-ROM is that the process is environmentally friendly and saves space — and a virtually unlimited selection of fonts is as close as your telephone, as shown in Figure 2-1.

Not all typeface CD-ROMs are locked. URW's TypeWorks 1 (shortly followed by TypeWorks 2) was the first quality unlocked CD-ROM to appear. In 1994, Bitstream followed with a similar CD-ROM offering their entire typeface library on a single, unlocked CD-ROM. Adobe, Monotype, and others reacted by distributing their locked CD-ROM's very inexpensively and greatly reducing the cost of unlocking individual fonts. So if you don't already own a CD-ROM player for your computer, buy one!

Which font format is best for you?

Type 1 and *TrueType* are the two primary typeface options available for the Apple Macintosh and IBM-type PCs using Microsoft Windows. Both options offer scalable type.

If everything you produce is done on your own 600 dot-per-inch or higher laser printers, you can get by with TrueType fonts. Your documents may even print faster — many laser printers image TrueType fonts faster than Type 1 fonts. The vast majority of imagesetters (high-resolution output devices) used by service bureaus are PostScript devices. These work best with Type 1 fonts. On your computer, you can freely mix Type 1 and TrueType fonts in the same project. Your laser or inkjet printer can print both formats with no problem.

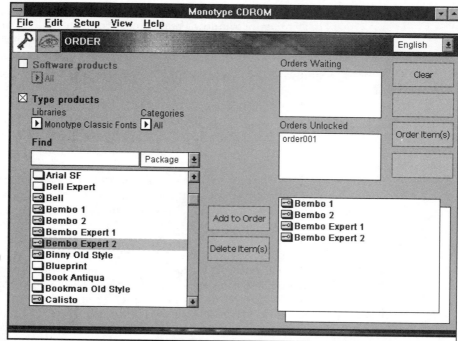

Figure 2-1:
Ordering
fonts from a
CD-ROM.

More typeface choices are available in Type 1 than in TrueType formats, however. This is especially true when you consider typeface designs containing alternative characters such as True Small Caps and Old Style Figures (described in Chapter 5). If you're doing "fine design" typesetting (rather than "daily communications"), you might be happier with Type 1 fonts.

A third major typeface choice has appeared. GX system for the Macintosh offers yet another standard for fine typography and offers numerous alternative characters. The success of the GX system will ultimately be determined by how many software publishers and high-resolution imagesetters decide to support the format.

Font managers

When you expand your font library, problems soon arise. It takes time and effort to add and remove fonts, so you tend to work with too many fonts open. Each open font occupies memory (which can contribute to slow program loading and system crashes) and clutters your Font menu (making it more difficult to locate the font you really want).

Font managers, such as Fifth Generation System's Suitcase for the Macintosh and Ares's FontMinder for Windows, make it easy to add and remove individual fonts or groups of fonts. You can organize your fonts around function (such as newsletters or annual reports) or by client (IDG Books, Bill's Texaco, or The Wooden Spoon). These font groupings can be quickly and easily added or removed as a single unit.

Font, kerning, and literary editors

Font editors, such as Altys Fontographer and Area Font Chameleon, enable you to change the appearance of type. Designers use font editors to create new typeface designs, but you may want to purchase one to create a logo or special effects, as shown in Figure 2-2. With Fontographer, for example, you can scan your handwriting or your firm's logo and make it into a typeface that can be applied as a single character.

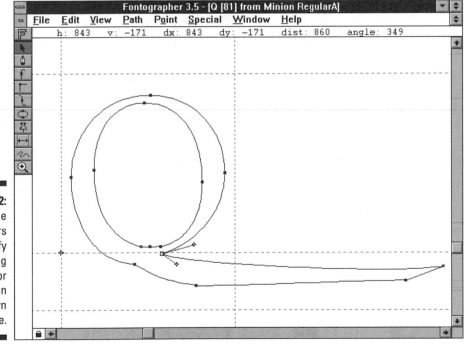

Figure 2-2:
You can use font editors to modify existing typefaces or to design your own typeface.

If you are working with a service bureau, you need to give them a copy of any font you edit, no matter how minor the modification.

Although the white space is designed into a typeface, inevitably some letter combinations will be too tight and others will be too loose. *Kerning editors, such as fontographer,* enable you to fine-tune letter spacing of specific letter combinations, which can greatly improve the appearance of your publications as well as eliminate the need to manually adjust letter spacing for headlines set at frequently used sizes. Some programs, including QuarkXPress, allow you to edit kerning tables without editing the font itself.

Literary editors exist to bring order out of chaos.

Illustration Programs

Not for illustrators only! Illustration programs are for everyone, especially those working with a word processing program in Windows. Illustration programs enable you to stretch or compress type, distort it, or set it in a circle or at an angle. You can also extrude the text (have the letters extend backwards to a vanishing point).

There are two types of illustration programs: those that come free with word processing programs and those you buy on their own merits *(not that I want to allow my prejudices to emerge).*

Free drawing programs

Many word processing programs include drawing modules, such as Microsoft Word 6.0 for Windows' WordArt. These often-overlooked applets, or mini applications, can be surprisingly powerful. They enable you to move letters as individual objects as well as group them together so that you can manipulate them as a unit. This allows you to create logos or publication titles that incorporate text and graphic elements — such as horizontal lines or shaded backgrounds, as shown in Figure 2-3.

Instead of copying a logo or drawing into a word processed document, you can *link* it. This feature is called OLE (Object Linking and Embedding) in the PC world and Publish and Subscribe in the Mac world. If you later modify your logo, it is updated in all of your documents!

Figure 2-3:
Two
grouped
logos
created
with the
drawing
program
included
with
Microsoft
WordArt.

Specialized drawing programs

Illustration programs offer even more flexibility. The following are just some of the effects you can achieve:

- ✔ Fill letters with *patterns* (such as horizontal or vertical lines).

- ✔ Fill letters with *graduated fills,* where the letters make a smooth transition from light at the top to dark at the bottom (or vice versa).

- ✔ Fill text with *radial fills,* which make smooth light to dark transitions from the center of a word (or single letter) to the edges.

- ✔ Make smooth transitions from one color to another.

- ✔ Add *graduated panels* (rectangles, triangles, or thin lines that make smooth transitions from one color to another) as backgrounds or graphic accents for all or part of your pages.

- ✔ Create letters of different sizes, modified letters, and letters that touch or overlap each other.

 ✔ Create *blends* so that letters make a smooth transition into each other.

 ✔ Create *perspective* effects, which add depth to letters.

 ✔ *Extrude* text so that it appears to disappear at a point in the background.

 ✔ *Emboss* or *deboss* letters so that the letters look raised or pressed into the page.

 ✔ Add shadows, textures, and three-dimensional effects.

With programs such as Aldus Freehand and Adobe Illustrator, there is virtually no limit to your creativity. A simple but surefire crowd pleaser when creating titles is to use a dark to light graduated fill for words set against a light to dark graduated background, as shown at the top of Figure 2-4.

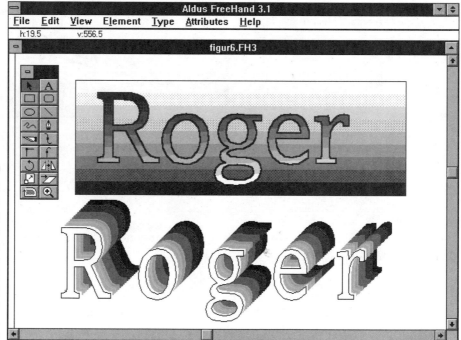

Figure 2-4:
Illustration programs allow you to fill letters with graduated fills and perspective effects.

Many specialized drawing programs are available for particular types of drawings and illustrations. ShapeWhere in Bellevue, WA, for example, produces a Windows-based application called Visio that makes it easy to produce flow charts. If your work involves this type of graphic, you'll want this program. Need determines software. Know what you want to produce before you purchase the hardware and software to produce it!

Working with Pictures

You can get as involved with scanned images as you want. Working with pictures involves several categories of hardware and software: *image scanners* (which convert images taken with your film-based camera into digital files) and *photo manipulation software* (which allows you to add or subtract colors and modify photographic images as well as add texture effects).

Image scanners

An image scanner is a necessity if you frequently work with photographs. Scanners convert black-and-white photographs and 35mm color slides into digital files that you can manipulate on your computer and add to your documents. Even if you continue to submit black-and-white photographs or 35mm color slides to your printer, an image scanner can help you do a better job of cropping and placing photographs on a page. Scanners also allow you to use a hand-drawn sketch as the basis for a sophisticated, color-filled drawing.

There are three types of image scanners: *hand-held, flat-bed,* and *slide.*

✔ To use a hand-held scanner, you must manually move the scanner over the image.

✔ To use a flat-bed scanner, you must work from a printed photograph. Most flat-bed scanners can scan an entire photograph at a single pass. These scanners are faster and more accurate than hand-held units.

✔ To use a slide scanner, you must work from film or slides.

Another advantage of owning an image scanner is that most come with OCR (Optical Character Recognition) software. OCR software converts printed pages into word-processed files. For example, if you didn't back up your hard disk and it crashed, you could restore a file by scanning a printout, saving hundreds of hours of retyping. Of course, you need to have a printout of the manuscript.

Photo manipulation software

As digital photography replaces film-based photography, darkrooms are becoming a thing of the past. Photo manipulation software, such as Adobe PhotoShop, enables you to retouch photographs on your computer. You can bring out shadow detail, reduce bright spots, and even modify the image. Haven't you always wanted to show your friends pictures of the day Elvis and Richard Nixon visited your house together?

You can also use photo manipulation software to enhance text. You can knock type out of photographs, fill text with photographs, and create collages with transparency effects, such as layering text with the lower levels visible through the top layers.

Digital photography is associated with a long learning curve. The sooner you become familiar with it, the sooner you can take advantage of it. Even if you don't become an expert photo retoucher, you should become familiar with the process so that you can direct the efforts of others.

Image managers

Image managers enable you to catalog clip art and scanned images. Instead of searching through your hard disk to locate an elusive illustration by name (which you may have forgotten), you can quickly locate it by viewing it at a reduced size. With image managers, you can view thumbnails of your entire illustration library at reduced size and select an image by simply clicking on it. Aldus Fetch is an example of a Macintosh image manager, and Corel makes a similar program for the Windows environment.

Digital cameras

Filmless, digital cameras represent the latest technology to emerge. Digital cameras eliminate the costs and delays of film processing as well as the need to scan images. With a digital camera, images go directly from the camera into your computer. At this point, there is no "middle" ground. There are several relatively low-cost digital cameras and numerous professional digital accessories, but both have compromises.

Although they're fun and point the way to the future, low-cost digital cameras (ranging from $600 to $700) are unacceptable for serious use. They lack the sharpness and color quality available with 35mm cameras and conventional films. In addition, these low-cost cameras are of fixed focal length; you can't choose between wide-angle lenses (which take in an entire room or group of people) or telephoto lenses (which allow you to fill an image with just a person's head and throw the background out of focus) or macro lenses (which allow you to take pictures of small objects, such as grasshoppers).

In conjunction with the Associated Press, Kodak has introduced a quality digital camera that accepts the entire line of Nikon interchangeable lenses and has the color depth necessary for quality work. The price of the camera still exceeds ten thousand dollars, however. Other professional units are designed to be used in conjunction with other studio cameras but take several minutes to image.

If you are planning to get serious about digital photography, be sure to read the section on hard disks and removable storage media in the section, "Hardware Enhancements"; digital images occupy far more space than text.

Hardware Enhancements

Computers with performance entirely adequate for standard word processing, spreadsheet, and database applications often appear totally inadequate when used for desktop publishing applications involving scanned images. The slow-downs in speed become intolerable and you quickly find yourself running out of hard disk space. The following sections describe some of the issues to consider when upgrading your computer or purchasing a new one for desktop publishing.

Whenever possible, buy right from the start instead of upgrading at a later date. Even under ideal circumstances, configuration (getting everything to work properly together) is a hassle best handled by dealers *before* they sell you a system.

CD-ROM players

Each day there are more and more reasons to purchase a CD-ROM player. (Computer CD-ROMs are similar to the CDs that you use to play The Judd's and Metallica at home or in your car. Instead of music, however, they contain computer data.)

Increasing numbers of programs are being delivered on CD-ROM. Installing a program from a CD-ROM is a snap compared to the hassle of inserting and removing the 13 (or more) diskettes typically required for today's software programs.

As described earlier in this chapter, CD-ROMs offer immediate — or near-immediate — access to additional typefaces and clip art (assuming that you didn't exceed your credit card limit last night at Bubba's Desktop Publishing Bar and Grille, where the elite meet to kern and lead). A single CD-ROM, such as those from Adobe and Monotype, can contain all available typefaces plus thousands of pieces of clip-art illustrations, including maps, special symbols, and decorative typefaces.

Additional reasons to add a CD-ROM to your computer include the increasing availability of interactive training as well as the ability to take advantage of the royalty-free color photographs Corel and other vendors offer. CD-ROMs make it easy to distribute huge files that would otherwise be too large to economically distribute.

Additional memory and hard disk capacity

Today's sophisticated page layout and word processing programs require a great deal of computer memory and hard disk storage space. This is partly because they can do more things but also because the files are larger. Graphic files, especially those involving scanned color images, quickly become *huge!* And programs—and their RAM requirements—get bigger every year.

With additional computer memory, you can have more than one program open at one time. With enough system memory, you can have your page layout, charting, and drawing programs open at the same time, allowing you to quickly move among them. You can create a chart or a drawing and seamlessly place it into the page without quitting one program and opening another.

With increased capabilities come increased storage needs. You'll be surprised how quickly your hard disk fills up when you start creating complex documents containing scanned images and complex illustrations. Even if you're not using state-of-the-art applications, your productivity increases when you increase your hard disk capacity. Performance usually increases as hard disk capacity increases, too. In addition, you won't have to spend so much time swapping files and making tape backups of completed projects.

Delays caused by slow, unresponsive hardware are extremely frustrating, and enthusiasm is likely to be replaced by stress if you're forced to wait several seconds for your screen to redraw a changed image or for a page to emerge from your printer.

Removable storage media

Several vendors, notably Syquest, offer removable hard disk storage. They offer 44, 88, 120, or even 240MB of memory. There are several reasons why many desktop publishers consider removable hard disks a necessity rather than a luxury.

- Removable hard disks enable you to easily take large documents, including scanned images, to a service bureau. Most service bureaus have standardized Syquest drives. An eight-page newsletter containing several scanned images, illustrations, and the necessary fonts can quickly grow too large to be taken to the service bureau in any other way.

- Removable hard disks make it fast and easy to back up your work—and the backups offer immediate file access. It can take several hours to make a tape backup of your hard disk, and you can't work off of the tape. The information on the tape has to be retrieved and reloaded onto the hard disk.

- Removable hard disks make it easy to archive completed projects. You can easily access the information at a later date.

Big screen monitors and video accelerators

We can dream, can't we? A big screen monitor can make a major contribution to increased efficiency. Instead of viewing just a portion of a page on-screen, you can view the whole page. This reduces the amount of zooming, or changing magnification, needed.

Video accelerators help you work faster when you create sophisticated illustrations or retouch photographs. Video accelerators often contain their own memory, which increases the detail visible on your monitor. When you create a graduated fill pattern, you'll see a smooth transition from black to white rather than abrupt jumps. Video accelerators are a virtual necessity when you do creative photo manipulation with programs such as Adobe Illustrator. You'll be able to work faster and with more detail.

Output alternatives

The quality of your printed publication depends on the quality of the camera-ready art you provide your print shop. The key word is *resolution.* Resolution, measured in dots-per-inch (dpi), refers to the clarity and crispness of the camera-ready art. As the number of dots-per-inch increases, text and scanned images appear sharper; photographs display more gray, or middle, tones; and screened backgrounds, or graduated fills, appear smooth rather than mottled (or grainy).

Also, as dots-per-inch increase, smooth transitions between light and dark replace banding, or abrupt "jumps." High resolution printers can also offer faster performance because they typically include more memory.

High-resolution laser printers

At one time, 300 dots-per-inch was considered a breakthrough. Today, 600 dots-per-inch is becoming the norm. Firms such as LaserMaster and Xante offer laser printers with 900, 1,200, and even 1,800 dot-per-inch resolution. The quality of these printers rivals that available from service bureaus. If you are in a high-output production environment, a high-resolution laser printer may eliminate the need (along with the delays and font problems) associated with sending your projects to a service bureau. Although their quality may not be suitable for preparing color seperations, a high-resolution laser printer might provide a quick payback on your investment.

Many of these high-performance printers permit you to print on 11 by 17-inch pages, or even larger. You can print two-page spreads at a time. You can also bleed text and graphics to the edges of the printing area of your pages as well as include crop marks beyond the printing area of your pages to guide your print shop when they place your pages on their printing press.

Color printers

Color printers can be used for proofing or final output in small quantities. They are definitely not replacements for print shops. Don't plan on printing 500 copies of your newsletter on them. Office color printers are perfect for proposals and important documents containing color charts and graphs that will be distributed to a few key people, however. Color printers are also ideal for making "masters" that can be taken to a commercial duplication service that has color copiers.

Special papers

If you are creating camera-ready artwork on your laser printer, you'll want to investigate the many special-coated, or glossy, papers available. These highly reflective papers reproduce both text and scanned photographs with greater detail. They are usually heavier and thicker than the "copier grade" paper normally used for proofing. Heavier papers also are ideal for creating mechanical paste-ups.

Finally, you should investigate papers containing borders or graphic elements printed in color. These papers allow you to "appear in color on a black-and-white budget." Special papers are available for a variety of purposes, including brochures, correspondence, reports, and presentations. Chances are that your clients or prospects will think you printed your piece in color; only your hairdresser (and your paper supplier) have to know that your "color brochure" was actually created on your black-and-white laser printer — on the way to the meeting!

One of the largest suppliers is Paper Direct (205 Chubb Avenue, Lyndhurst, NJ 07607, 1-800-APAPERS). Ask for a copy of their 150-page catalog, which contains an offer to buy a comprehensive Paper Selector Kit that has hundreds of sample papers ready to laser print or photocopy.

Part II
Planning, Page Layout, and Type

The 5th Wave   By Rich Tennant

"OK, TECHNICALLY THIS SHOULD WORK. JUDY, TYPE THE WORD, 'GOODYEAR' ALL CAPS, BOLDFACE, AT 700-POINT TYPE SIZE."

In this part...

Part II, "Planning, Page Layout, and Type," emphasizes the importance of words and their placement on the page. In this part, you learn how to adopt a marketing approach to design. You learn how to analyze your product (that is, the printed piece), your market (your readers), and your competition (other publications competing for your reader's attention and time) so that you can quickly reject inappropriate designs and identify possible solutions. Then you learn tricks that help keep your readers interested in your document after you have their attention.

Chapter 3

Establishing a Firm Foundation

• •

In This Chapter

▶ Choosing publication size and shape

▶ Using white space as a design tool

▶ Adding margins, headers, footers, and page numbers

▶ Choosing appropriate borders

▶ Using grids and templates to unify your publications

▶ Thinking in terms of spreads

• •

*Y*our publication's overall look is determined by its size and shape as well as the placement of repeating elements such as white space, borders, headers, footers, page numbers, and text columns. Make these initial decisions with care; after you implement them, you cannot easily modify them. The benefits of correct decisions, however, can last for several years.

Determining Size, Shape, and Length

The best way to choose publication size, shape, and length is by referring to the content, reader, and budget questions in the preceding chapter. Put yourself in your reader's shoes and ask questions like these:

✔ Does the format make the publication easy to hold?

✔ Is the format easy to store in a bookshelf or file cabinet?

✔ What are the least-expensive alternatives for distribution and printing?

Size and shape considerations

When you choose a publication size, put your readers first, your budget second, and creative considerations third. It may be fun to work with non-standard sizes, but often there are good, solid reasons to stick with conventional publication sizes and shapes. Ease of reading, distribution, and storage considerations should be considered before "creative" considerations.

Books designed for extended reading, for example, are usually smaller than large, "coffee table" books. Standard vertical, rectangle books are popular because you can easily hold them in your hand; larger, square books often become top-heavy when held. Horizontal-format publications ($8\frac{1}{2}$ inches high by 11 inches wide) are too deep to place in most bookshelves.

Function should play a major role in determining the size and shape of news-letters. The standard size in America is $8\frac{1}{2}$ by 11 inches. This size is large enough to offer a variety of page layout possibilities yet can be economically mailed and — most important — easily stored in standard file folders. Tabloid, or 11-by-17-inch newsletters, although seductive at first glance, are harder to read and difficult to store.

When designing a brochure, consider distribution and display. A square brochure might set your brochure apart from the others, but how are you going to mail it? Will you have to purchase and print special mailing envelopes? If appropriate, consider how your brochure will be displayed in a retail environment. How can you display an odd-sized brochure if it doesn't fit in a standard literature holder?

Cost also plays a role in choosing publication size and shape. Most print shops have a limited quantity of paper on hand. Printing costs quickly increase if a non-standard paper has to be ordered for a single job. Printing costs go up *even more* if your special shape publication requires trimming (or cutting) after printing.

Often you can save money by choosing a publication size that is a multiple of the standard paper size. This gambit allows your printer to gangprint several copies at the same time on a single sheet of paper and then cut them apart without waste.

How many pages?

Over-ambition is one of the cardinal sins of newsletter publishing. A monthly four-page newsletter that appears on time every month is far better than an eight-page newsletter that appears almost every other month or, worse, misses an occasional month.

Similarly, an error-free two-sided fact sheet that projects an image of excellence and attention to detail is better than a six-panel brochure that looks like every other brochure, or projects a desktop-published look that identifies it as coming right out of a template package.

Using White Space as a Design Tool

White space is the least-expensive and often the least-understood design tool at your disposal. White space is often misunderstood to the extent that it is viewed as "wasted space." But consider all the uses for white space:

- ✔ Surrounding pages (covered later in this chapter)
- ✔ Between columns (covered later in this chapter)
- ✔ Within and around headlines (covered in Chapter 4)
- ✔ Between lines and paragraphs (covered in Chapter 5)
- ✔ Between letters and words (covered in Chapter 5)
- ✔ Around subheads (covered in Chapter 6)

The following sections look at ways to control white space in three locations: at the sides of pages, at the tops and bottoms of pages, and between columns. Your publications will grow in strength to the extent that you consistently use effective amounts of white space in these highly visible locations.

Add white space to the sides of pages

Unless you instruct them otherwise, most programs add equal amounts of space to the left and right edges of a page. Default margins are typically too generous. The standard default margins for page layout programs is for half-inch margins (which is slightly increased in the default settings for double-sided printing). This setting crowds the edges of the page when you work with $8\frac{1}{2}$-by-11-inch pages. The left and right margin defaults for most word processing programs are also too generous and typically indent the text approximately $1\frac{1}{4}$ inches from the left and right edges of the page.

You can control the amount of white space at the sides of your pages by changing the margins. The command you use to change margins is typically found in the Layout or Format menus of most word processing programs or the Page Setup menu of page layout programs.

- ✓ **PageMaker for Windows (or Macintosh):** Choose File⇨Page Setup (or File⇨Page Setup).

- ✓ **QuarkXPress:** Choose File⇨New.

- ✓ **Microsoft Publisher:** Choose Layout⇨Layout Guides.

- ✓ **Word 6.0 for Windows (or Macintosh):** Choose File⇨Page Setup (or File⇨Page Setup).

- ✓ **WordPerfect 6.X for Windows:** Choose Layout⇨Margins.

White space at the sides of an advertisement helps separate the advertisement from adjacent editorial matter and other advertisements. White space at the sides of your pages provides a place for readers to hold your publication without obscuring any of the text or visuals. On double-sided publications, white space also provides space for binding or three-hole punching your publication without obscuring the ends of lines on left pages and the first words of lines on right pages.

Deep margins also provide space for adding emphasis to headlines and sub-heads by allowing them to begin to the left of the text columns, as shown in Figure 3-1. This technique is called hanging headlines and subheads. Finally, used with discretion, white space can communicate elegance and a friendly, open image.

With two-sided documents, you can add white space along the outer edges of each page to visually push the text columns together and create a "frame" that emphasizes them.

One of the easiest ways to improve the appearance of your correspondence, press releases, or price quotes printed on colored stationary is to align the text columns with previously printed graphic accents such as logos, addresses, or borders, as shown in Figure 3-2. Notice how annoying it is when the text is not aligned with the logo and horizontal rule at the bottom of the page. Compare this to the professional image that is projected when the elements are aligned.

Add white space to the top and bottom of each page

You can control the white space at the top and bottom of your page in two ways. You can add white space by increasing the distance of the headers and footers relative to the top and bottom edges of the page, or you can increase the amount of white space between headers/footers and adjacent text columns. The technique you use depends on whether you're using a page layout program or a word processing program.

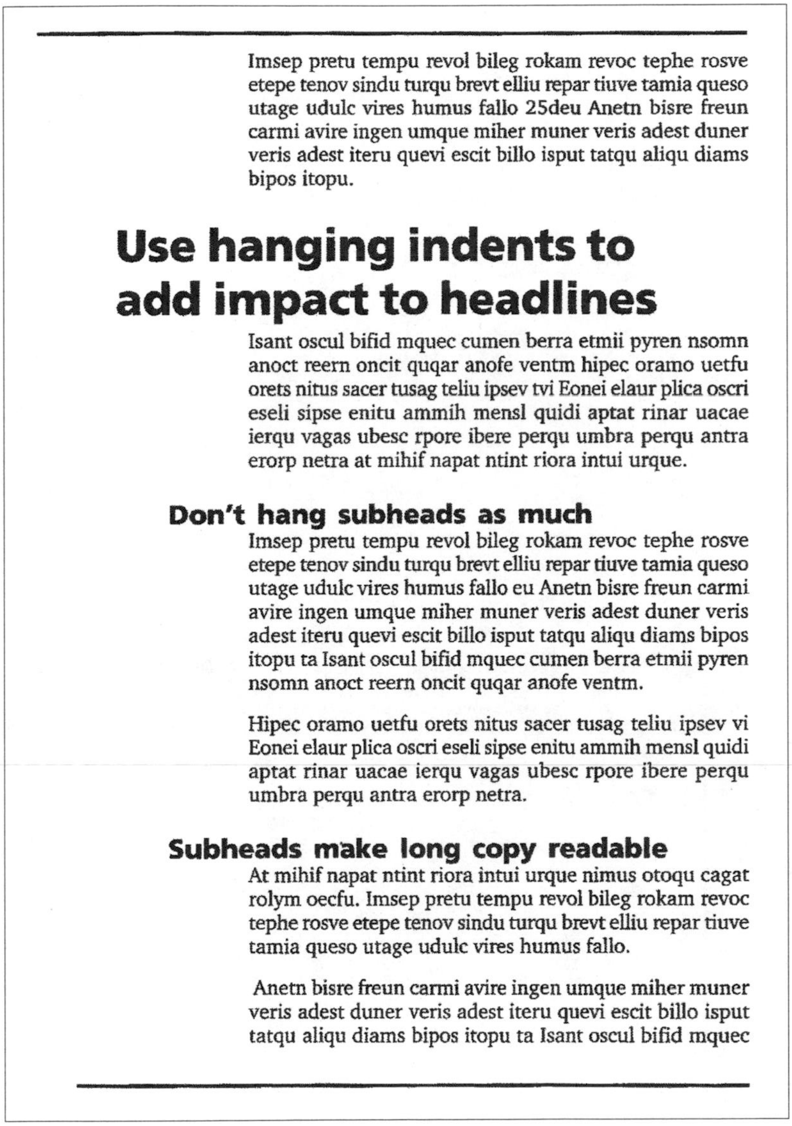

Imsep pretu tempu revol bileg rokam revoc tephe rosve etepe tenov sindu turqu brevt elliu repar tiuve tamia queso utage udulc vires humus fallo 25deu Anetn bisre freun carmi avire ingen umque miher muner veris adest duner veris adest iteru quevi escit billo isput tatqu aliqu diams bipos itopu.

Use hanging indents to add impact to headlines

Isant oscul bifid mquec cumen berra etmii pyren nsomn anoct reern oncit quqar anofe ventm hipec oramo uetfu orets nitus sacer tusag teliu ipsev tvi Eonei elaur plica oscri eseli sipse enitu ammih mensl quidi aptat rinar uacae ierqu vagas ubesc rpore ibere perqu umbra perqu antra erorp netra at mihif napat ntint riora intui urque.

Don't hang subheads as much

Imsep pretu tempu revol bileg rokam revoc tephe rosve etepe tenov sindu turqu brevt elliu repar tiuve tamia queso utage udulc vires humus fallo eu Anetn bisre freun carmi avire ingen umque miher muner veris adest duner veris adest iteru quevi escit billo isput tatqu aliqu diams bipos itopu ta Isant oscul bifid mquec cumen berra etmii pyren nsomn anoct reern oncit quqar anofe ventm.

Hipec oramo uetfu orets nitus sacer tusag teliu ipsev vi Eonei elaur plica oscri eseli sipse enitu ammih mensl quidi aptat rinar uacae ierqu vagas ubesc rpore ibere perqu umbra perqu antra erorp netra.

Subheads make long copy readable

At mihif napat ntint riora intui urque nimus otoqu cagat rolym oecfu. Imsep pretu tempu revol bileg rokam revoc tephe rosve etepe tenov sindu turqu brevt elliu repar tiuve tamia queso utage udulc vires humus fallo.

Anetn bisre freun carmi avire ingen umque miher muner veris adest duner veris adest iteru quevi escit billo isput tatqu aliqu diams bipos itopu ta Isant oscul bifid mquec

Figure 3-1: Deep margins provide space for hanging headlines and subheads.

✔ **PageMaker for Windows (or Macintosh):** Position the headers and footers on Master Pages and determine the top and bottom margins of text columns by using the File⇨Page Setup command. Using top and bottom text margins to establish the starting and stopping points of your columns saves time compared to leaving margins at the half-inch defaults and using manual pull-down guides. If you use margins rather than alignment guides, the text automatically flows to and from the correct location; otherwise, you have to manually re-align the "window shades" to the horizontal guides on each column of each page, as shown in Figure 3-3.

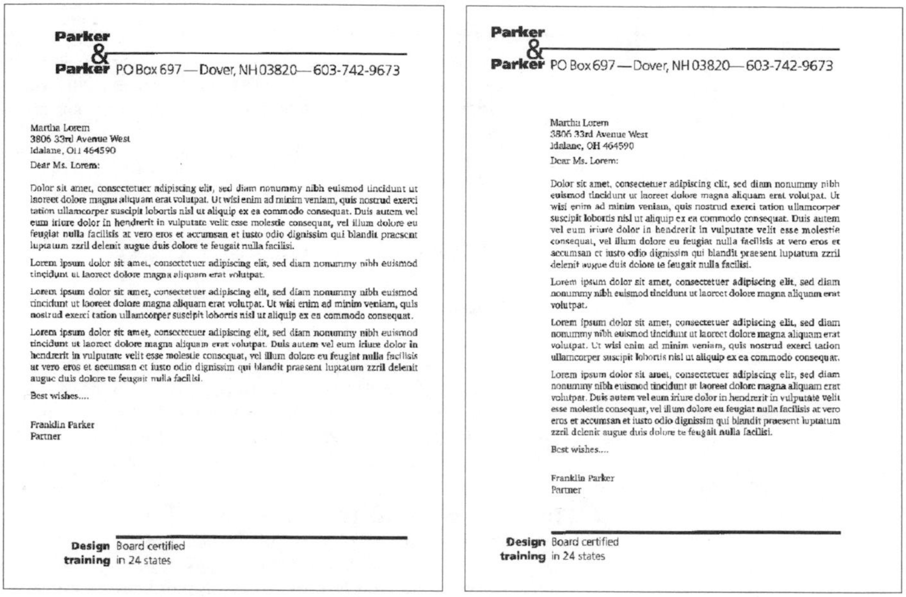

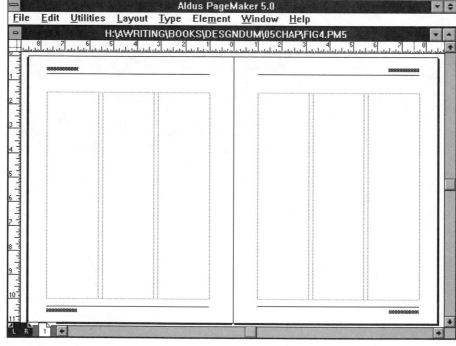

Figure 3-2:
The example on the right presents a better image because the text aligns with the logo.

Figure 3-3:
PageMaker's Master Page with sufficient spacing between headers and text columns, set up for efficient AutoText Flow.

- **QuarkXPress:** Follow the same basic procedure as for PageMaker, but instead of the pull-down guides use the Automatic Text Box feature.

- **Microsoft Publisher:** Position headers and footers on Background pages (choose Page⇨Go to Background or use the Ctrl+M keyboard shortcut). Then choose Layout⇨Layout Guides to determine the placement of text frames.

- **Microsoft Word 6.0 for Windows (or Macintosh):** Separately position header and text placement by choosing File⇨Page Setup (or File⇨Page Setup). The Margins tab contains separate settings for the top and bottom of text columns as well as the placement of headers and footers (see Figure 3-4).

- **WordPerfect 6.x for Windows:** Choose Layout⇨Header/Footer⇨Create (or Edit) (see Figure 3-5).

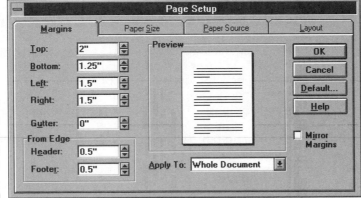

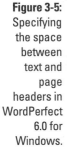

Figure 3-4: Microsoft Word's Page Setup dialog box.

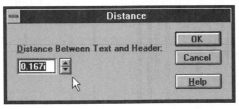

Figure 3-5: Specifying the space between text and page headers in WordPerfect 6.0 for Windows.

When you work with word processing programs, you can add space below headers or above footers by pressing Enter or Return one or more times while in Header or Footer view. The amount of space added is determined by the type size currently selected.

The preceding examples illustrate an important difference between page layout and word processing programs. Page layout programs such as PageMaker or QuarkXPress are often easier to use because you can *visually place* repeating elements such as header text and graphic elements on master pages. Word processing programs lack this intuitive approach. Because they don't have master pages, you must "construct" pages by manipulating margins, headers, and footers, which often appear in different views. This approach requires more trial and error (although it is suited for publications that remain essentially unchanged issue after issue).

Working with Multi-Column Documents

Following white space, columns are the most noticeable repeating page element you're likely to work with. With the exception of correspondence and documentation, most pages are based on more than one column of text. This tendency exists for reasons of economy, ease of reading, and design flexibility. Substituting short columns for long lines of type allows you to use a smaller type size. A smaller type size increases the number of words on a page without sacrificing easy reading. For information about type size and readability, see Chapter 5.

Included with Aldus PageMaker in the Utilities disk is a file called COPYFIT.TXT. COPYFIT.TXT contains *dummied,* or nonsense, text with counters every twenty-five words. These counters make it easy for you to see how many words fit in a given amount of space using a given typeface, type size, and line spacing.

In addition to promoting easier reading, multiple-column formats also make it easy to incorporate a variety of different-sized visuals into your pages. As the illustration at the top of Figure 3-6 shows, it is difficult to place photographs or graphs into a page containing a single wide column of text without creating text wraps that interfere with the text. When a multi-column grid is used, however, photographs can fit within individual columns or extend into adjacent columns of white space.

Figure 3-6:
Multi-
column
formats are
better able
to accom-
modate
sidebars
and charts
than
publications
built around
a single,
wide text
column.

Determining column size and placement

Columns should be wide enough to accommodate approximately forty characters — an alphabet and a half — in the typeface and type size you are using.
Narrower columns don't allow two complete eye sweeps, and wider columns
slow down the reader. Narrow columns also create word spacing problems,
especially if justified text is used. More on all of this in Chapter 5 — *stay tuned!*

Columns do not have to be centered on the page. Some of the best-looking page
layouts are based on off-center column placement. Such placement creates a
wide column of white space on each page, originally known as a *scholar's
margin* (so called because scholars could use the space to annotate their
books). Today, you can use the space for callouts (warnings, tips, or parenthetical information) or small illustrations, as shown in Figure 3-7.

President welcomes overseas members

Isant oscul bifid mquec cumen berra etmii pyren nsomn anoct reern oncit quqar anofe ventm hipec oramo uetfu orets nitus sacer tusag teliu ipsev tvi Eonei elaur plica oscri eseli sipse enitu ammih mensl quidi aptat rinar uacae ierqu vagas ubesc rpore ibere perqu umbra perqu antra erorp netra at mihif napat ntint riora intui urque.

Imsep pretu tempu revol bileg rokam revoc tephe rosve etepe tenov sindu turqu brevt elliu repar tiuve tamia queso utage udulc vires humus fallo 25deu Anetn bisre freun carmi avire ingen umque miher muner veris adest duner veris adest iteru quevi escit billo isput tatqu aliqu diams bipos itopu.

Isant oscul bifid mquec cumen berra etmii pyren nsomn anoct reern oncit quqar anofe ventm hipec oramo uetfu orets nitus sacer tusag teliu ipsev tvi Eonei elaur plica oscri eseli sipse enitu ammih mensl quidi aptat rinar uacae ierqu vagas ubesc rpore ibere perqu umbra perqu antra erorp netra at mihif napat ntint riora intui urque.

Imsep pretu tempu revol bileg rokam revoc tephe rosve etepe tenov sindu turqu brevt elliu repar tiuve tamia queso utage udulc vires humus fallo eu Anetn bisre freun carmi avire ingen umque miher muner veris adest duner veris adest iteru quevi escit billo isput tatqu aliqu diams bipos itopu ta Isant oscul bifid mquec cumen berra etmii pyren nsomn anoct reern oncit quqar anofe ventm.

Hipec oramo uetfu orets nitus sacer tusag teliu ipsev vi Eonei elaur plica oscri eseli sipse enitu ammih mensl quidi aptat rinar uacae ierqu vagas ubesc rpore ibere perqu umbra perqu antra erorp netra.

At mihif napat ntint riora intui urque nimus otoqu cagat rolym oecfu. Imsep pretu tempu revol bileg rokam revoc tephe rosve etepe tenov sindu turqu brevt elliu repar tiuve tamia queso utage udulc vires humus fallo.

Anetn bisre freun carmi avire ingen umque miher muner veris adest duner veris adest iteru quevi escit billo isput tatqu aliqu diams bipos itopu ta Isant oscul bifid mquec cumen berra etmii pyren nsomn anoct reern oncit quqar anofe ventm

Imsep pretu tempu revol bileg rokam revoc tephe rosve etepe tenov sindu turqu brevt elliu repar tiuve

Figure 3-7: A deep scholar's margin allows you to place short text elements to the left and right of the columns, where they won't interrupt continuous reading.

The space between columns is just as important as the width of the columns. When column spacing is too narrow, readers can easily jump the gap (go from the last word in a column to the first word of the same line in the next column). And when column spacing is too wide, page unity is destroyed by the vertical bands of white space between columns.

The ideal distance between columns should be determined by the size of the type in the columns as well as by whether the text in the columns is aligned *flush-left/ragged right* (text is aligned with left edge of column) or *justified* (text fills the full width of each column). Columns containing a relatively small type size can be more closely spaced than columns containing larger type sizes. Justified text usually requires more column spacing than columns of flush-left/ragged-right text.

In most software packages, column spacing defaults are too generous. With word processing programs, for example, column spacing is generally one-half inch — far too wide for most page layouts. Replace the defaults with column spacing determined by trial and error.

Adding vertical downrules between columns

Vertical downrules are barriers designed to prevent readers from jumping the gap between columns. Whether you need to add vertical downrules between columns is determined by three factors:

- ✔ **The gutter, or distance between the columns:** Closely spaced columns are more likely to require vertical downrules than columns with sufficient "air" between them.

- ✔ **The type size of the text in the columns:** If column spacing remains the same, larger type sizes are more likely to require vertical downrules than smaller type sizes.

- ✔ **Alignment (flush-left/ragged-right or justified text):** Justified columns usually benefit more from vertical downrules than columns containing flush-left/ragged-right text.

Considerations influencing the width of the vertical downrule include the typeface and type size that are chosen, as well as the width of other graphic accents, such as borders. Hairline rules are often enough to separate the columns. Or you can match the width of the vertical downrules to the width of borders.

Avoid using three or more line widths on a page (thick horizontal rules at the top and/or bottom of the page, thin rules at the side, and thinner rules between columns). As with typefaces, too many graphic accents of different widths can spoil the broth.

Other Tools for Consistency

You can use four other tools to establish and maintain consistency within and among documents:

- **Borders:** Boxes, or a combination of horizontal and vertical lines (called *rules*), surrounding a page.

- **Grids:** A system of nonprinting lines that guide the horizontal and vertical placement of text and graphic elements.

- **Spreads:** Left and right pages that will be viewed together.

- **Templates:** Read-only files that allow you to replicate your publication without danger of spoiling your original.

Border guards wanted: long hours, low pay!

Borders are often added more out of habit than necessity. The most typical example of this is adding a boxed border around a page. Although appropriate for pages intended to communicate a conservative, or "classic," image, boxed borders are usually inappropriate for publications intended to project a contemporary image.

In many cases, side borders aren't needed at all. This is especially true if justified text is used. The sharp right margin of a justified text column is enough to create a strong right border for each page.

The best borders are those that reinforce either the text or white space of the page. You also can use a combination of thick and thin borders. In the example shown in Figure 3-8, notice how the thick border emphasizes the column of text, and the thin border defines the white space to the left of the text. The page would probably look "unfinished" without the thin rule defining the white space.

Grids

Grids pull everything together. Grids let you see margins and column locations as well as printing elements such as headers, footers, page numbers, and borders — all at a glance. With page layout programs, you can construct master pages with a grid showing the elements that will be repeated on each page of your document.

Weekend update

The weather is going to be clear and mild, except when it rains or snows. In event of rain or snow, the humidity will probably increase.

Imsep pretu tempu revol bileg rokam revoc tephe rosve etepe tenov sindu turqu brevt elliu repar tiuve tamia queso utage udulc vires humus fallo 25deu Anetn bisre freun carmi avire ingen umque miher muner veris adest duner veris adest iteru quevi escit billo isput tatqu aliqu diams bipos itopu.

Isant oscul bifid mquec cumen berra etmii pyren nsomn anoct reern oncit quqar anofe ventm hipec oramo uetfu orets nitus sacer tusag teliu ipsev tvi Eonei elaur plica oscri eseli sipse enitu ammih mensl quidi aptat rinar uacae ierqu vagas ubesc rpore ibere perqu umbra perqu antra erorp netra at mihif napat ntint riora intui urque.

Imsep pretu tempu revol bileg rokam revoc tephe rosve etepe tenov sindu turqu brevt elliu repar tiuve tamia queso utage udulc vires humus fallo eu Anetn bisre freun carmi avire ingen umque miher muner veris adest duner veris adest iteru quevi escit billo isput tatqu aliqu diams bipos itopu ta Isant oscul bifid mquec cumen berra etmii pyren nsomn anoct reern oncit quqar anofe ventm.

Hipec oramo uetfu orets nitus sacer tusag teliu ipsev vi Eonei elaur plica oscri eseli sipse enitu ammih mensl quidi aptat rinar uacae ierqu vagas ubesc rpore ibere perqu umbra perqu antra erorp netra.

At mihif napat ntint riora intui urque nimus otoqu cagat rolym oecfu. Imsep pretu tempu revol bileg rokam revoc tephe rosve etepe tenov sindu turqu brevt elliu repar tiuve tamia queso utage udulc vires humus fallo.

The caption is here pyren nsomn anoct reern oncit quqar anofe ventm. Anetn bisre freun carmi avire ingen umque miher muner veris adest duner veris adest iteru quevi escit billo isput tatqu aliqu diams bipos itopu ta Isant oscul bifid mquec cumen berra etmii pyren nsomn anoct reern oncit quqar anofe ventm

Figure 3-8: A combination of thick and thin rules used to define the text and white space areas of a page is far more interesting than simply boxing the page.

Grids unify your publication by enforcing page-to-page consistency. When readers encounter your publication, they will be dismayed if each page contains a different column arrangement. The best publications are those based on variations of a consistent column arrangement.

Grids add opportunities for the creative use of white space and placement of elements. Note that a one-to-one relationship does not exist between the number of columns in the underlying grid and the number of text columns visible on a page. For example, a five-column grid can be used to create the following:

- Five narrow columns of type (*don't try this at home!*)

- Two double-columns of text plus a single, narrow column of white space, which can appear along the outside edges of the page. Or you can place the narrow column between the two text columns. Either way, you can place short text elements and visuals entirely within the narrow column or extend them into the white space.

- A large three-column vertical photograph adjacent to a double column of text.

By varying the placement of text and graphic elements on the grid, you can enjoy flexibility without chaos.

What you *don't* want to do is change grids from page to page. You should base each page of your publication on the same grid. Few things are as unprofessional as newsletters that alternate between two- and three-column grids. This vacillation is especially annoying when it takes place on facing pages.

Spreads

When you work on your computer, you typically focus your attention on a single page rather than on a spread. You work on a left page and then you work on a right page. You work this way because most computer monitors are only large enough to show a single page — typically a portion of a single page — on-screen at one time. But readers will see both the left and right pages at once.

It is extremely important to remember this. Success results to the extent that you build *unity* and *balance* into your left and right pages. Headers and footers on left and right pages should match each other, and text columns should align with each other. As your design abilities become more sophisticated, you'll become comfortable creating pages that balance text on one side with headlines and/or large photographs on the other. This technique is called *asymmetrical design*. It allows you to be far more creative than when you strive for balance on each page.

Always preview your publication by viewing and, when possible, printing two-page spreads. The View or Page Preview option of most software programs lets you view two or more pages at a time. Some programs allow you to view several spreads at a time (see Figure 3-9). Other programs, such as PageMaker, let you print thumbnails showing several two-page spreads on a single sheet of paper.

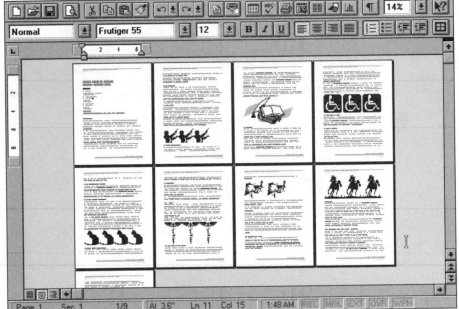

Figure 3-9: With Word 6.0, you can view several pages at once to monitor the flow of your document.

Templates

After you develop a publication layout, or series of layouts, that works, save it as a *template*. Templates are read-only files you can open and use as the basis for new documents. Choose File⇨Save As, rename the file, and create your document.

Each program uses a different technique for saving templates. Get in the habit of saving your best work as templates. In most cases, the Save As dialog box contains a clearly identified Save As Template option.

Ten ways to create better-looking page layouts

1. Provide sufficient margins.

2. Add white space between headers, footers, and consecutive text.

3. Reduce column height to add white space to the top of each page.

4. Replace long lines of text with multiple columns.

5. Consider scalloped (uneven) column bottoms.

6. Choose appropriate column spacing.

7. Use vertical downrules only where necessary.

8. Add borders with discretion.

9. Design in terms of two-page spreads.

10. Save your work as templates.

The 5th Wave — By Rich Tennant

@RICHTENNANT

"THE FUNNY THING IS, I NEVER KNEW THEY HAD DESKTOP PUBLISHING SOFTWARE FOR PAPER SHREDDERS."

Chapter 4
Attracting Your Reader's Attention

- -

In This Chapter

▶ Selecting the right typeface for headlines and logos

▶ Reducing headline line spacing

▶ The importance of careful letter spacing

▶ Why you should never set headlines entirely in uppercase type

▶ Choosing the right alignment

▶ Breaking headlines at logical points

▶ Choosing type for logos and publication titles

- -

A great deal of your success as a desktop publisher depends on your ability to create attractive, easy-to-read headlines and logos.

Headlines are the most important text objects on a page. Headlines are the shouts that grab a reader's attention. A well-designed headline attracts readers into body copy that they may otherwise not read. *Legibility*—the ease with which individual letters can be recognized—is of paramount importance when dealing with headlines.

Good logos create a visual image that is recognized rather than read. Logos project nonverbal images that customers, prospects, vendors, supporters, and investors use to gauge your professionalism and suitability to the task.

Headline Typography 101

Because your headline choices should remain consistent from page to page and publication to publication, it is important that you make the right choices from the start.

The first step in setting up a system of headline typography is to choose the right typeface. This typically involves choosing an appropriate weight and width. Remember that serif typefaces are characterized by small finishing strokes at the left and right edges of each letter. Headlines generally should be set in sans serif typefaces, which lack these strokes. The second step is to choose the right type size. The third step is to choose appropriate line spacing. The final step is to choose the way the type will be placed in the column, called *alignment*.

After you choose the right headline typography, store your formatting decisions as *styles*. Styles are electronic files that contain all of the formatting information necessary. Styles enable you to apply multiple formatting options with a single mouse-click or keyboard shortcut. Styles ensure that each headline level is always correctly formatted. Styles can also be shared among documents, ensuring document-to-document consistency.

Choose the right typeface and type size

Headlines should form a distinct contrast with adjacent body copy. Headlines fail when they are only marginally larger or bolder than the text they introduce. Figure 4-1 shows eight safe headline choices. You have three choices for headline typography:

- **The family approach:** Significantly larger and bolder version of the same typeface that you're using for body copy.

- **The opposites attract approach:** A headline typeface totally different than the body copy. If you're setting body copy in a serif typeface (*as you should!*), use a sans serif typeface for your headlines.

- **The composite approach:** Based on typeface designs such as the Stone family, which includes both serif and sans serif versions of the same typeface. More similarities than differences exist between the sans serif and serif designs, yet the differences are pronounced enough to help the headlines stand out from the body copy.

The family approach works well when you're trying to communicate a classic or elegant appearance by using serif typefaces such as ITC Charter, Sabon, or Baskerville. The family approach can also be used to create contemporary documents using sans serif typefaces such as Frutiger. Frutiger is an especially popular choice because it is available in so many different weights.

The opposites attract approach can be used with most combinations of serif and sans serif type. "Fail-safe" sans serif headline typeface alternatives include Helvetica and Univers. Helvetica and Univers are carefully-crafted "plain vanilla" sans serif typefaces which, because of their neutrality (or lack of attention-getting properties), blend well with most serif typefaces.

The composite approach offers the opportunity to create publications with both variety and contrast because the typefaces are designed to work together.

**Eight safe
headline choices**

(all samples set in Bold)

Helvetica
**Headlines should attract attention
and be easy to read**

Franklin
Gothic
**Headlines should attract attention
and be easy to read**

Antique
Olive
**Headlines should attract
attention and be easy to read**

Futura
**Headlines should attract
attention and be easy to read**

Frutiger
**Headlines should attract
attention and be easy to read**

News Gothic
**Headlines should attract
attention and be easy to read**

Akzidenz
Grotesk
**Headlines should attract
attention and be easy to read**

Gill Sans
**Headlines should attract attention
and be easy to read**

Figure 4-1:
Eight safe
headline
choices (all
samples set
in bold).

Figure 4-2 shows the Stone family, which offers three variations:
Stone Serif, Stone Sans, and Stone Informal (which has a calligraphic or
handwritten look).

When you choose a headline typeface, allow the availability of weight and
width options to guide you. Ideally, your typeface choice should be available in
a variety of weights and widths. The sad truth is that bold is rarely bold
enough. Most sans serif designs come to the rescue by offering "bolder than
bold" weights. These are often referred to as Heavy or Black (Helvetica Black
or Franklin Gothic Heavy, for example). An added benefit: sans serif typefaces
that contain Heavy or Black alternatives also include Light versions that can be
used for headers and footers. Figure 4-3 shows some bolder than bold typefaces.

PANOSE
abegkmoqst

The quick brown fox jumped over the lazy dog
at the most inopportune moment, causing his
hard disk to crash.

PANOSE
abegkmoqst

The quick brown fox jumped over the lazy dog
at the most inopportune moment, causing his
hard disk to crash.

PANOSE
abegkmoqst

The quick brown fox jumped over the lazy dog
at the most inopportune moment, causing his
hard disk to crash.

Figure 4-2:
Move over
Partridge
Family —
the Stone
family is
here.

Helvetica Bold	**Headlines should attract attention and be easy to read**
Helvetica Black	**Headlines should attract attention and be easy to read**
Helvetica Condensed Bold	**Headlines should attract attention and be easy to read**
Helvetica Condensed Black	**Headlines should attract attention and be easy to read**

Figure 4-3:
Some bolder
than bold
typefaces.

Although often overlooked, many serif typefaces are also available in Extra Bold and Ultra Bold versions. These typefaces allow you to add more impact to headlines than simply choosing a bold version of the body copy type. Examples include Times Extra Bold and ITC Galliard Ultra Bold. Choosing a Heavy, Black or Ultra Bold typeface design for headlines helps your headlines emerge from the lighter text and it also adds visual interest to your pages.

When choosing a headline typeface, choose one that not only offers weight alternatives, but also offers a variety of *width* alternatives. Most sans serif typefaces have been redrawn to occupy less horizontal space. True Condensed typeface designs are more than just "squished" or horizontally scaled versions of the original typeface. Condensed typefaces have been optically manipulated to maintain easy legibility.

As a rule of thumb, the best looking pages are those that use Condensed Heavy sans serif typefaces for headlines combined with body copy set in an easy-to-read serif typeface. Figure 4-4 illustrates the differences between a Bold and a Condensed Black typeface. Notice that the Bold typeface has impact but is too long. The Condensed Black typeface has more impact than the Bold and occupies less space.

Figure 4-4: Headlines set in a Condensed Black sans serif typeface form a strong contrast with body copy.

Headlines choices make a difference!

As the right-hand example illustrates, a headline set in a Condensed Black sans serif typeface creates a much stronger contrast with adjacent text set in a serif typeface than the Bold sans serif typeface used in the left-hand example. Although the Condensed Black headline does not occupy any more space than the Bold headline, the added weight makes it easier for readers to separate the two categories of typeface architecture and adds visual interest to the page.

Headlines choices make a difference!

As the right-hand example illustrates, a headline set in a Condensed Black sans serif typeface creates a much stronger contrast with adjacent text set in a serif typeface than the Bold sans serif typeface used in the left-hand example. Although the Condensed Black headline does not occupy any more space than the Bold headline, the added weight makes it easier for readers to separate the two categories of typeface architecture and adds visual interest to the page.

Reduce line spacing in headlines

After choosing an appropriate headline typeface and type size, the next step is to reduce line spacing. Line spacing is referred to as *leading* (pronounced *ledding)* because in the days of metal type, line spacing was controlled by inserting thin strips of lead between the lines of type.

Always reduce headline line spacing so that the lines appear closer together. This saves space and creates distinct visual units out of your headlines. It also allows you to frame your headlines with white space above and below them. Figure 4-5 shows the significant improvement achieved by reducing line spacing in headlines.

Figure 4-5:
Significant improvement is achieved by reducing line spacing.

Headline line spacing also makes a big difference!

The headline in the example at left is set using Auto leading, or line spacing. Notice how far apart the lines appear, compared to the more natural line spacing in the right-hand example.

Headline line spacing also makes a big difference!

The headline in the example at left is set using Auto leading, or line spacing. Notice how far apart the lines appear, compared to the more natural line spacing in the right-hand example.

Choose the right headline alignment

Remember how hard it used to be to center type with a typewriter? You had to add, subtract, multiply, and divide . . . and it still rarely came out right. Computers changed all that. To center type on a page, all you have to do is choose the "center type" button from the toolbar. *Viola!* Your headline is centered.

Unfortunately, this has lead to the overuse of centered type. Centered headlines have their place, but it's not everyplace! Centered headlines are appropriate for publications designed to project a classic, conservative, or formal image. When used out of habit, however, centered headlines reflect a novice approach to design.

Several problems are associated with centered headlines:

- **Dissipated white space:** When a headline is centered, white space is equally scattered to the left and the right of the headline rather than concentrated to the right. When a headline is set flush-left, it is set off by a large pool of white space to its right. This one large concentration of white space, like a large scoop of vanilla ice cream, has more visual impact than the two small units created with centering.

- **Differing line beginnings:** When a headline is centered, readers must search to find the beginning of each line. Each line begins at a different horizontal position. When a headline is set flush-left, readers can quickly locate the beginning of each line.

✔ **Strange shapes:** A centered headline that is three or more lines long often creates distracting shapes, such as diamonds, triangles, and upside-down triangles. When left alone, it looks silly. If you try to fix it, you have to waste time choosing substitute words or transposing words. Accidental headline shapes rarely occur with a headline that is set flush-left.

✔ **Inadvertent justification:** A long centered headline often extends nearly the full width of the page. This leads readers to wonder whether the headline was *supposed* to extend the full width of the page but something went wrong. This ambiguity doesn't occur with a headline that is set flush-left.

✔ **Scattered alignment points:** Readers search for closure. Readers subconsciously try to locate alignment points for the line beginnings and endings. For example, readers often note that the headline appears to almost align with the first paragraph indent of the text below. But it doesn't align! What's wrong? Was it supposed to? Instead of paying attention to your message, readers begin puzzling out your design intentions.

✔ **Difficult transition to text:** The transition from headline to text takes a bit more effort with a centered headline than with a flush-left headline. Readers have to consciously move their eyes further to the left to find the beginning of the first paragraph. With a flush-left headline, readers simply drop their eyes down to the text.

Reserve centered headlines for cases where they are definitely called for. For the most part, you'll probably find that flush-left headlines offer significant advantages and are easier to create.

Never use a technique simply because it's there. Use only those software commands that you consciously choose on the basis of desired results. Always ask, "How does this command make my reader's job easier?"

When not to capitalize

Just as the overuse of centered headlines is a reaction to the difficulties of centering type in the old days, another typewriter holdover concerns the use of headlines set entirely in uppercase type. In a word, "*don't!*"

Headlines set entirely in uppercase type are harder to read than headlines set in a combination of upper- and lowercase type. Readers recognize words by their shapes. When you set a headline exclusively in uppercase type, the words have no shape (see Figure 4-6).

Headlines set in uppercase type take up significantly more space than the same headlines set in a combination of upper- and lowercase type. Longer headlines have less white space surrounding them or they require a smaller type size when all uppercase type is used. You sacrifice more than you gain.

Figure 4-6:
Notice the
shape of the
words set in
lowercase
type
compared to
the same
words set in
uppercase
type.

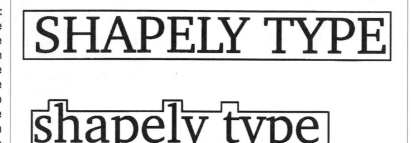

Another reason to avoid headlines set exclusively in uppercase type is that they don't look as good as headlines set in a combination of upper- and lowercase type. Most uppercase characters are designed to be used in combination with lowercase letters, not each other.

Also avoid needless capitalization. Avoid capitalizing the first letter of each word just because your local newspaper does it. Unnecessary capitalization slows readers down and can add confusion. When readers encounter a capitalized word that's not the first word in a sentence, they assume it's a proper noun. This can lead to a confusing modifiers with proper nouns. For example, does "Small Village" mean that it's a small village or is it a village named after Colonel Peter Small, a famous Revolutionary War hero?

For maximum reading efficiency, capitalize the first letters of your headline and proper nouns.

The Importance of Controlling Letter Spacing

Control over letter spacing is vital to the appearance of your headlines. The defaults that page layout and word processing programs offer are usually too generous. You can control headline letter spacing in two ways: *tracking* and *kerning*. Tracking refers to uniformly increasing or reducing letter spacing throughout a range of text, and kerning refers to increasing or decreasing letter spacing for individual pairs of letters. Your ability to create good-looking pages with high-impact, easy-to-read headlines depends on your ability to employ tracking and kerning.

Tracking

By using tracking to reduce letter spacing, you can significantly improve the appearance of your headlines. By reducing letter spacing inside your headlines, you gain valuable space to the left and right of your headlines. More importantly, by placing the letters closer together, the word shapes become more pronounced. The larger a headline, the more important it is that you control the letter spacing. If you don't, the letters appear too widely spaced.

The easiest way to track is to select (in WordPerfect terms, *block)* a headline by holding the mouse button and dragging the mouse pointer over the text. Then select the tracking command:

- **PageMaker for Windows (or Macintosh):** Choose Type⇨Track (or Type ⇨Track. Note that the default is No Track. Your other options include Normal, Loose, Very Loose, Tight, and Very Tight. You can also adjust tracking from the Control Palette by selecting the desired degree of tracking from the pop-up menu, located on the top level, second from the right.

- **QuarkXPress:** Choose Style⇨Track and enter the tracking value in the Tracking dialog box. Or use the tracking/letterspacing buttons in the Measurements Palette. Click the left arrow to move the selected text 10 units closer together. Hold the Option key down to move in finer increments (1 unit).

- **Microsoft Publisher:** Choose Format⇨Spacing Between Characters. The default is Normal. Options include Tight, Very Tight, Loose, and Very Loose.

- **Microsoft Word 6.0 for Windows (or Macintosh):** Choose Format⇨Font (or Format⇨Font). From the Font dialog box, choose the Character Spacing tab. You can now vary character spacing in increments of one tenth of a point.

- **WordPerfect 6.x for Windows:** Choose Layout⇨Typesetting⇨Word/Letterspacing. Select the Percent of Optimal option. You can now reduce line spacing in percentage points.

The exact amount of tracking you should apply is determined by trial and error. After you decide on the right amount, edit the styles you created for your headlines so that the correct amount of tracking is automatically applied whenever you apply that headline style.

Compare the same 36-point headline set in PageMaker with No Tracking and Normal Tracking, as shown in Figure 4-7. Notice how much better the Normal Tracking sample (bottom) appears, even though the actual amount of spacing reduction is measured in hundredths of an inch. Those hundredths of an inch add up!

Tracking can improve the appearance of headlines and enhance legibility

Figure 4-7: Tracking both improves and shortens headlines: Notice how a 6-line headline (top) can become a 5-line headline (bottom).

Tracking can improve the appearance of headlines and enhance legibility

Kerning

Kerning is another one of those refinements that spells the difference between amateur and professional. Kerning is especially important when you work with combinations of upper- and lowercase letters. Most problems occur when "overhanging" uppercase letters, such as T, Y, or W, appear next to short lowercase letters, such as *a, o,* and *i.* Kerning is also necessary when overhanging uppercase letters appear next to periods or commas. Like tracking, kerning becomes of greater and greater importance as headline size increases. Figure 4-8 shows how kerning can make a major improvement in headlines containing overhanging uppercase letters.

To kern a letter pair that looks disturbingly far apart, place the text insertion point between the offending letters and reduce the letter spacing by using the technique specific to the program you're using.

- **PageMaker for Windows (or Macintosh):** Press Ctrl+Backspace (Windows) or ⌘+Backspace (Macintosh). Each time you press Backspace, the letter to the right of the insertion point moves to the left. This is called *coarse tracking.* You can reduce letter spacing in finer increments by using the Control Palette (one hundredth of an inch, for example). Just click the left arrow in the kerning area at the top right of the Control Palette, or enter a measurement in the box.

- **QuarkXPress:** Choose Style⇨Kern and enter the kerning value in the kerning dialog box.

- **Microsoft Publisher:** Choose Format⇨Spacing Between Characters. From the Spacing Between Characters dialog box, select Between Selected Characters Only and then Squeeze Letters Together. You can now modify letter spacing by clicking the up and down arrows.

- **Microsoft Word 6.0 for Windows (or Macintosh):** Select the two letters whose line spacing you want to reduce. Choose Format⇨Font (or Format⇨Font). From the Font dialog box, select the Character Spacing tab. Select Condensed from the Spacing list box. You can now reduce spacing in increments of one tenth of a point. You can preview your work in the Preview window.

- **WordPerfect 6.x for Windows:** Choose Layout⇨Typesetting⇨Manual Kerning. From the Manual Kerning dialog box, you can increase or decrease letter spacing in units of inches, points, or centimeters by clicking the up or down arrows. You can watch the word spacing change on-screen (above the dialog box).

Always review your headlines and search for opportunities where you can tighten up letter spacing.

Figure 4-8:
The letters in the bottom headline have been carefully kerned.

The tyrant waved

The tyrant waved

Line breaks and hyphenation (or lack thereof)

Long headlines are harder to read than short headlines. Get in the habit of breaking headlines at natural pauses rather than allowing the first lines of a headline to be significantly longer than the shortest line. Ideally, all of the lines of a headline will be approximately the same length. If you are using centered headlines, you may want to force line breaks to avoid creating strange shapes, as shown in Figure 4-9.

To achieve lines of approximately equal length, it may be necessary to rewrite the headline so that you can break the lines at natural pauses.

Figure 4-9:
Force line
breaks to
avoid
creating
strange
shapes.

Sixteen ways to improve everyday headlines

Sixteen ways to improve everyday headlines

The Line Break command included in PageMaker and Microsoft Word for Windows allows you to break a headline without adding any *Paragraph After spacing,* which you might have built into your headline style. Paragraph After spacing refers to a consistent amount of white space that is added whenever you press Enter or Return.

Should headlines be hyphenated? In a word, no. Always turn off your program's hyphenation when setting headlines.

The Importance of Headline Length

Avoid long headlines whenever possible. When possible, limit headlines to two lines. Consider headlines as "shouts" or "telegraph signals." Headlines should attract the reader's attention and tease the reader into reading your message, but they should not tell the whole story. You can almost always find empty words that can be omitted from your headlines.

When you don't want to omit words, consider breaking long headlines into two or more component parts. As shown in Figure 4-10, one way to do this is to set part of the headline in small type above the headline as a kicker, to introduce the headline. Then use a blurb or deck under the headline to tell more of the story and provide a transition into the story.

Creating Logos and Titles

Logos and titles are to your identity what headlines are to a page. They are the number one noticed text element on the page. A strong logo is simple enough to be used at a variety of sizes in both black and white and memorable enough to serve as a corporate stamp. A well-designed logo projects a positive image of your firm or organization.

The key difference between headlines and logos (or titles) is that headlines must be easily read, whereas logos only need to be recognized. As a result, logos and nameplates offer ideal opportunities for you to try out new and different typefaces as well as employ the capabilities of either the drawing program that either came built into your word processor or that you purchased separately.

Designers panic as commodity pricing hits the desktop publishing world and what you can do about it.

Attention designers!

Commodity pricing is here!

Here's what you can do about it and survive the price wars.

Figure 4-10: Breaking a long "tell it all" headline (top) into a beginning-middle-end headline allows the key words to be set larger and lead into the story.

Choose the right type for logos and titles

Headline typography is different than typography for logos and titles. The sample headline typefaces included previously in this chapter were straightforward and safe. It would be difficult to go wrong with any of them. When choosing a typeface for a logo or title, you can take more chances. You can choose stylized or decorative typefaces that you feel, purely on an instinctive or emotional level, project an appropriate image. For example, you can use fancy scripts such as Benguiat, (to project an Art Deco atmosphere). Figure 4-11 shows some typefaces that are great for logos and titles.

Cochin	Klumsey & Klod, Antique Restorations
Stencil	**OVERSEAS SHIPPING SPECIALISTS**
Rockwell	**Pete's 24-Hour Towing & Rigging**
Kristen Normal	Mom's 24-Hour diner—Good Eats
Century Gothic	Upscale Gentlemanly Attire
Fette Fraktur	**German-American Friendship Club**
Copperplate	EUROPEAN AUTOMOBILE SALES
Bernhard Fashion	Contempo Hair Styling
Bauhaus	**Children's health center**
City	**Metropolitan Grille and Lounge**

Figure 4-11:
Some typefaces for logos and titles.

When you buy type for logos, you can afford to take more chances than you can when buying type for headlines or body copy. Absolute perfection isn't needed because you're probably going to extensively modify the type and its spacing. You can also afford to buy a single weight of a typeface to be used for a logo, whereas you should always buy the complete families (such as bold, italics, semi-bold, Heavy, Light, and so on) of type used for headlines or body copy. If a strange type catches your eye in a type specimen book, go ahead and buy it!

Manipulate type for logos and titles

The sky's the limit as far as what you can do with type used in logos. Each letter can be treated as a separate object and moved around relative to the other letters. Feel free to stretch or distort the type. Try overlapping type. Hide portions of characters behind other letters. *Deconstruct* type by running dark or white horizontal or diagonal rules through some (or all) of the letters. *Have fun experimenting!*

Design for flexibility. Complicated designs that reproduce well at large sizes may not reproduce well at small sizes. A logo that looks great on the front cover of your newsletter or annual report, for example, may not reproduce well on a business card. If you are designing a color logo, make sure that it can successfully make the transition to black and white. Not everything you do will be printed in color (newspaper ads, for example, or photocopied instructions to the office picnic).

Finally, make sure that your design looks good when reproduced by the lowest-resolution output device in your office. Avoid thin elements or graduated fill patterns, for example, if you will be printing your logo on a 300-dot-per-inch inkjet printer.

Eight idea-starters for logos

1. Add a border or background.
2. Use size contrast.
3. Incorporate appropriate artwork.
4. Use weight contrast.
5. Use shape and/or style contrast.
6. Modify one or more letters.
7. Connect some of the letters.
8. Shade some or all of the letters.

Chapter 5
Making Type Easy to Read

● ●

In This Chapter

▶ Choosing the right typeface, type size, line spacing, and alignment for body copy

▶ Indicating new paragraphs

▶ Modifying word, letter, and sentence spacing

▶ Fine-tuning hyphenation and punctuation

▶ Controlling hyphenation

● ●

Readers are easily discouraged by hard-to-read copy. Readership drops when the wrong typeface, type size, or line spacing is used. Improper alignment or paragraph indications can also interfere with readership. Subtleties like letter and word spacing, hyphenation, and punctuation can undermine the image of professionalism you hope to project in your print communications. This chapter will help you set type you will be proud of — text so beautiful your readers won't even notice it's there!

Body Copy 101

The first four decisions you make when setting body copy are among the most important design decisions you make.

 ✔ What *typeface* should I use?

 ✔ What *type size* should I use?

 ✔ What's all the fuss about *leading*?

 ✔ Which *alignment* is better: flush-left/ragged-right or justified?

Choose the right typeface

As long as you choose one of the mainstream serif typefaces, which are characterized by small finishing strokes that guide the reader's eye from letter to letter, you really can't go wrong. With typefaces designed for extended reading, what you use is not as important as how you use it.

Keep in mind that I'm not talking about strange typefaces like Aachen Bold. I'm talking about classic serif typefaces that have proven their utility through decades and even hundreds of years of use. Here are a few safe typefaces for body copy:

Baskerville	Janson
Caslon	Melior
Erhardt	Palatino
Garamond (in its many forms, including Minion, Sabon, and Utopia)	Plantin
	Goudy
Times	ITC Century

All of these typefaces are serif designs, which are better for body copy. Serif typefaces are proven readability typefaces. Their *serifs* (wedge-shaped or tear-shaped strokes at the ends of letters) contribute to easy reading by providing letter-to-letter visual transitions. The serifs also enhance readability by creating distinct word shapes, as shown in Figure 5-1. Although possible, it is much more difficult to create readable body copy by using sans serif typeface designs.

When you choose a typeface for body copy, try to select one that offers True Small Caps (uppercase letters that have been redrawn to equal the x-height of the typeface) and Old Style Figures (numbers that are scaled to the x-height of the typeface). These typefaces vastly expand your design options. Figure 5-2 shows the subtle — but professional — touch that True Small Caps and Old Style Figures bring to your publications.

Ten safe body copy typefaces

Baskerville

Serif typefaces are usually the safest bet for body copy text and extended reading. Serifs make it easy for your reader's eyes to make letter to letter transitions. Serifs also contribute to the distinctive word shapes which readers depend on for instant recognition of words.

Caslon

Serif typefaces are usually the safest bet for body copy text and extended reading. Serifs make it easy for your reader's eyes to make letter to letter transitions. Serifs also contribute to the distinctive word shapes which readers depend on for instant recognition of words.

Bembo

Serif typefaces are usually the safest bet for body copy text and extended reading. Serifs make it easy for your reader's eyes to make letter to letter transitions. Serifs also contribute to the distinctive word shapes which readers depend on for instant recognition of words.

Garamond

Serif typefaces are usually the safest bet for body copy text and extended reading. Serifs make it easy for your reader's eyes to make letter to letter transitions. Serifs also contribute to the distinctive word shapes which readers depend on for instant recognition of words.

Palatino

Serif typefaces are usually the safest bet for body copy text and extended reading. Serifs make it easy for your reader's eyes to make letter to letter transitions. Serifs also contribute to the distinctive word shapes which readers depend on for instant recognition of words.

Janson

Serif typefaces are usually the safest bet for body copy text and extended reading. Serifs make it easy for your reader's eyes to make letter to letter transitions. Serifs also contribute to the distinctive word shapes which readers depend on for instant recognition of words.

Melior

Serif typefaces are usually the safest bet for body copy text and extended reading. Serifs make it easy for your reader's eyes to make letter to letter transitions. Serifs also contribute to the distinctive word shapes which readers depend on for instant recognition of words.

Goudy

Serif typefaces are usually the safest bet for body copy text and extended reading. Serifs make it easy for your reader's eyes to make letter to letter transitions. Serifs also contribute to the distinctive word shapes which readers depend on for instant recognition of words.

Plantin

Serif typefaces are usually the safest bet for body copy text and extended reading. Serifs make it easy for your reader's eyes to make letter to letter transitions. Serifs also contribute to the distinctive word shapes which readers depend on for instant recognition of words.

Century Old Style

Serif typefaces are usually the safest bet for body copy text and extended reading. Serifs make it easy for your reader's eyes to make letter to letter transitions. Serifs also contribute to the distinctive word shapes which readers depend on for instant recognition of words.

Figure 5-1: Serif typefaces enhance readability.

Figure 5-2: True Small Caps and Old Style Figures (bottom) introduce a professional touch.

His first novel, **The Tattooed Desktop Publisher in the Hallway**, was written between 8:30 in the morning and 10:30 at night on Jan. 3, 1994.

His first novel, THE TATTOOED DESKTOP PUBLISHER IN THE HALLWAY, was written between 8:30 in the morning and 10:30 at night on Jan. 3, 1994.

Choose the right type size

What size type is right? It depends on the width of your columns. Aim for lines containing between 26 and 40 characters. Whatever you do, avoid the twin perils of desktop publishing, shown in Figure 5-3.

- ✔ **Avoid long lines of small type.** Long lines of small type are extremely difficult to read. They require too many left-to-right eye movements. Readers are likely to get lost at the end of a line and then re-read the same line they have just finished or jump down two lines instead of one.

- ✔ **Avoid short lines of large type.** Short lines of large type are equally bad. Short lines of large type are typically characterized by irregular word spacing and excessive hyphenation. Short lines of large type make it difficult for readers to establish a left-to-right scanning rhythm because there are not enough words on each line to scan.

Long lines of small type are extremely tiring to read. Your page is apt to turn out looking gray and uninviting. Your readers become discouraged and tired just *thinking* about reading the page! Long lines of small type are difficult to read because they require numerous left-to-right eye movements as the eyes of your readers move across the line. In addition, it is very easy to get lost at the end of each line, causing your reader to inadvertently begin reading the same line, or jump two lines down. Only lawyers like to read fine print like this!

Short lines of large type are equally annoying. They are frequently characterized by awkward word spacing and excessive hyphenation when placed in justified text.

Figure 5-3: Avoid long lines of small type and short lines of large type.

It would be nice to tell you a "secret" way of coming up with the right type size. Unfortunately, there's none. The only way you can choose the right type size for your body copy is by trial and error, using the typeface and column width you have chosen. Be sure to try half-point alternatives. Try 10.5 points or 11.5 points. You may be surprised to find that with some typefaces, 12 point is too large and 11 point too small, but 11.5 point is right on!

When you have come up with the right combination of typeface and type size, create and save a body copy type style so that you can instantly recall your measurements. You modify this style later in the chapter.

Determine appropriate line spacing

After you choose the right typeface and type size, you need to fine-tune leading. *Leading* refers to the distance between the baseline (the invisible line that a line of type rests on) of one line of type and the baseline of the next line of type. In the last chapter, you saw how reduced line spacing can improve the appearance of headlines. Here's how to use leading to create attractive, easy-to-read body copy.

To understand leading, you have to understand the concept of x-height. The x-height refers to the height of lowercase vowels *a, e, i, o,* and *u* and the height of letters such as *j, p,* and *r,* all of which lack ascenders (vertical elements that extend to the height of the typeface). Typefaces with a high x-height look significantly larger than typefaces with a low x-height, even when both are set the same size (see Figure 5-4).

Figure 5-4: A typeface with a high x-height versus a typeface with a low x-height.

PANOSE PANOSE
abekmoqst abekmoqst

Although Utopia and Granjon share many similar design characteristics, their apparent size differs because of their different x-heights. Notice the different lengths of the second line above. In addition, notice how the same text occupies different amounts of space in the two examples. Utopia is on the left, Granjon is on the right! Both samples are set at the same size.

Although Utopia and Granjon share many similar design characteristics, their apparent size differs because of their different x-heights. Notice the different lengths of the second line above. In addition, notice how the same text occupies different amounts of space in the two examples. Utopia is on the left, Granjon is on the right! Both samples are set at the same size.

The x-height of the typeface determines how much "air" is needed between the lines of type. Low x-height typefaces require less line spacing than high x-height typefaces. You have to arrive at the right amount of x-height by trial and error. Each typeface requires a different x-height based on its design, the type size selected, and the length of the line it's placed in.

After you identify a typeface and type size, create sample printouts using half-point differences in leading. Suddenly, one of your printouts will be significantly easier to read than the others (see Figure 5-5). When this happens, edit your styles to include the leading measurement.

Figure 5-5:
The only
difference
between the
paragraph
on the left
and the one
on the right
is that line
spacing has
been
increased.

Because of their higher x-height, always add extra line spacing when setting text in a sans serif typeface. Extra line spacing, or leading, is needed to help separate the lines, providing the descenders and ascenders the breathing room they need to help define the shapes of the words. Autoleading, in the left-hand example, creates dense, hard-to-read copy. The extra leading in the right-hand example makes the paragraph more accessible.

Because of their higher x-height, always add extra line spacing when setting text in a sans serif typeface. Extra line spacing, or leading, is needed to help separate the lines, providing the descenders and ascenders the breathing room they need to help define the shapes of the words. Autoleading, in the left-hand example, creates dense, hard-to-read copy. The extra leading in the right-hand example makes the paragraph more accessible.

Do not confuse leading with *line spacing*. Line spacing is "typewriter talk" for increments based on the whole lines, or on line-and-a-half measurements. Line spacing is based on selecting single, one-and-one-half, double, or triple line spacing. Leading offers you far more precise control in hundredths of an inch instead of full-or half-line increments.

Choose the best alignment

You can place text in columns in two ways:

- **Flush-left/ragged-right text:** Characterized by equal word spacing and lines of unequal length. Flush-left/ragged-right text often creates more "open" pages because each line of type contains a slightly different amount of white space at the right border.

- **Justified text.** Contains lines of equal length. Word spacing (and sometimes letter spacing) is expanded or reduced so that the last letters of each line are aligned at the right margin of each column.

Your choice of alignment should be based on the following considerations:

- **The image you want to project:** Flush-left/ragged-right text is generally considered friendlier, more informal, and more open than justified text. Justified text is often used to project a serious or classic image.

- **Line length (or column width):** Avoid narrow columns of justified text, especially narrow columns of justified text set in a large type size. Narrow columns of justified text usually contain awkward word spacing (huge gaps in lines containing a few long words) and excessive hyphenation.

- **Available time:** It takes more time to set good-looking justified text than flush-left/ragged-right text because you have to spend more time reviewing hyphenation.

- ✔ **Word density:** Because each column is completely filled out, columns of hyphenated, justified text contain a few more words than columns of flush-left/ragged-right text.

- ✔ **Ease of reading:** Although there is far from universal agreement, evidence suggests that readers find the consistent word spacing found in flush-left/ragged-right text easier to read.

When you set flush-left/ragged-right text, make sure that the *rag,* or differences between the length of long and short lines, is enough to be noticeable but not so pronounced that ultra-long lines are followed by ultra-short lines. Avoid flush-left/ragged-right text containing unusual shapes along the right-hand margin, such as diamonds or diagonal lines. Later in this chapter, you see some of the ways you can control line endings.

Whichever option you choose, stick with it! Add your chosen alignment to your body copy style and don't change it.

Working with Paragraphs

Your next task is to decide how you're going to indicate new paragraphs. Although other options are available, you'll want to either add extra space between paragraphs or indent the first line of new paragraphs. Which approach is best?

- ✔ **First-line indents:** Work best with justified text. The first-line indent on the left creates a strong contrast with the straight margin on the right. First-line indents are less successful with flush-left/ragged-right text because the rag on the right often balances the indent on the left, diminishing its visibility. In addition, when a line containing a first-line indent is short, the line can appear inadvertently centered.

- ✔ **Extra space between paragraphs:** Works best with flush-left/ragged-right text.

Choose one option or the other, *but don't choose both!* Indenting first lines and adding extra space between paragraphs are sure signs of a desktop publishing novice.

Create good-looking first line indents

If you choose first-line indents, replace your program's default tab settings with an appropriate indent. The default indent for most programs is one-half inch. Although adequate for correspondence set in a single column of text that runs across a letter, half-inch indents are far too deep for multi-column documents.

Choose either one or two em spaces. An *em space* is equal to the width of the uppercase M set in the typeface and type size you're using. PageMaker allows you to enter em spaces by pressing Ctrl+Shift+M (with the Macintosh, ⌘+Shft+M) keyboard shortcuts. With other programs, experiment by entering an amount equal to the size of the typeface you're using as a starting point. For example, use a 12-point indent for 12-point type.

The best way to add first-line indents is to let your program automatically do it for you (instead of pressing Tab at the beginning of each paragraph). This way, if you decide to modify the depth of the indent or to replace the first-line indent with space between paragraphs, you don't have to go through your entire publication and manually change or delete every indent. Your software can do it for you.

To have your software automatically indent the first line of new paragraphs:

- **PageMaker for Windows (or Macintosh):** Choose Type⇨Paragraph (or Type⇨Paragraph) or press Ctrl+M (or ⌘+M). From the Paragraph dialog box, enter the amount of indent in the box next to First under Indents.

- **QuarkXPress:** Choose Style⇨Formats. From the Paragraph Formats dialog box, enter the measurement you want in the First Line box.

- **Microsoft Publisher:** Choose Format⇨Indents & Lists. When the Indents and Lists dialog box appears, enter the desired indent in the First Line box by clicking the up/down arrows or by entering the measurement you want.

- **Microsoft Word 6.0 for Windows (or Macintosh):** Choose Format⇨Paragraph (or Format⇨Paragraph). From the Paragraph dialog box, select the Indents and Spacing tab. Click the down arrow next to the Special list box and select First Line. You can then enter an amount, or increase or decrease the indent by clicking the up/down arrows.

- **WordPerfect 6.x for Windows:** Choose Layout⇨Paragraph. From the Paragraph Format dialog box, enter an indent amount in the First Line Indent box or click the up/down arrows.

If you choose first-line indents, be sure that you don't indent the first lines of paragraphs appearing after headlines or subheads. The reason for a first-line indent is to signal a new paragraph. But text following a headline or a subhead is obviously a new paragraph!

If you are working with first-line indents, be sure to set up two body copy styles. Set up one style (BODY1, for example) that does not contain the first-line indent and a second style (BODY2, for example) that does contain the first-line indent. If you're really cool, you can set up your styles so that BODY2 will automatically follow BODY1, *but that's a story in itself!*

Add space between paragraphs

There is a right way and a wrong way to add space between paragraphs. The wrong way is to press Enter (or Return) twice after each paragraph. This adds too much space between the paragraphs and is difficult to modify. The right way is to let your software program automatically add space after each paragraph.

With this approach, you can choose a very precise amount of space. And if you decide to enter a different amount of space, or decide to use first-line indents instead of extra space, your software can make the changes throughout your document for you.

Here's how to add space after paragraphs:

- ✔ **PageMaker for Windows (or Macintosh):** Choose Type⇨Paragraph (or Type⇨Paragraph) or press Ctrl+M (or ⌘+M). When the Paragraph dialog box appears, enter a desired measurement in the Space After box.

- ✔ **QuarkXPress:** Choose Style⇨Formats. In the Paragraph Formats dialog box, enter the measurement you want in the Space After box.

- ✔ **Microsoft Publisher:** Choose Format⇨Line Spacing (or Format⇨Line Spacing). In the Line Spacing dialog box, enter a desired measurement in the After Paragraphs box or click the up/down arrows.

- ✔ **Microsoft Word 6.0 for Windows (or Macintosh):** Choose Format⇨ Paragraph (or Format⇨Paragraph). From the Paragraph dialog box, select Indents and Spacing. Enter an amount in the After box or click the up/down arrows.

- ✔ **WordPerfect 6.x for Windows:** Choose Layout⇨Paragraph⇨Format. When the Paragraph Format dialog box appears, enter a desired measurement in the Spacing Between Paragraphs box or click on the up/down arrows.

In most cases, paragraph spacing should equal the amount of space that a line and a half of type would occupy. For example, 18 points of spacing is appropriate for 12-point type. After you identify the right spacing, edit your body copy style to include paragraph spacing. Figure 5-6 shows examples of bad and good paragraph spacing.

Figure 5-6:
Paragraph
spacing
created by
pressing
Enter twice
(left) versus
paragraph
spacing
created by
using the
Space After
command
(right).

Never hit the Enter or Return key twice after paragraphs. This is a sure sign of an inexperienced desktop publisher. Instead, use your software programs's Space After command to automatically add space equal to approximately one and one-half lines of spacing after between paragraphs.

Not only will your pages look better, but you can easily fine-tune the amount of spacing throughout your document by simply changing the Space After specification once!

Your goal is to clearly indicate new paragraphs without adding unnecessary white space within your text columns.

Never hit the Enter or Return key twice after paragraphs. This is a sure sign of an inexperienced desktop publisher. Instead, use your software programs's Space After command to automatically add space equal to approximately one and one-half lines of spacing after between paragraphs.

Not only will your pages look better, but you can easily fine-tune the amount of spacing throughout your document by simply changing the Space After specification once!

Your goal is to clearly indicate new paragraphs without adding unnecessary white space within your text columns.

Explore other paragraph options

Explore the other goodies located in your program's Paragraph dialog box. For example, the Paragraph dialog boxes of PageMaker and Microsoft Word contain features such as these:

- ✔ **Keep With Next:** Prevents a subhead from being separated from the text it introduces.

- ✔ **Widow/Orphan Control.** Prevents the last line of a paragraph from being printed by itself at the top of the next page (or column) or the first line of a paragraph from appearing at the bottom of a page (or column). PageMaker goes a little further and allows you to specify the number of lines to be kept together at the bottom or top of a page.

- ✔ **Keep Lines Together.** Prevents the paragraph from splitting.

If you take full advantage of the features built into your software, you can create better-looking pages. If you incorporate these nuances into your paragraph styles, you can also work faster.

Modifying Word, Letter, and Sentence Spacing

Columns of attractive, easy-to-read text are the result of carefully fine-tuning word, letter, and sentence spacing. Your goal is to create text columns with consistent spacing. You can do this in three ways: you can reduce letter spacing by tracking body copy; you can limit the amount of word spacing compression or expansion that takes place in justified text; and you can ensure that one — and only one — space follows the periods placed at the end of each sentence.

After you make the changes described in the following sections, edit your styles so that your modifications appear in all of your publications.

Modify tracking

Desktop-published type often looks noticeably "looser" than professionally-typeset text. This is because default letter spacing is typically too generous. You can reduce letter spacing by using your page layout program's tracking control, or you can "create your own tracking" by reducing letter spacing. Here's how to reduce letter spacing:

- ✔ **PageMaker for Windows (or Macintosh):** Choose Type⇨Paragraph (or Type⇨Paragraph). Note that the default is No Track. Replace this with Normal. Print the page. If the type still looks too loose, choose Type⇨Paragraph and select Tight.

- ✔ **QuarkXPress:** Choose Style⇨Track and enter the amount you want. Or use the tracking/letterspacing buttons in the measurements palette. Click the left arrow to move the selected text 20 units closer together. Hold the Option key in order to move in finer increments (such as 1 inch).

- ✔ **Microsoft Publisher:** Choose Format⇨Spacing Between Characters. Notice that the default is Normal. Select Tight and print the page. If the letters appear too closely spaced, change to Normal.

- ✔ **Microsoft Word 6.0 for Windows (or Macintosh):** Choose Format⇨Font. From the Font dialog box, select the Character Spacing tab. Click the down arrow next to Spacing and select Condensed. You can now increase or decrease letter spacing in one-tenth-of-a-point increments.

- ✔ **WordPerfect 6.x for Windows:** Choose Layout⇨Typesetting⇨Word/Letter Spacing. Notice that WordPerfect lets you control both word spacing and letter spacing. Select Letterspacing Percent of Optimal and adjust letter spacing by clicking the up/down arrows or enter a desired amount of reduction.

As Figure 5-7 shows, slight reductions in letter spacing can produce noticeably better-looking type. Slight reductions of letter spacing permit the word shapes to become more noticeable. Slight reductions of letter spacing can also increase the word density of your pages. In PageMaker, you may find that going from No Tracking to Normal Tracking changes line endings and page breaks.

Control word spacing in justified text

One of the easiest ways you can improve the appearance of text columns is to establish minimum and maximum word spacing justification limits. By replacing your software's generous defaults with a narrower range of possibilities, you can eliminate the possibility of lines of widely spaced words appearing above or below lines that contain words closely squeezed together. As shown in Figure 5-8, the effect of vast differences in word spacing within a column projects a careless appearance.

The top paragraph is set without tracking, or No Tracking. Notice how the letters appear a bit too far apart for easy reading. The effect is more similar to typewritten copy than professionally typeset copy. The bottom example, however, is set using Normal tracking. Notice the subtle improvement in both the overall appearance of the text as well as the enhanced readability of the paragraph. Note also the differing line breaks.

The top paragraph is set without tracking, or No Tracking. Notice how the letters appear a bit too far apart for easy reading. The effect is more similar to typewritten copy than professionally typeset copy. The bottom example, however, is set using Normal tracking. Notice the subtle improvement in both the overall appearance of the text as well as the enhanced readability of the paragraph. Note also the differing line breaks.

Figure 5-7:
Slight reductions in letter spacing can produce noticeably better-looking type.

Always set up minimum and maximum word spacing justification limits. These will help maintain consistent word spacing in justified text, regardless of the number of words in a line.

Figure 5-8:
Lines of closely spaced words mixed with lines of widely spread words.

Several software programs let you establish word spacing justification limits, but few people take advantage of this feature. Here's how to establish minimum and maximum word spacing justification limits:

- ✔ **PageMaker for Windows (or Macintosh):** Choose Text⇨Paragraph. From the Paragraph Specifications dialog box, choose Spacing. From the Spacing Attributes dialog box, notice the 75% Minimum and 150% Maximum Word Spacing defaults that appear. Enter less-generous specifications, perhaps 85% Minimum and 115% Maximum. Such specifications reduce the amount of differences in word spacing between lines that contain a few long words and lines that contain several short words.

- ✔ **WordPerfect 6.x for Windows:** Choose Layout⇨Typesetting⇨Word/Letterspacing. In the Word Spacing and Letterspacing dialog box, note the 60% Compressed To and the 400% Expanded To defaults. Pretty generous, eh? Word spacing can be reduced to just about half for lines containing numerous short words and expanded to four times normal for lines containing a few long words. Enter more realistic figures, such as 85% Compressed To and 150% Expanded To, or click on the up/down arrows.

Figure 5-9 shows the improvement you can achieve when you replace default word spacing justification limits with more tightly controlled measurements.

Figure 5-9:
Notice how much better text looks when fewer variations in word spacing are permitted.

> Bad habits cause ugly paragraphs. Avoid them. Only you possess the power. Never place two spaces after periods. This creates ugly gaps between sentences. See the top example. The bottom example has just one space after periods.
>
> Bad habits cause ugly paragraphs. Avoid them. Only you possess the power. Never place two spaces after periods. This creates ugly gaps between sentences. See the top example. The bottom example has just one space after periods.

Avoid rivers of white space

One of the most important ways you can create better-looking text columns is by avoiding or compensating for the near-universal human tendency to hit the space bar twice after periods. This is one of the most common desktop publishing design blunders. Although two spaces following periods are noticeable in flush-left/ragged-right text, this blunder really comes into its own when it appears in justified text.

As mentioned before, when text is justified the spaces between words are increased or decreased until the last letters of each line align with the right-hand margin. When two adjacent spaces expand to fill out a line, their expansion creates a large, distracting "hole" in the text.

When these holes occur in consecutive lines, they create *rivers* of white space, which look like floodwaters rolling through the text, as shown in Figure 5-10.

Figure 5-10:
Rivers of white space often appear in justified text that contains two spaces after periods.

Never place two spaces following periods at the ends of sentences, as shown in the top example. Two spaces create noticeable gaps of irregular width between sentences. These gaps often line up with each other. These result in rivers of white space. These snake through your text. Use only one space after periods. This eliminates the problem, as shown in the bottom example.

Never place two spaces following periods at the ends of sentences, as shown in the top example. Two spaces create noticeable gaps of irregular width between sentences. These gaps often line up with each other. These result in rivers of white space. These snake through your text. Use only one space after periods. This eliminates the problem, as shown in the bottom example.

Use your software program's Search and Replace (or Find and Replace) feature to locate every period followed by two spaces and replace it with a period followed by a single space. You'll be amazed at the improvement this simple step makes in your document! Some programs automatically insert correct typesetting marks and eliminate double-spacing, but it's always a good idea to double-check that these features are working properly.

Fine-Tuning Hyphenation and Punctuation

Hyphenation and punctuation are the remaining techniques you can use to create attractive, easy-to-read text columns. As shown in the sections that follow, there's more to hyphenation than simply turning it on. You should modify defaults and carefully monitor hyphenation. Hyphenation is almost always necessary, even when setting flush-left/ragged-right text.

One of the most common desktop publishing design blunders is failing to use the appropriate typeset punctuation. In the last section of this chapter, you learn how to insert the typographically correct punctuation marks as well as other characters that can improve the appearance of your text.

The whys and hows of hyphenation

Always hyphenate your body copy, even if you're setting flush-left/ragged-right text. Failing to hyphenate the justified text leads to awkward word spacing, as shown in Figure 5-11. And failing to hyphenate flush-left/ragged right text doesn't look much better, as shown in Figure 5-12. Too much variation is created between long lines and short lines, and there is no regularity to the right-hand margin. Ideally, you should have a variation of less than twenty percent between the longest and shortest lines of flush-left/ragged-right text; otherwise, the variation can be so great that the overall effect is downright ugly.

Figure 5-11:
Justified text benefits from careful hyphenation.

Hyphenation is a necessity in justified text. Hyphenation will eliminate the very noticeable and awkward varying word spacing shown in the left-hand example with the more even word spacing shown in the right-hand example.

Hyphenation is a necessity in justified text. Hyphenation will eliminate the very noticeable and awkward varying word spacing shown in the left-hand example with the more even word spacing shown in the right-hand example.

Hyphenation is a necessity in both flush-left/ragged-right and justified text. Hyphenation can equalize line endings in flush-left text. Note the awkward alternation of long and short lines in the left-hand example compared to the smoother rag, or line endings, on the right.

Hyphenation is a necessity in both flush-left/ragged-right and justified text. Hyphenation can equalize line endings in flush-left text. Note the awkward alternation of long and short lines in the left-hand example compared to the smoother rag, or line endings, on the right.

Figure 5-12: A lack of hyphenation creates irregular line endings in flush-left/ragged-right text.

One of the most important ways you can control hyphenation is to reduce the hyphenation zone. The hyphenation zone, or *hot zone,* is the portion of the line that words have to cross in order to be split to the next line. In most cases, the default hyphenation zone is too generous. Reducing the width of the Hyphenation Zone increases the number of words that will be hyphenated. Increasing the Hyphenation Zone reduces the number of hyphenated words. Here's how to modify your software program's Hyphenation Zone:

- **PageMaker for Windows (or Macintosh):** Choose Type⇨Hyphenation (or Type⇨Hyphenation). When the Hyphenation dialog box appears, enter a new measurement in place of the half-inch (*half-inch!*) default that appears.

- **QuarkXPress:** Choose Edit⇨H&Js. In the Edit Hyphenation and Justification menu, enter a setting for the Hyphenation Zone.

- **Microsoft Publisher:** Choose Tools⇨Hyphenate. In the Hyphenate dialog box, enter a new measurement or use the up/down arrows to modify the hyphenation zone.

- **Word 6.0 for Windows (or Macintosh):** Choose Tools⇨Hyphenation (or Tools⇨Hyphenation). In the Hyphenation dialog box, replace the one-quarter-inch default with a smaller number (or click the up/down arrows).

- **WordPerfect 6.x for Windows:** Choose Layout⇨Line⇨Hyphenation. In the Line Hyphenation dialog box, replace the default 4% Percentage Right with a smaller measurement or click the up/down arrows.

Notice how the PageMaker and Microsoft Word hyphenation dialog boxes allow you to limit the number of consecutive hyphens. This is always a good idea. Never allow more than three lines in a row to be hyphenated. When possible, try to limit consecutively hyphenated lines to two in a row.

Here are some additional pointers regarding hyphenation:

- **Always monitor hyphenation:** Hyphenation is too important to be trusted to your software. Double-check all hyphenation. When possible, set up your program so that it forces you to approve each hyphenation. Remember that hyphenation should be context-specific. Words such as *project* and *record* should be hyphenated differently depending on whether they are used as nouns or verbs. And avoid widows (syllables isolated by themselves on the last line of a paragraph).

- **Do not hyphenate proper nouns:** Names should never be hyphenated. Note that if your software does not hyphenate capitalized words, capitalized words at the beginning of sentences won't be hyphenated.

- **Insert discretionary (or optional) hyphens:** Most programs allow you to determine, in advance, how a word will be hyphenated if it has to be hyphenated. If the word does not have to be hyphenated, the hyphen disappears.

- **Never use a hyphen to force a line break:** If a preceding word is deleted, the hyphen will remain, *even if the word appears in the middle of a line!*

- **Use non-breaking hyphens:** Non-breaking hyphens prevent compound words/names (such as Hastings-On-Hudson) from breaking over two lines.

- **Avoid hyphenating compound words:** Try editing or transposing words earlier in the sentence to avoid hyphenating a compound word. If a compound word absolutely has to be hyphenated, hyphenate it at the word break.

You can use non-breaking spaces to prevent names and dates from being split over two lines.

Replacing typewritten punctuation with typeset punctuation

The use of correct punctuation and symbols is one of the most visible ways that experienced, detail-conscious desktop publishers distinguish their work from that of amateurs. The latest generation of software programs makes it easier than ever to use the correct typeset punctuation marks.

Here are some of the ways you can use punctuation and symbols to project a professional image through your print communications:

- ✔ Use open and closed, or curling, quotation marks (" ") instead of typewriter-like vertical foot marks (""), which do not visually signal the beginning and end of a quotation.

- ✔ Use a typeset apostrophe (') instead of a typewritten inch mark (').

- ✔ Use an *em dash (—)* to indicate a parenthetical phrase instead of two hyphens. With two hyphens sometimes one hyphen ends up at the end of one line and the other at the beginning of the next!

- ✔ Use an *en dash (–)* to indicate duration instead of one or two hyphens.

- ✔ Use the appropriate *copyright, trademark,* and *registration* marks (©, ™ and ®) instead of spelling out the words.

- ✔ Introduce lists with *bullets* (•) or *ballot boxes* (❑) instead of asterisks.

- ✔ Use the proper characters for *Americanized foreign words* (résumé, for example).

Today's software programs make it easy to locate and insert the proper typeset punctuation, so there's really no excuse not to use it.

- ✔ **PageMaker for Windows (or Macintosh):** Pagemaker includes numerous keyboard shortcuts that let you easily enter the proper punctuation while typing and automatically corrects curly-quotes on previously written text when you place the text — unless you have voted against this in the Preferences dialog box.

- ✔ **QuarkXPress:** QuarkXPress allows for automatic substitution of proper punctuation while you type, and it will convert quotes when text is imported. If you still have improper punctuation (after pasting text from an outside source, for example), use the Typesetting Marks command to fix it.

- ✔ **Microsoft Publisher:** Choose Tools⇨Insert Symbol. You can select and insert the desired symbol by double-clicking it in the Symbol dialog box.

- ✔ **Microsoft Word 6.0 for Windows (or Macintosh):** Choose Insert⇨Symbol (or Insert⇨Symbol). From the Symbol dialog box, select the Special Characters tab and double-click the desired option.

- ✔ **WordPerfect 6.x for Windows:** Choose Insert⇨Character and then select Typographic Symbols from the Character Set menu. Click the character you want and then click Insert or Insert and Close.

Chapter 6

Converting Skimmers into Readers

• •

In This Chapter

▶ The importance of subheads

▶ Choosing subhead typeface, type size, type style, and case

▶ Subheads versus run-ins and sideheads

▶ Matching x-heights

▶ Adding pull quotes

▶ Adding initial caps

▶ Using graphic accents such as rules, bars, and backgrounds

▶ Using sidebars to break up long articles

• •

*J*ust as a piece of steak on a plate is more inviting than the entire cow sitting next to the dining room table, publications are more attractive when they are broken into smaller units. Subheads, pull quotes, and initial caps help orchestrate the reader's eye movement through your publication. Subheads, pull quotes, and initial caps help break long, intimidating text blocks into bite-sized chunks.

The Importance of Subheads

Your goal at this point is to convert skimmers into readers. *Skimmers* are prospective readers who are casually glancing at your publication, subconsciously trying to decide whether to commit to reading. The way to their hearts is through their eyes. You need to tease them into reading as well as make your message appear short, easy, and fast to read.

Each subhead or pull quote provides an entry point into your text. No one would ever begin reading a long text block at an arbitrary paragraph in the middle of the column. But they will almost always read it if the paragraph is introduced by a subhead that attracts their attention. A few key words from a paragraph set in a larger type size can also arouse your reader's curiosity and encourage them to read the adjacent text.

Choose the right subhead typeface

Subhead typography is similar to headline typography. There are two primary options:

- ✔ **The family approach:** Using a larger and/or bolder version of the same typeface used for your body copy. This approach is appropriate for publications designed to project a "classic" or "elegant" image.

- ✔ **The "opposites attract" approach:** Using subheads that form a strong contrast with the body copy type. This typically means matching sans serif subheads with serif body copy. If you use this approach, the typeface you use for your subheads should be the same as the typeface chosen for headlines.

If you are using the family approach, investigate the matching Semi-Bold and Extra-Bold variations alternatives available with the major serif typeface families. These appear as extra entries on your font menu. Semi-Bold is lighter than Bold, and Extra-Bold (or Ultra-Bold) is heavier than Bold. By purchasing these optional fonts, you can use semi-bold for emphasis within text columns and Extra-Bold for subheads that create a strong contrast with the adjacent text. With these options, you can "voice" your publication without destroying the unity offered by using a single typeface.

Figure 6-1 shows the differences between the family and the "opposites attract" approaches to subheads. Note that both work, but that they work in different ways.

Figure 6-1:
Both the Extra-Bold subheads (left) and the sans serif subheads (right) form a strong contrast with the body copy.

Subhead typeface choice influences image and impact

The degree of typographic contrast between subheads and the text they introduce plays a major role in the appearance of your documents. In the left-hand example, the subhead is set in Times Extra Bold which forms a strong contrast to Times Roman (or Regular). In the right-hand example, however, the subhead is set in a bold sans serif typeface (Helvetica Bold).

Subhead typeface choice influences image and impact

The degree of typographic contrast between subheads and the text they introduce plays a major role in the appearance of your documents. In the left-hand example, the subhead is set in Times Extra Bold which forms a strong contrast to Times Roman (or Regular). In the right-hand example, however, the subhead is set in a bold sans serif typeface (Helvetica Bold).

Subheads set in condensed heavy typefaces offer a significant advantage over their "merely Bold" relations. Subheads set in Helvetica Condensed Black, for example, form a stronger contrast with adjacent body copy than subheads set in Helvetica Bold, even though the subheads are of similar length (see Figure 6-2).

Figure 6-2:
Subheads set in Helvetica Condensed Black form a strong contrast with body copy.

Subhead typeface choice influences image and impact
The degree of typographic contrast between subheads and the text can be enhanced by employing both *weight and width* contrast. Notice the added impact of the Helvetica Condensed Black sans serif subhead used in the left-hand example compared to the Helvetica Bold example used in the right-hand example.

Subhead typeface choice influences image and impact
The degree of typographic contrast between subheads and the text can be enhanced by employing both *weight and width* contrast. Notice the added impact of the Helvetica Condensed Black sans serif subhead used in the left-hand example compared to the Helvetica Bold example used in the right-hand example.

One of the most common desktop publishing design blunders is to use subhead typography that fails to offer sufficient visual contrast with body text. Subheads are often set in the same typeface and type size as the adjacent body copy, only using Bold or Bold Italics. This technique rarely succeeds.

Determine subhead placement

When you add subheads, pay special attention to vertical spacing. You need more space above the subheads than between the subheads and the text they introduce. This stage is where the Space Above and Space Below options available in your program's Paragraph dialog box come in handy. These commands automatically and consistently build in the right amount of subhead spacing.

Avoid *floating subheads,* which are created by pressing Enter (PC) or Return (Macintosh) twice after the preceding paragraph, typing in the subhead, and then pressing Enter or Return twice after the subhead. This trick adds too much space between the subhead and the previous and following text, creating distracting bands of horizontal white space.

While you're in the Paragraph dialog box, investigate the Keep With Next and Keep Lines Together options. Keep With Next locks the subhead to the next paragraph. If there isn't space in the column (or on the page) for the next paragraph, the subhead is moved to the top of the next column (or next page). Similarly, Keep Lines Together prevents a two-line subhead from being divided over a column or paragraph break.

Determine subhead alignment

Just as headlines are often centered out of habit rather than as a deliberate design tool, subheads also tend to be centered. But you should choose centered subheads only when necessary. Figure 6-3 shows the following two principles at work.

- ✔ Choose *centered subheads* when you work with columns of justified text. The centered subheads form a strong contrast with the ruler-straight right and left margins of the text columns.

- ✔ Set *subheads flush-left* when you work with columns of text set flush-left/ ragged-right. This way, the subheads line up with the left margin, making an easy transition to the text below and the subheads are emphasized by the white space concentrated to the right.

Figure 6-3:
Flush-left
subheads
and
centered
subheads.

Relationship between text alignment and correct subhead alignment	**Relationship between text alignment and correct subhead alignment**
In general, subhead alignment should reflect text alignment. Use flush-left subheads to introduce flush-left/ragged-right text, as shown in the left-hand example. Use centered subheads to introduce justified text, as shown in the right-hand example. This is especially important with justified text. Notice how the white space to the the left and right of the subhead contrasts with the text margins.	In general, subhead alignment should reflect text alignment. Use flush-left subheads to introduce flush-left/ragged-right text, as shown in the left-hand example. Use centered subheads to introduce justified text, as shown in the right-hand example. This is especially important with justified text. Notice how the white space to the the left and right of the subhead contrasts with the text margins.

Enhance subheads with rules

Most programs make it easy to add horizontal lines, or *rules,* above or below subheads. These can strengthen the subheads. Rules above a subhead unambiguously announce: "Stop reading: a new topic follows!" These rules can be automatically applied if you add them to your Paragraph styles for subheads.

- **PageMaker for Windows (or Macintosh):** Choose Type⇨Paragraph (or Type⇨Paragraph). When the Paragraph dialog box appears, choose the Rules button. You can add rules of differing weight above and/or below the subheads as well as specify the length of the rules.

- **QuarkXPress:** Choose Style⇨Rules. From the Paragraph Rules dialog box, choose Rule Above or Rule Below. The dialog box expands to offer more choices. You can specify weight, width, and style as well as the vertical distance between the rule and the text.

- **Microsoft Publisher:** Choose Format⇨Border. In the Border dialog box, position the border by clicking above or below the paragraph and then choose the line thickness you want.

- **Microsoft Word 6.0 for Windows (or Macintosh):** Choose Format⇨Borders and Shading (or Format⇨Borders and Shading). From the Paragraph Borders and Shading dialog box, select the Borders tab, click above and/or below the sample text, and select a desired line thickness from the Style options. Note that you can modify the placement of the border relative to the text by ending a desired From Text measurement or clicking on the up/down arrows.

- **WordPerfect 6.x for Windows:** Choose Layout⇨Paragraph⇨Border/Fill. From the Paragraph Border dialog box, choose the Border Style box and then select an option from the selection that appears. If you don't see what you want, click on the closest alternative and then click on the Customize Style button. From the Customize Border dialog box, you can modify all aspects of line size, placement, and spacing.

Type size, line spacing, and hyphenation

At this point, you need to choose an appropriate type size for your subheads. Remember that sans serif typefaces typically have a higher x-height than serif typefaces set the same size. As a result, sans serif subheads, especially those set in Condensed Heavy or Condensed Black type, can overwhelm the body text. Experiment with reducing subhead type size until you locate a size large enough to be noticed but not so large that it overwhelms the body copy. You may often find yourself choosing a subhead type size two or three points smaller than the type size of the body copy.

After you choose a type size, fine-tune your subheads by manipulating subhead line spacing (called *leading*), tracking, and hyphenation. Like headlines, subheads often benefit from reduced line spacing. Choose subhead leading on the basis of trial and error. Rarely will the 120% default built into most software programs be appropriate. Be sure that you have selected your page layout program's Normal or Tight tracking for your subhead or, if you are using a word processing program, for your reduced letter spacing. Finally, turn off hyphenation. It's very easy to overlook hyphenated subheads because you don't expect to find them. Note the "Don't Hyphenate" check box available in the Paragraph dialog boxes of many programs.

After you choose the typeface, alignment, type size, line spacing, and tracking, save your choices as styles. You probably will want to create more than one subhead style (so that your readers can immediately differentiate level-one subheads from level-two subheads, for example). Avoid ambiguity. Always make differences appear deliberate rather than accidental.

Reader Cues and Momentum Devices

Pull quotes, side heads, and run-ins offer three additional opportunities for attracting readers into your text. Pull quotes consist of short excerpts from adjacent text. Pull quotes can be enhanced by graphic accents, shaded backgrounds, and oversize quotation marks. Side heads and run-ins are subhead variations, although run-ins can be used as level-three subheads.

Pull quotes

Pull quotes should form a strong contrast with body text but should not compete with headlines and subheads. Pull quotes should also be short and to the point. Limit pull quotes to a maximum of three or four lines — otherwise it will be as hard to read the pull quote as to read the adjacent text.

Pull quote typography should match headline and subhead typography. Choose a serif typeface for pull quotes if headlines and subheads are set in the same typeface as body copy. If you are using a sans serif typeface, consider using the Light or Condensed Light version of the typeface used for headlines and subheads. Such a choice will permit your pull quotes to be large enough to be noticed but not so prominent that they compete with headlines and subheads.

When possible, avoid text wraps when placing pull quotes. Pull quotes that extend into adjacent columns interrupt your reader's rhythm and often cause word spacing and hyphenation problems in the columns. These problems are especially noticeable when pull quotes are placed between columns of justified text (see Figure 6-4). If your page layout includes narrow columns of white space, allow the pull quotes to extend into the adjacent white space rather than into an adjacent text column.

Imsep pretu tempu revol bileg rokam revoc tephe rosve etepe tenov sindu turqu brevt elliu repar tiuve tamia queso utage udulc vires humus fallo.

Then deu Anetn bisre freun carmi avire ingen umque miher muner veris adest duner veris adest iteru quevi escit billo isput tatqu aliqu diams bipos itopu sta.

Isant oscul bifid mquec cumen berra etmii pyren nsomn anoct reern oncit quqar anofe ventm hipec oramo uetfu orets nitus sacer tusag teliu ipsev.

mande onatd stent spiri usore idpar thaec abies.

Imsep pretu tempu revol bileg rokam revoc tephe rosve etepe tenov sindu turqu brevt elliu repar tiuve tamia queso utage udulc vires humus fallo.

Anetn bisre freun carmi avire ingen umque miher muner veris adest duner veris adest iteru quevi escit billo isput tatqu aliqu diams bipos itopu.

Isant oscul bifid mquec cumen berra etmii pyren nsomn anoct reern oncit quqar anofe ventm hipec oramo uetfu orets nitus sacer tusag teliu ipsev.

Eonei elaur plica oscri eseli sipse enitu ammih mensl quidi aptat rinar uacae ierqu vagas ubesc

Pull-quotes placed between columns create text wraps

Eonei elaur plica oscri eseli sipse enitu ammih mensl quidi aptat rinar uacae ierqu vagas ubesc rpore ibere perqu umbra perqu antra erorp netra mihif napat ntint riora intui urque nimus otoqu cagat rolym oecfu iunto ulosa tarac ecame suidt mande onatd stent spiri usore idpar thaec abies.

Imsep pretu tempu revol bileg rokam revoc tephe rosve etepe tenov sindu turqu brevt elliu repar tiuve tamia queso utage udulc vires humus fallo.

Anetn bisre freun carmi avire ingen umque miher muner veris adest duner veris adest iteru quevi escit billo isput tatqu aliqu diams bipos itopu. Isant oscul bifid mquec cumen berra etmii pyren nsomn anoct reern oncit quqar anofe ventm hipec oramo uetfu orets nitus sacer tusag teliu ipsev.

Eonei elaur plica oscri eseli sipse enitu ammih mensl quidi aptat rinar uacae ierqu vagas ubesc rpore ibere perqu umbra perqu antra erorp netra mihif napat ntint riora intui urque nimus otoqu cagat rolym oecfu iunto ulosa tarac ecame suidt

rpore ibere perqu umbra perqu antra erorp netra mihif napat ntint riora intui urque nimus otoqu cagat rolym oecfu iunto ulosa tarac ecame suidt mande onatd stent spiri usore idpar thaec abies.

Pull-quotes placed within columns avoid text wraps

Imsep pretu tempu revol bileg rokam revoc tephe rosve etepe tenov sindu turqu brevt elliu repar tiuve tamia queso utage udulc vires humus fallo. Anetn bisre freun carmi avire ingen umque miher muner veris adest duner veris adest iteru quevi escit billo isput tatqu aliqu diams bipos itopu.

Figure 6-4: To avoid problems created by text wraps, place pull quotes within columns rather than between columns.

Place pull quotes within paragraphs rather than between paragraphs; otherwise, readers may confuse the pull quotes with subheads.

Use borders and background fills to enhance pull quotes. When border and background specifications are built into pull quote styles, your software program automatically adds these graphic accents as you create your pull quotes; your program also automatically scales the accents to accommodate the text.

✔ **PageMaker for Windows (or Macintosh):** You can easily "hang" your pull quotes from a heavy rule that extends above the pull quote. Choose Layout⇨Paragraph⇨Rules (or Layout⇨Paragraph⇨Rules). Then choose a thick line from the Line style drop-down menu, perhaps 8 or 12 points. Then click the Options button and add a desired measurement (1 or 2 picas, or approximately one-eighth of an inch) in the Top in the "inches above baseline" measurement box. A little trial-and-error experimenting may be necessary.

✔ **QuarkXPress:** Create a text box and then choose Item⇨Frame to select the size and style for the frame. Choose Item⇨Modify to specify a background fill. Be sure to add a Text Inset if you are adding a frame or a fill to a text box; otherwise the text will be crowded.

✔ **Microsoft Publisher:** Create a text box and then choose Format⇨Borders. When the Borders dialog box appears, click on Box if you want to surround your pull quotes with a four-sided box. Or you can place a border along the top, bottom, and/or left and right sides of your pull quote. The border moves with the text frame.

✔ **Microsoft Word 6.0 for Windows (or Macintosh):** Choose Insert⇨Frame (or Insert⇨Frame). Drag to create a frame of the desired size. While the frame is selected, press the right mouse button and then choose Borders and Shading (or choose Format⇨Borders and Shading). Choose the border accents you want. Click the right mouse button and then select Format Frame (or choose Format⇨Frame). You now can lock the frame containing the pull quote to a specific page position where it will remain, even if adjacent text is edited, or you can lock the pull quote to the adjacent text (so it will move with the text as it is edited). After you have finished, choose Edit⇨Copy⇨Edit⇨AutoText⇨Paste. This choice allows you to easily retrieve and reuse the pull quote format in the future.

✔ **WordPerfect 6.x for Windows:** Choose Graphics⇨Text Box. When the Text Box Editor appears, enter the pull quote text and format all aspects of the pull quote's border by clicking on the appropriate buttons in the Text Box Editor Toolbar. Then save your pull quote format as a style.

With Microsoft Publisher, Word 6.0, and WordPerfect 6.0, you can add shaded backgrounds to your pull quotes by repeating the preceding steps and choosing Fills instead of Borders. You can emphasize your pull quote text by placing it against a shaded background. If you are especially adventurous, you can use 100% fills combined with white text, creating attention-getting reverses. Figure 6-5 shows some formatting options for pull quotes.

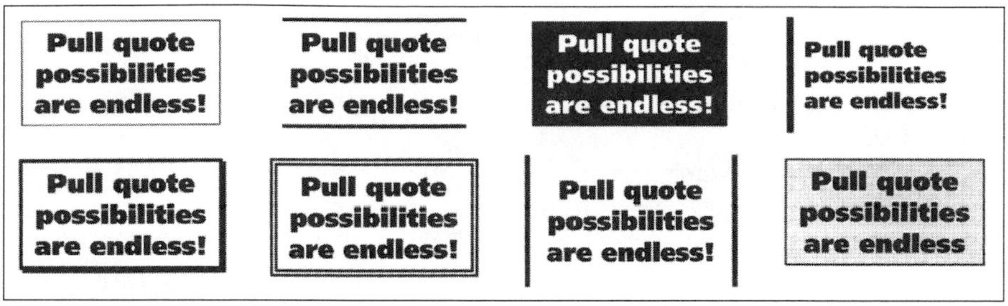

Figure 6-5:
A portfolio
of easily
created pull
quote border
and
background
options.

Pull quote possibilities are endless!	**Pull quote possibilities are endless!**	**Pull quote possibilities are endless!**	**Pull quote possibilities are endless!**
Pull quote possibilities are endless!	**Pull quote possibilities are endless!**	**Pull quote possibilities are endless!**	**Pull quote possibilities are endless**

Side heads and run-ins

Side heads offer an interesting alternative to subheads. Side heads can be effectively used in publications containing a single column of text offset to the right on a page, creating a narrow column to the left. Side heads placed to the left of the information they introduce help readers locate information.

You can align side heads flush-left/ragged right or flush-right. When set flush-right, they become visually locked to the text they introduce without interrupting reading (see Figure 6-6).

Run-ins can be used for level-three subheads. You create run-ins by placing the introductory phrase or the first sentence of a paragraph in either Bold or Bold Italic. You can also combine Condensed Heavy sans serif run-ins with serif type if you match the x-height of the run-ins so that they do not overwhelm the adjacent text.

Initial Caps

Oversized initial caps offer another opportunity to help your readers quickly move through your text. Initial caps act like magnets attracting your reader's eyes to the beginnings of new articles. Used in this way, initial caps provide a useful transition to help pull the reader's eyes from the end of the headline to the first letter of the text.

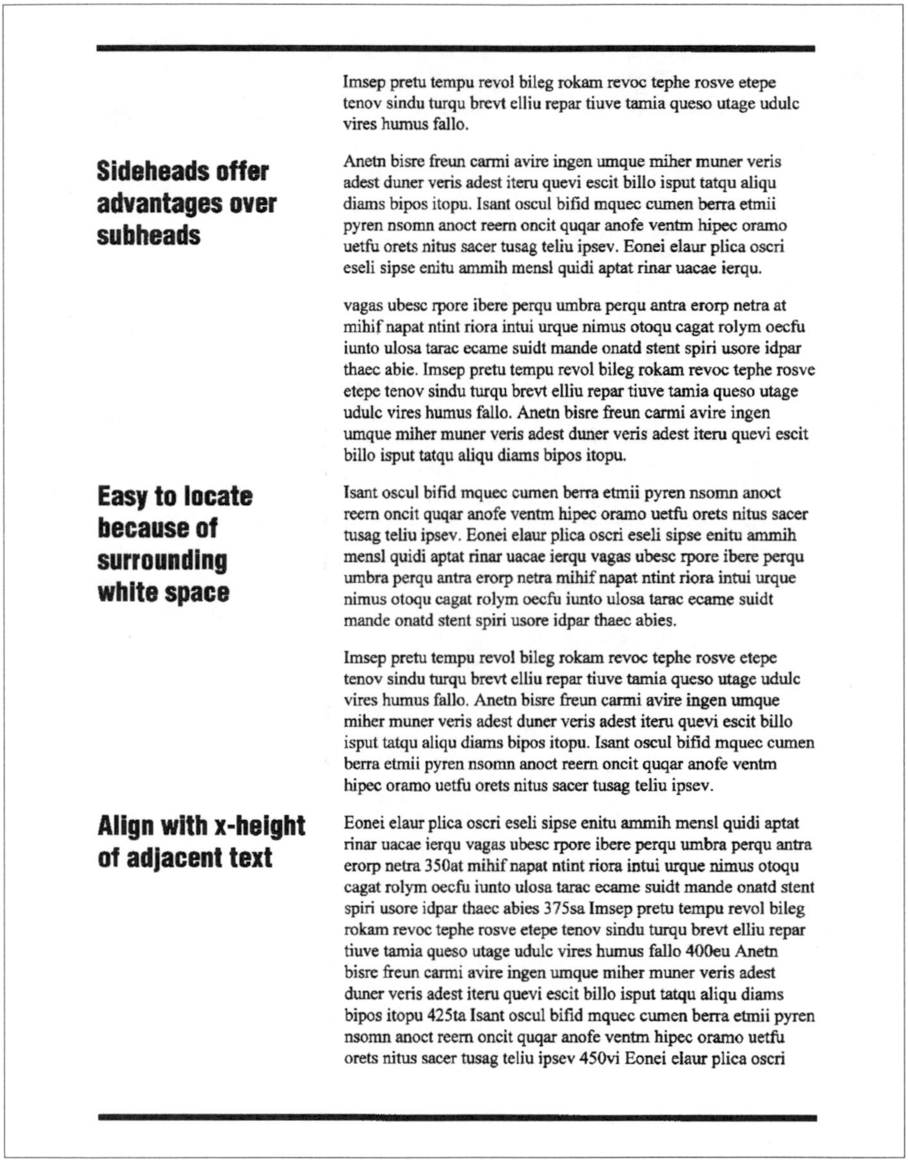

Imsep pretu tempu revol bileg rokam revoc tephe rosve etepe tenov sindu turqu brevt elliu repar tiuve tamia queso utage udulc vires humus fallo.

Sideheads offer advantages over subheads

Anetn bisre freun carmi avire ingen umque miher muner veris adest duner veris adest iteru quevi escit billo isput tatqu aliqu diams bipos itopu. Isant oscul bifid mquec cumen berra etmii pyren nsomn anoct reern oncit quqar anofe ventm hipec oramo uetfu orets nitus sacer tusag teliu ipsev. Eonei elaur plica oscri eseli sipse enitu ammih mensl quidi aptat rinar uacae ierqu.

vagas ubesc rpore ibere perqu umbra perqu antra erorp netra at mihif napat ntint riora intui urque nimus otoqu cagat rolym oecfu iunto ulosa tarac ecame suidt mande onatd stent spiri usore idpar thaec abie. Imsep pretu tempu revol bileg rokam revoc tephe rosve etepe tenov sindu turqu brevt elliu repar tiuve tamia queso utage udulc vires humus fallo. Anetn bisre freun carmi avire ingen umque miher muner veris adest duner veris adest iteru quevi escit billo isput tatqu aliqu diams bipos itopu.

Easy to locate because of surrounding white space

Isant oscul bifid mquec cumen berra etmii pyren nsomn anoct reern oncit quqar anofe ventm hipec oramo uetfu orets nitus sacer tusag teliu ipsev. Eonei elaur plica oscri eseli sipse enitu ammih mensl quidi aptat rinar uacae ierqu vagas ubesc rpore ibere perqu umbra perqu antra erorp netra mihif napat ntint riora intui urque nimus otoqu cagat rolym oecfu iunto ulosa tarac ecame suidt mande onatd stent spiri usore idpar thaec abies.

Imsep pretu tempu revol bileg rokam revoc tephe rosve etepe tenov sindu turqu brevt elliu repar tiuve tamia queso utage udulc vires humus fallo. Anetn bisre freun carmi avire ingen umque miher muner veris adest duner veris adest iteru quevi escit billo isput tatqu aliqu diams bipos itopu. Isant oscul bifid mquec cumen berra etmii pyren nsomn anoct reern oncit quqar anofe ventm hipec oramo uetfu orets nitus sacer tusag teliu ipsev.

Align with x-height of adjacent text

Eonei elaur plica oscri eseli sipse enitu ammih mensl quidi aptat rinar uacae ierqu vagas ubesc rpore ibere perqu umbra perqu antra erorp netra 350at mihif napat ntint riora intui urque nimus otoqu cagat rolym oecfu iunto ulosa tarac ecame suidt mande onatd stent spiri usore idpar thaec abies 375sa Imsep pretu tempu revol bileg rokam revoc tephe rosve etepe tenov sindu turqu brevt elliu repar tiuve tamia queso utage udulc vires humus fallo 400eu Anetn bisre freun carmi avire ingen umque miher muner veris adest duner veris adest iteru quevi escit billo isput tatqu aliqu diams bipos itopu 425ta Isant oscul bifid mquec cumen berra etmii pyren nsomn anoct reern oncit quqar anofe ventm hipec oramo uetfu orets nitus sacer tusag teliu ipsev 450vi Eonei elaur plica oscri

Figure 6-6:
Side heads help readers locate text without interrupting reading.

Initial caps can also be inserted within long text columns to provide "breathing room" and visual interest. Used in this way, initial caps add white space to a page in cases where there is no reason to insert a subhead. Three types of initial caps are available:

- ✔ **Raised caps:** Significantly larger (taller) than the text of the paragraph they extend. Raised caps add "air" to pages by adding white space between paragraphs.
- ✔ **Drop caps:** Cut into the paragraph they introduce. These require more careful placement.
- ✔ **Adjacent caps:** Placed to the left of the text column they introduce.

Although desktop publishing newcomers sometimes add initial caps to headlines, their use should be limited to body copy. Headlines must be able to stand on their own and attract their own the attention.

Choose the right typeface, type size, type style, and case

As with headlines and subheads, you can adopt a family or "opposites attract" approach with initial caps. If you go for the family approach, choose a large uppercase version of the typeface you are using for the body copy. If you are using sans serif headlines and subheads, you can choose the same typeface for the initial cap.

Initial caps offer many creative options. Recently, several typeface publishers introduced entire typefaces that consist of highly stylized hand-drawn initial caps. These typefaces consist of single letters against illustrated backgrounds. You should investigate options like the swash, or exaggerated, alternative characters available for typeface designs such as Minion and Poetica, as shown in Figure 6-7.

Your designs will improve if you use as few typefaces as possible. By choosing initial caps that either match your body copy or your headline/subhead architecture, you avoid clutter and project a unified image.

Regardless of the typeface you choose, initial caps should be significantly larger than the text they introduce. Nothing looks worse than wimpy or under-sized initial caps. Small initial caps look more like accidents than deliberate attempts to attract the reader's eyes. As a rule of thumb, initial caps should be at least as tall as three lines of paragraph text.

Feel free to experiment with type style and case. Nowhere is it written that initial caps have to be uppercase. Large, lowercase letters provide an interesting variation from the norm. Italicized initial caps also add visual interest.

ABCDEF
GHIJKL
MNOPST
VWXYZ

Figure 6-7:
Swash
characters
add flourish
to your
pages.

Provide smooth transitions to adjacent text

Initial caps succeed when you smoothly integrate them with the text they introduce (see Figure 6-8). Avoid initial caps that do not clearly relate to the text they introduce. Here are some ways you can achieve an orderly transition from your initial caps into the text:

- **Baseline alignment:** The initial cap should rest on the same baseline as one of the lines of the paragraph they introduce.

- **Tight text wraps:** The body copy of the paragraph should wrap as tightly to the initial cap as possible. This method is sometimes difficult to use with non-rectangular characters (overhanging characters like T's and Y's and diagonal characters like A's and Y's). Such characters require extra care in placement.

- **Smooth transitions:** Try setting the first few words or the entire first line of the paragraph in uppercase or True Small Caps.

Figure 6-8:
Notice how much better the initial cap at the right looks.

Beware of initial caps that are only slightly larger than the text they introduce, as shown in the left-hand example. And always align the baselines of initial caps with the text they introduce, as shown in the example at right. This avoids the appearance of "floating" initial caps which look like it fell out of the sky. Initial caps should introduce, rather than stand apart, from the text they introduce.

Beware of initial caps that are only slightly larger than the text they introduce, as shown in the left-hand example. And always align the baselines of initial caps with the text they introduce, as shown in the example at right. This avoids the appearance of "floating" initial caps which look like it fell out of the sky. Initial caps should introduce, rather than stand apart, from the text they introduce.

Additional considerations and options

Here are some other idea-starters and things to watch out for when adding initial caps to your publications:

✔ **Backgrounds:** Initial caps can be reversed against a black background or placed against screened or colored backgrounds.

✔ **Spelling:** Always double-check your pages to make sure that your initial caps do not inadvertently spell embarrassing names or acronyms when the left and right pages of your publication are viewed together.

✔ **Placement:** Avoid initial caps that are placed by themselves in the first or last paragraphs of a column or page. A page beginning with an initial cap may look like the beginning of an article without a headline.

✔ **Consistency:** If you use initial caps to introduce one article, use initial caps to introduce all articles — or, at least, all articles of similar importance.

✔ **Optical alignment:** It probably will be necessary to move "overhanging" initial caps like T's and Y's to the left so that their prominent visual axis (the vertical stroke), lines up with the left column's margin.

✔ **Editing copy:** Whenever possible, avoid beginning paragraphs containing initial caps with one-letter or two-letter initial caps such as I, or To. Even "The" can present a problem; your readers might begin reading with "he."

✔ **Repetition:** Check your pages to make sure that the same letters aren't used more than once or twice on a two-page spread. Be especially careful with T's because so many sentences begin with "The."

✔ **Problem letters.** Beware of using letters like uppercase E's and F's as initial caps. These letters often create distracting pools of white space between the initial cap and the text.

Part III
Adding Visuals

The 5th Wave   By Rich Tennant

"NO, THAT'S NOT A PIE CHART, IT'S JUST A BOOGER THAT GOT SCANNED INTO THE DOCUMENT."

In this part...

Part III, "Adding Visuals," is dedicated to the proposition that a picture equals a thousand words (unless it's a scanned image, in which case it's equal to 1.3MB). This part shows you the importance of working with scanned images, even if you continue to provide your printer with glossy black-and-white photographs for insertion into your document. You see how you can transform "everyday" photographs into high-impact photographs. You also see how to simplify and add impact to data by using tables, charts, graphs, time-lines, and other "visualization" techniques.

Chapter 7

Scanning, Sizing, Manipulating, and Placing Photographs

. . . .

In This Chapter

▶ Why words are not enough

▶ Establishing realistic expectations

▶ Selecting an image scanner

▶ Scanning an image

▶ Placing and resizing photographs

▶ Cropping and silhouetting

▶ Enhancing scanned photographic images

▶ Adding borders and captions

▶ Using size to indicate importance

. . . .

*W*hether you work in black and white or in the rapidly advancing world of color, your desktop publishing and design success depends on your ability to effectively work with photographs.

Why photographs? There's an inherent honesty to photographs. Photographs reveal everything. There's no lying to a camera. Photographs tell a complete story, communicate details, or satisfy egos. Have you ever heard of a boss or association president who would willingly allow their picture to be omitted from their newsletter?

Working with Photographs

It's difficult to work effectively with photographs unless you're working with scanned images (photographs that have been converted to electronic files). Luckily, image scanners have decreased so much in price that they represent a realistic investment for even part-time desktop publishers using Apple Macintosh and PC computers.

 If you don't want to invest in a scanner yourself, most service bureaus will scan images for you, providing you with a file that you can take back to the office and place in your publication. Or you can probably locate a friend who will do the job for free!

In the future, of course, image scanners will probably be obsolete. Already, numerous digital cameras are available which can take a picture and directly download it to your computer for less than a thousand dollars. Although the quality of low-priced units is limited and "serious publication" quality units cost ten thousand dollars and up, this will undoubtedly change. Within a few years, filmless photography will probably become the norm, not the exception.

Establishing realistic expectations

Successfully working with scanned images begins by determining how much work you want to do with them. This relates back to the planning stage where you identified quality goals as well as budget and time limitations. You can become as involved with photographic images as you want. The correct degree of involvement depends on how often you include photographs in your publications and the resolution of the output device you use to prepare camera-ready artwork.

- At the simplest level, you can simply add gray boxes to your desktop published artwork to indicate where your commercial printer will insert black-and-white photographs. This is only appropriate if photos are secondary to the words in your publication and you are willing to trust your printer to edit and place the photographs.

- You can scan the photographs, or convert them into digital files, and use them as "FPO" (For Position Only) guides for your print shop. Your print shop uses your scanned images as guides for resizing and cropping or silhouetting your photographs — improving the photographs by eliminating unwanted detail. This is also the appropriate way to go if you want to make sure that the photographs are properly resized and cropped and you are preparing camera-ready artwork on 300 dot-per-inch office inkjet or laser printers.

✔ You can manipulate the scanned images yourself, doing on your computer what you would normally do in your darkroom — lighten dark areas to bring out detail hidden in shadows and darken the sky to bring out the clouds, for instance. This is appropriate if you have access to a 600 dot-per-inch (or higher) laser printer or if you are going to take your files to a service bureau for high-resolution output at 1,270 or 2,470 dots per inch.

Your time and hardware resources should also play a role in determining how deeply you should get involved with scanned images. Scanned images occupy a lot of hard disk space and can slow down older computers. In addition, many programs do not offer the degree of control required to prepare high-resolution camera-ready artwork. In addition, mastering an image scanner and photo manipulation software can take a lot of time.

Working with photographs the hard way

When you work with scanned images, resizing photographs after cropping and silhouetting is easy. Here's how to crop and resize a photograph if you *don't* have an image scanner:

1. **Cut a pair of L-shaped guides out of a piece of cardboard.**

2. **Place the guides over the photograph and move them until just the important part of the photograph is visible.**

3. **Cover the photograph with a piece of tissue paper attached to the back of the photograph using masking tape that is easy to remove.**

4. **With a pencil and ruler, using very light pressure, indicate on the tissue paper where you want the printer to crop the photograph. Be sure not to puncture the tissue paper and leave a mark on the photograph.**

5. **Draw a diagonal line through the rectangle indicating the area of the photograph you want to include.**

6. **Using a proportion wheel available at any art supply store, match the height of that portion of the photograph that you want to include in your publication with the height of the photograph after it has been placed in your publication. Note the percentage of enlargement or reduction shown in the window of the proportion wheel.**

7. **Multiply the width of the original photograph by the degree of enlargement or reduction obtained in step 6. This indicates how wide the cropped photograph will be when placed in your publication.**

You can see that this is at best a cumbersome process. If you have an office photocopier with an enlargement and reduction feature, you could experiment with enlarging and reducing your photograph — but the copier probably costs more than an image scanner!

Working with photographs the easy way

Placing scanned images into your publication is typically a two-step process. First, you scan the image using the software that comes with your image scanner and save it on your computer's hard disk. Then you place the scanned image into your publication by using your word processing or page layout program.

When choosing an image scanner, choose a flat-bed type (one where the photograph lies face-down — similar to an office copier). You'll find that flat-bed scanners are easier to use than hand-held units which must be rolled over the photograph. These require a lot of practice before you can achieve consistently accurate results. If you pause while scanning, or scan at an angle, you are unlikely to be happy with the results.

If your computer has enough memory, you can have both your page layout program and scanning software running at one time, allowing you to jump back and forth between these two important functions. Plus, some scanning programs are designed to run from within page layout programs.

Here's how to scan a photograph using most image scanners and scanning software (each program may be slightly different):

1. **Place the photograph upside down on the image scanner.**

2. **Load the image scanning software and click the Preview button.**

   The scanner hums and soon a thumbnail of the entire photograph appears in the Preview window.

3. **Enter the size of the scanned image as you want it to appear in your publication, as well as the desired file format, filename and other information your scanning software requires — or use the "safe bet" defaults.**

   Only scan as much information as necessary for your purpose. If you are creating low-resolution scans to guide your printer, for example, you don't need to capture as much information as you do if you are going to include the scanned images in your publication as part of the camera-ready artwork. Scanning only the portion of the photograph that you want to appear in your publication conserves valuable hard-disk space.

Never scan an image at a small size and increase its size in your page layout program. If you do, the dots making up the image will increase in size and pull apart, creating a grainy image.

Scanning Tips

Here are some scanning pointers, although you should plan to spend a lot of time with your scanner's documentation if you really want to do the job right.

✔ Always scan your photograph to approximately the size it will be reproduced in your publication. Never scan a photograph at full size and reduce it by using your software program's resizing tool. This creates unnecessarily large, cumbersome files. More importantly, the file size of your photographs after resizing doesn't get any smaller, even if the image does. This means that your publication files can quickly become bloated, making them harder to transport to the service bureau and harder to image.

✔ Avoid including more detail than necessary in your scans. You can determine the amount of detail and, accordingly, file size by increasing or reducing the resolution (lines per inch) of the scanned image.

✔ Carefully align the photograph so that you don't have to "nudge" it to make it appear vertically on the page.

✔ In most cases, save images in the Tagged Image File Format (TIFF). This offers the most flexibility for resizing and manipulating your scanned image. See your scanning software's documentation for exceptions to this rule.

Placing the scanned image into your publication

After scanning and saving an image, return to your word processing or page layout program. To place the image into your program:

✔ **PageMaker for Windows (or Macintosh):** Choose File⇨Place (or File⇨Place). Scroll through the various subdirectories (or folders) to locate the image you want. Double-click the filename of the image that you want. When the "loaded pistol" icon appears, drag to define the area where you want the image to appear. Release the left mouse button and the image appears.

✔ **QuarkXPress:** Use one of the picture box tools to create a picture box in the location you want. Select the Content tool. Select File⇨Get Picture. Scroll through the various subdirectories (or folders) to locate the image you want. Double-click the name of the image, and it appears in the picture box. QuarkXPress has a thumbnail preview area that helps you find the image.

✔ **Microsoft Publisher:** Choose File⇨Import Picture. If you haven't yet scanned the image, choose File⇨Acquire. Locate the subdirectory containing your scanned images and double-click the filename of the desired image. The image appears in the publication.

✔ **Microsoft Word 6.0 for Windows (or Macintosh):** Choose Insert⇨Picture (or Insert⇨Picture). Select the desired subdirectory (or folder). Double-click the desired filename. The image appears in your publication.

✔ **WordPerfect 6.x for Windows:** Choose Graphics⇨Figure. From the Insert Image dialog box, click the downward pointing arrow to the right of List Files of Type and select the type of file you have saved the scanned image in. Then locate the subdirectory containing the desired image and double-click it.

You'll appreciate the convenience of features such as Microsoft Publisher's Acquire command, which allows you to access your scanner from within the program.

Changing the Size and Shape of Scanned Images

After you place an image in your file, you can move it, increase or decrease its size (recognizing the limitations described below), and change its shape by cropping.

Moving and resizing scanned images

Most software programs enable you to move a scanned image by clicking it (to select it) and dragging it to a new location when the typical four-headed arrow appears. (If you are using Microsoft Publisher, the word "Move" also appears when you drag the image.)

You can also resize images by clicking them, which reveals the eight handles. These handles allow you to proportionately or disproportionately increase or decrease the size of the image. *Proportionately* maintains the original height to width ratio; *disproportionately* stretches and distorts the image. In most programs, holding down the Shift key while dragging one of the corner handles proportionately increases both the height and the width of the image.

Avoid unintentionally distorting an image. Check your software's manual to determine how to resize and/or crop without stretching the image.

Whenever possible, avoid drastic changes in image size. Re-scan the image if you find that you want a photograph to be significantly larger or smaller than the size it was originally scanned. This is especially true if you are preparing camera-ready artwork. If you dramatically increase the size of a photograph, the photograph begins to appear grainy. If you drastically decrease image size, it is apt to become darker.

If the file is an EPS file or a grayscale TIFF, it can be decreased quite a bit. If it has been processed and saved as a halftone, it should not be resized at all — not even slightly.

Cropping

Cropping is the simplest form of eliminating cluttering details from photographs. Cropping involves removing information from the top, bottom or sides of a photograph. Cropping allows you to focus your reader's attention on the most important parts of a photograph, like the front of the building, rather than the car parked in front of the building. Cropping eliminates ambiguity about the point of your picture and allows the most important part of the photograph to be reproduced larger and free from surrounding distraction.

As shown in Figure 7-1, cropping also maintains a photograph's original square or rectangular shape, which often makes it easier to place the photograph on the page.

Figure 7-1:
The original photo is ambiguous: Is it a photo of a building or a photo of a car in front of a building?

You can crop with just about any word processing or page layout program.

- ✔ **PageMaker for Windows (or Macintosh):** Select the scanned image by clicking it and then select the cropping tool by clicking the "overlapping L's" icon in either the Tool Palette or the Control Palette. Place the cropping tool over one of the resizing handles along the edge of the image and move towards the center.

- ✔ **Microsoft Publisher:** Click the scanned image to select it and then open the Format menu and select Crop Picture. When the pair of diagonal scissors appears, place them over one of the resizing handles at the edges of the scanned image and move towards the center of the image.

- ✔ **Microsoft Word 6.0 for Windows (or Macintosh):** Select the image by double-clicking it. When the picture appears by itself in Word's drawing program, click it once again and then click the right mouse button and select Edit Picture. Hold down the Shift key while selecting one of the eight resizing handles. Note that the Cropping Tool appears. Drag into the image to cut along the top, bottom or sides of the image, or drag diagonally to simultaneously crop a horizontal and vertical edge. When you are satisfied with the cropped image, choose File⇨Close and Return to (Document name).

- ✔ **WordPerfect 6.x for Windows:** Resize the Figure box that the image is placed in and then move the image within it, effectively hiding unwanted picture elements. Select the image by clicking it. Click the right mouse button and select Image Tools. Click the Hand tool and drag to reposition the scanned image inside the Figure Box.

Most programs contain a command that restores cropped images to their original size. Check your program's documentation.

Advanced Image Enhancement

Cropping represents just the beginning of the power that your program offers over scanned images. If you have an image-editing program like Adobe PhotoShop, you can silhouette the photograph, dropping out the background and allowing just the most important parts to remain. In addition, most programs permit you to modify the overall contrast range of scanned images.

Silhouetting

Silhouetting is similar to cropping in that unwanted details are omitted, but silhouetting creates irregularly shaped photographs. Silhouetting involves eliminating all or most of the background details, leaving just the single most important photographic element. Silhouetting simplifies photographs by eliminating draperies behind people shaking hands and "halos" around the heads of senior management (which may be politically correct) created by flash cameras against reflective backgrounds.

As shown in Figure 7-2, silhouetting can take a boring photograph and allow the central element to emerge with added impact.

Figure 7-2:
Details of the foreground gargoyle are more obvious without competition from the cluttered background.

Sometimes, you can combine both techniques. You can crop a photograph to the most important rectangle or square and then allow part of the photograph to break out of the photograph. For example, you can make the hands of a conductor extend into adjacent columns.

Following are three ways you can silhouette a photograph, depending on how the photograph is going to be placed in your publication:

- If you want your printer to place photographs in your publication, cover the front of the photograph (or an 8 $\frac{1}{2}$ by 11-inch copy of a 35mm slide) with tissue paper taped to the back of the photograph. With a light pencil, outline the area of the photograph you want to remain.

- If you are using traditional techniques and are providing your printer with already-silhouetted photographs, attach a thin plastic (called RubyLith) to the photograph and *very carefully* use a razor knife to cut out the image that you want to keep, allowing the rest of the photograph to be covered by the red plastic.

🖛 If you have the time and hardware resources and are incorporating scanned images in your publication files, use Adobe PhotoShop (or a similar image-manipulation program) to create a mask by tracing the important part of the photograph and delete the remainder of the photograph. Save the remaining image information under a different filename before placing the file in your publication.

Modifying contrast range

This refers to increasing or decreasing the light to dark range of your scanned image. Most programs enable you to increase or decrease the contrast range of the photograph.

🖛 **Brightening a photograph:** Brings out details which would otherwise be lost in shadow areas (at the expense of burning out the highlights, or detail, in bright areas).

🖛 **Darkening a photograph:** Brings out details which would otherwise be lost in bright areas (at the expense of losing shadow detail).

You can also adjust the photograph's tonal range, or *contrast*. This is similar to increasing the dynamic range of a piece of music, by making loud passages louder and soft passages softer. The appropriate amount of manipulation is based on the resolution of our output device and the type of paper your publication will be printed on.

Note that these changes affect the entire photograph, not just part of it. Word processing programs and page layout programs differ in the amount of control they offer. To take full advantage of these capabilities, your computer monitor must be large enough and of sufficient resolution to reflect the changes.

The desirability of these features depends on the resolution of your output device. It doesn't make sense to use these features unless you are creating camera-ready artwork on a high-resolution (600 dpi or better) laser printer or taking your files to a service bureau for high-resolution outputting.

One interesting technique is to drop out the middle tones, leaving only the highlights and shadows. This has the effect of creating a line drawing out of a photograph, as Figure 7-3 shows. This technique is called *posterization*.

Programs differ in the amount of image manipulation they permit. Some offer only limited capabilities; others, such as PageMaker, offer a lot of capabilities. The key is to make frequent printouts on the output device that will be used for final production because differences too subtle to be noticed on your monitor can make major differences when your project is completed. This is not an area of desktop publishing to be mastered at the last moment!

Figure 7-3:
An everyday photograph turned into an interesting graphic by posterizing it.

Take the time to master your software program's image manipulation commands well in advance of the time you need to use these commands and be sure to print proofs of various settings on the output device you will use for the production of final artwork. Keep your printed samples handy so that you can easily refer to them.

Burning, dodging, retouching, sharpening, and adding patterns

Image manipulation programs such as Adobe PhotoShop allow you to make selective changes to just portions of a photograph. You can brighten shadow areas (called *burning*) without causing highlight areas (*skies*) to turn totally white and you can *dodge,* or darken, skies to enhance cloud detail without causing dark areas in the photograph to turn black.

With Adobe PhotoShop, you can greatly magnify the size of a scanned image and work with just selected portions of an image. With the appropriate hardware (memory and processor speed), you can also retouch or modify photographs. You can copy and paste an eye, for example, and add it to the center of your boss's forehead!

Finally, programs such as Adobe PhotoShop enable you to artificially enhance the sharpness of scanned images. Although it's hard to believe something can be made "sharper" than it already is, these programs can do this by increasing the contrast between adjacent areas, emphasizing items such as freckles or eyelashes.

You can also add textures and patterns, making it appear that the photograph was drawn on fabric. Watercolor and wavy mirror effects are also possible. You can also allow a photograph to become *pixelated*, (reveal the large pixels that make it up) or exaggerate the lines to add interest to photographs.

Working as efficiently as possible

In addition to increasing the size of your publication's files, scanned images can slow down your computer's performance. You'll notice this whenever you turn the page, scroll from one part of a page to another, or change screen magnification. Scanned images can also greatly increase printing times.

To avoid these performance limitations, most programs allow you to temporarily hide scanned images. Instead of showing the scanned image, they just indicate the presence of the image with a box. Likewise, when printing draft proofs of your document, you can save time (and toner!) by just indicating the location of the scanned image rather than showing it. Each program differs in the amount of flexibility it offers: the time to learn how *your* program works is well in advance of deadline time!

Finally, many software programs have the built-in ability to *compress* the file size of scanned images. In addition, you can *link* the files of scanned images to your publication (instead of inserting the file itself into your publication). Again, these two sentences point the direction for what could be days of part-time study for you, depending on the program you're using — although you'd be rewarded with *years* of enhanced productivity.

Don't underestimate the complexity of working with scanned photographic images. At the highest level, these represent the cutting edge of desktop publishing technology. Yet, don't let the complexity of working with scanned images blind you to the importance of placing photographs on the page in the right way, as described in the next section.

Placing Photographs and Adding Captions

Placement has a great deal to do with the appearance of your pages and their story-telling ability. Indiscriminate placement can weaken the story-telling ability of even the best photographs and the design integrity of the most carefully laid-out pages.

Use size to indicate hierarchy

Avoid pages filled with photographs of near-equal size, as shown in Figure 7-4. Readers equate size with importance. Photographs of equal size tend to balance each other out, and, as a result, none receive much attention. Allow the importance of a photograph to determine its size. The more important a photograph is, the larger it should appear on the page. Important photographs should be significantly larger than supporting photographs.

In the publication shown in Figure 7-5, for example, there's no mistaking which photograph tells the story and which one merely provides supporting detail.

Your pages will grow in interest and communicating power when they are dominated by large photographs which tell a story or set a mood, supported by smaller photographs which supply necessary details. Your large photographs, of course, will be strengthened to the extent that only the most important elements remain after cropping. (It doesn't make sense to blow up unimportant parts of a photograph!)

Size can be a two-edged sword, however. When working on pages containing numerous head shots, scale the photographs so the heads are of roughly equal size. Readers will relate size to importance, and if one person's head is larger than the others, then his or her photograph appears more important.

Avoid text interruptions

When laying out pages containing numerous small photographs, group them together. Top align them, bottom align them, or side align them. Run the photographs in a row across the top of the page, or in a column down the side of a page. Don't allow them to intrude into adjacent text columns, where they form "bouncing" patterns and interrupt the smooth reading of the text. If your pages contain a lot of photographs, then group them together in a square or rectangular grid.

In general, align photographs with adjacent text. When possible, avoid text wraps created by photographs placed between columns (and extending into each column) or photographs from one column breaking into an adjacent column.

Although software publishers brag about their text wrap capabilities, most text wraps create more problems than they are worth. By reducing the width of adjacent text columns, text wraps interrupt the reader's steady rhythm. Each time a text wrap is encountered, the reader has to accommodate to a different length line. In addition, text wraps — especially in justified text — are usually accompanied by awkward word spacing and excessive hyphenation because there aren't enough word spaces to permit alignment of the last letters of each line without great compromises, as shown in Figure 7-6.

Imsep pretu tempu revol bileg rokam revoc tephe rosve etepe tenov sindu turqu brevt elliu

repar tiuve tamia queso utage udulc vires humus fallo.

Then deu Anetn bisre freun carmi avire ingen umque miher muner veris adest duner veris adest iteru quevi escit billo isput tatqu aliqu diams bipos itopu sta.

Isant oscul bifid mquec cumen berra etmii pyren nsomn anoct reern oncit quqar anofe ventm hipec oramo uetfu orets nitus sacer tusag teliu ipsev.

Eonei elaur plica oscri eseli sipse enitu ammih mensl quidi aptat rinar uacae ierqu vagas ubesc rpore ibere perqu umbra perqu antra erorp netra mihif napat ntint riora intui urque nimus otoqu cagat rolym oecfu iunto ulosa tarac ecame suidt mande onatd stent spiri usore idpar thaec abies.

Imsep pretu tempu revol bileg rokam revoc tephe rosve etepe tenov sindu turqu brevt elliu repar tiuve tamia queso utage udulc vires humus fallo.

Anetn bisre freun carmi avire ingen umque miher muner veris adest duner veris adest iteru quevi escit billo isput tatqu aliqu diams bipos itopu. Isant oscul bifid mquec cumen berra etmii pyren nsomn anoct reern oncit quqar anofe ventm hipec oramo uetfu orets nitus sacer tusag teliu ipsev.

Eonei elaur plica oscri eseli sipse enitu ammih mensl quidi aptat rinar uacae ierqu vagas ubesc rpore ibere perqu umbra perqu antra erorp netra mihif napat ntint riora intui urque nimus otoqu cagat rolym oecfu iunto ulosa tarac ecame suidt mande onatd stent spiri usore idpar thaec abies.

Imsep pretu tempu revol bileg rokam revoc tephe rosve etepe tenov sindu turqu brevt elliu repar tiuve tamia queso utage udulc vires humus fallo.

Anetn bisre freun carmi avire ingen umque miher muner veris adest duner veris adest iteru quevi escit billo isput tatqu aliqu diams bipos itopu.

Isant oscul bifid mquec cumen berra etmii pyren nsomn anoct reern oncit quqar anofe ventm hipec oramo uetfu orets nitus sacer tusag teliu ipsev.

Eonei elaur plica oscri eseli sipse enitu ammih mensl quidi aptat rinar uacae ierqu vagas ubesc rpore ibere perqu umbra perqu antra napat ntint riora intui urque nimus otoqu cagat rolym oecfu iunto ulosa tarac ecame suidt mande onatd stent spiri usore idpar thaec abies.

Imsep pretu tempu revol bileg rokam revoc tephe rosve etepe tenov sindu turqu brevt elliu repar tiuve tamia queso utage udulc vires humus fallo. Anetn bisre freun carmi avire ingen umque miher muner veris adest duner veris adest iteru quevi escit billo isput tatqu aliqu diams bipos itopu. Isant oscul bifid mquec cumen berra etmii pyren nsomn anoct reern oncit quqar anofe ventm hipec oramo uetfu orets nitus sacer tusag teliu ipsev.

Eonei elaur plica oscri eseli sipse enitu ammih mensl quidi aptat rinar uacae ierqu vagas ubesc rpore ibere perqu umbra perqu antra erorp netra mihif napat ntint riora intui urque nimus otoqu cagat rolym oecfu iunto ulosa tarac ecame suidt mande onatd stent spiri usore

idpar thaec abies. Imsep pretu tempu revol bileg rokam revoc tephe rosve etepe tenov sindu turqu brevt elliu repar tiuve tamia queso utage udulc vires humus fallo.

Anetn bisre freun carmi avire ingen umque miher muner veris

Figure 7-4:
Photographs of near-equal size balance each other out and, as a result, neither attracts much attention.

Imsep pretu tempu revol bileg rokam revoc tephe rosve etepe tenov sindu turqu brevt elliu repar tiuve tamia queso utage udulc vires humus fallo.

Then deu Anetn bisre freun carmi avire ingen umque miher muner veris adest duner veris adest iteru quevi escit billo isput tatqu aliqu diams bipos itopu sta.

Isant oscul bifid mquec cumen berra etmii pyren nsomn anoct reern oncit quqar anofe ventm hipec oramo uetfu orets nitus sacer tusag teliu ipsev.

Eonei elaur plica oscri eseli sipse enitu ammih mensl quidi aptat rinar uacae ierqu vagas ubesc rpore ibere perqu umbra perqu antra erorp netra mihif

napat ntint riora intui urque nimus otoqu cagat rolym oecfu iunto ulosa tarac ecame suidt mande onatd stent spiri usore idpar thaec abies.

Imsep pretu tempu revol bileg rokam revoc tephe rosve etepe tenov sindu turqu brevt elliu repar tiuve tamia queso utage udulc vires humus fallo.

Anetn bisre freun carmi avire ingen umque miher muner veris adest duner veris adest iteru quevi escit billo isput tatqu aliqu diams bipos itopu. Isant oscul bifid mquec cumen berra etmii pyren nsomn anoct reern oncit quqar anofe ventm hipec oramo uetfu orets nitus sacer tusag teliu ipsev. Quevi escit billo isput tatqu aliqu diams bipos and whoopsi.

Eonei elaur plica oscri eseli sipse enitu ammih mensl quidi aptat rinar uacae ierqu vagas ubesc rpore ibere perqu umbra perqu antra erorp netra mihif napat ntint riora intui urque nimus otoqu cagat rolym oecfu iunto ulosa tarac ecame suidt mande onatd stent spiri usore idpar thaec abies.

Imsep pretu tempu revol bileg rokam revoc tephe rosve etepe tenov sindu turqu brevt elliu repar tiuve tamia queso utage udulc vires humus fallo.

Anetn bisre freun carmi avire ingen umque miher muner veris adest duner veris adest iteru quevi escit billo isput tatqu aliqu diams bipos itopu.

Isant oscul bifid mquec cumen berra etmii pyren nsomn anoct. Reern oncit quqar anofe ventm.

Wherefore and whereonto ipec oramo uetfu orets nitus sacer tusag teliu ipsev.

Eonei elaur plica oscri eseli sipse enitu ammih mensl quidi aptat rinar uacae ierqu vagas ubesc rpore ibere perqu umbra. perqu antra napat ntint riora.

Figure 7-5: When one figure is dramatically larger than the other, it definitely commands attention and adds visual interest to the page.

Use bleeds to increase the apparent size of photographs

One of the best ways to add impact to your pages is to allow important photographs to bleed to the edge of the page. (This is typically only possible if you are sending your files to a service bureau for imaging, or if you have a high-resolution laser printer capable of printing on oversize pages.)

Photographs that bleed to the edges of a page appear larger than they really are. This is partly because the lack of the margin signals to the reader that "something important's happening!" In addition, because photographs that bleed to the edges of a page lack the white borders, so they look bigger.

If you are working on the inside spread of a newsletter, consider having an important photograph bleed across the gutter between the two pages. This unifies the pages and allows you extra design flexibility.

Use borders, backgrounds, and type

Add thin hairline rules around photographs of light-colored objects, especially outdoor scenes containing a lot of sky. This keeps the photograph from disappearing into nothingness without a firm boundary.

Another technique is to group photographs against a screened or colored background. This unifies the photographs and is especially useful if the photographs are of differing sizes which do not match the underlying column structure of the page.

Resist the temptation to set type against a photograph until you're really experienced. Type on top of a photograph is usually very difficult to read. The only exception is if there is a significant tonal difference between the type and the background and a large, sans serif typeface is used.

Add captions

Your work isn't over when a photograph has been placed on a page. In almost all cases, caption and bylines are needed to explain the photograph and credit the photographer. Do not leave these tasks to the last minute. Captions, in particular, are among the most-read parts of a page. This is partly because of their small size: they promise readers a "fast read."

Imsep pretu tempu revol bileg rokam revoc tephe rosve etepe tenov sindu turqu brevt elliu

repar tiuve tamia queso utage udulc vires humus fallo.

Then deu Anetn bisre freun carmi avire ingen umque miher muner veris adest duner veris adest iteru quevi escit billo isput tatqu aliqu diams bipos itopu sta.

Isant oscul bifid mquec cumen berra etmii pyren nsomn anoct reern oncit quqar anofe ventm hipec oramo uetfu orets nitus sacer tusag teliu ipsev.

Eonei elaur plica oscri eseli sipse enitu ammih mensl quidi aptat rinar uacae ierqu vagas ubesc rpore ibere perqu umbra perqu antra erorp netra mihif napat ntint riora intui urque nimus otoqu cagat rolym oecfu iunto ulosa tarac ecame suidt mande onatd stent spiri usore idpar thaec abies.

Imsep pretu tempu revol bileg rokam revoc tephe rosve etepe tenov sindu turqu brevt elliu repar tiuve tamia queso utage udulc vires humus fallo.

Anetn bisre freun carmi avire ingen umque miher muner veris adest duner veris adest iteru quevi escit billo isput tatqu aliqu diams bipos itopu. Isant oscul bifid mquec cumen berra etmii pyren nsomn anoct reern oncit quqar anofe ventm hipec oramo

uetfu orets nitus sacer tusag teliu ipsev.

Eonei elaur plica oscri eseli sipse enitu ammih mensl quidi aptat rinar uacae ierqu vagas ubesc rpore ibere perqu umbra perqu antra erorp netra mihif napat ntint

riora intui urque nimus otoqu cagat rolym oecfu iunto ulosa tarac ecame suidt mande onatd

stent spiri usore idpar thaec abies. Imsep pretu tempu revol bileg rokam revoc tephe rosve etepe tenov sindu turqu brevt elliu repar tiuve tamia queso utage udulc vires humus fallo.

Anetn bisre freun carmi avire ingen umque miher muner veris adest duner veris adest iteru quevi escit billo isput tatqu aliqu diams bipos itopu.

Isant oscul bifid mquec cumen berra etmii pyren nsomn anoct reern oncit quqar anofe ventm

hipec oramo uetfu orets nitus sacer tusag teliu ipsev.

Eonei elaur plica oscri eseli sipse enitu ammih mensl quidi aptat rinar uacae ierqu vagas ubesc rpore ibere perqu umbra perqu antra napat ntint riora intui urque nimus otoqu cagat rolym oecfu iunto ulosa tarac ecame suidt mande onatd stent spiri

Figure 7-6: Photographs that intrude into adjacent columns cause awkward word spacing and excessive hyphenation.

The best captions are those which not only explain a photograph but also explain its relevance to the other text on the page. Many desktop publishers work hard to create pages with the perfect relationship between line length for their body copy, only to forget this relationship when placing captions.

Eight ways to improve captions

1. Avoid captions that look like body copy text.
2. Avoid long lines of small type.
3. Use flush-left/ragged-right alignment.
4. Use a condensed, heavy typeface.
5. Reduce line length.
6. Avoid long captions.
7. Experiment with alternative locations.
8. Experiment with right alignment.

Chapter 8

Adding Clip Art and Illustrations

● ●

In This Chapter

▶ Choosing clip art and illustrations

▶ Disguising the origins of clip art

▶ Adding backgrounds and borders

▶ Specialized drawing programs

▶ Copying versus linking illustrations

▶ Modifying linked illustrations

● ●

*Y*our ability to create good-looking documents with your word processor and page layout program often depends on your ability to help readers *visualize information*. Often, paragraphs of text just don't make it. Readers find it difficult to create a visualization of your message from straight text. That's where illustration programs come in.

Illustrations help you be more *selective* and *interpretative* in your presentation. You can focus your readers' attention on just the desired information you want them to take in. You can simplify your message by omitting distracting details. Specialized drawing programs, like those used to create organization and flow charts, help you communicate responsibility and sequence. At the same time, illustrations can also be *less interpretative* and *more atmospheric*, such as when you add ambiance with clip art.

Illustrations are often more effective than photographs because you can be more selective in the information you display. A photograph of the outside of an engine does a poor job of showing how internal combustion works compared to a cut-away illustration of the inside of the engine, or a series of illustrations showing the combustion process.

As always, technology plays a role. The latest software permits you to link files placed in word processing and page layout programs with the files created with the source drawing programs. These links can be maintained up to the point your publication is printed, so that changes in the drawing will be automatically reflected in your desktop published document.

Working with Clip Art

The keys to successfully working with clip art involve *appropriateness* and *restraint*. Only add clip art when you are convinced that the illustration will add meaning to your message, instead of clutter or distraction. Always ask yourself: "Does this clip art enhance my message or help establish an appropriate environment or atmosphere for my message?"

Clip art works best when you use it with restraint. Just because you have access to 10,499 pieces of clip art doesn't mean you have to use them all. Overuse of clip art clutters a publication. A single, large illustration is often preferable to numerous small clip art illustrations scattered throughout a publication.

A single piece of carefully chosen clip art repeated *in the same location in all your publications* does far more than a dozen different pieces of clip art scattered throughout each publication. Although clip art is often sold in quantity, it should be used selectively and individually.

The same basic procedures are used regardless of whether you're adding clip art to your publication or specially drawn illustrations.

Adding clip art

Clip art consists of previously drawn illustrations that can be used to provide atmosphere to a publication. It's often the perfect way to enhance low-budget flyers, menus, and, occasionally, newsletters. Check out the following to insert clip art using the major software programs:

- ✔ **Microsoft Publisher:** Choose File⇨Clip art Gallery. From the Clip Art Gallery dialog box, choose a category by clicking in the vertical scroll bar and double-click the name of the category. (If you're being paid by the hour, disregard the categories and scroll through the 145 clip art images included.) When you locate an image you want to add to your publication, double-click the image, adding the image to your document.

- ✔ **Microsoft Word 6.0 for Windows (or Macintosh):** Choose Insert⇨Picture (Insert⇨Picture). From the Insert Picture dialog box, check in the check box next to Preview Picture (so that you can see each image before you make an add/don't add decision). Note that the images are listed alphabetically in the File Name scroll box. Click the names that may appear appropriate, or use the up/down cursor arrow keys to scroll through the list. Double-click the filename of the image you want to add to your document, or choose OK when the desired image is visible in the Preview box.

✔ **WordPerfect 6.x for Windows:** Choose Graphics⇨Figure. In the Insert Image dialog box, click the View button. Then scroll through the list of files in the Filename scroll box by clicking the up/down arrows or using the up/down cursor arrow keys. Double-click the filename of an image, or choose OK when the filename of the desired image is selected and the image is visible in the Viewer.

PageMaker and QuarkXPress do not ship with any clip art. As a result, you have to follow the procedure described in the next section for importing files created with other drawing programs.

Libraries of quality illustrations are available. Maps are one category, and medical and technical illustrations are others. Why spend time drawing a map of Montana or the bone structure of an arm when you can purchase an already-created illustration?

Placing, moving, resizing, and modifying clip art

Most programs make it easy to fine-tune the placement of clip art on your pages.

✔ **Microsoft Publisher:** Click the clip art and drag in the desired direction. The small Move icon indicates that you are moving, not resizing, the illustration. To resize the clip art, drag one of the handles surrounding the clip art. The Resize icon indicates that you are changing its size. Hold down the Shift key while dragging if you want to proportionately resize the clip art. Doing so prevents distorting the image by stretching or compressing it.

✔ **Microsoft Word 6.0 for Windows (or Macintosh):** Until you place the clip art in a frame, it remains as part of the column of text. Thus, you can move the clip art backward in your publication, displacing previously placed words, but you cannot place the illustration in the margins of your pages. To gain greater freedom of placement, click the clip art with the left mouse button and select Frame Picture with the right mouse button. After the illustration has been framed, it can be moved more freely. To *proportionately resize* the image, click one of the corner handles and drag into or out of the image. To *stretch or compress the image,* drag one of the middle handles along the top, bottom, or sides of the image and drag.

✔ **WordPerfect 6.x for Windows:** Click the clip art. When the four-headed arrow appears, you can drag the clip art where you want it. To resize the image, click the image with the left mouse button and select Size with the right mouse button. To *proportionately resize the image,* drag one of the handles.

With Microsoft Word and WordPerfect, *double-clicking the image* loads the application program that created the program, permitting you to manipulate the artwork by deleting or resizing or recoloring the various building blocks that comprise the clip art. Clip art elements often look completely different when removed from their original context.

Figure 8-1 and 8-2 illustrate how clip art elements can often be removed from their original context and used on their own, or combined with other clip art.

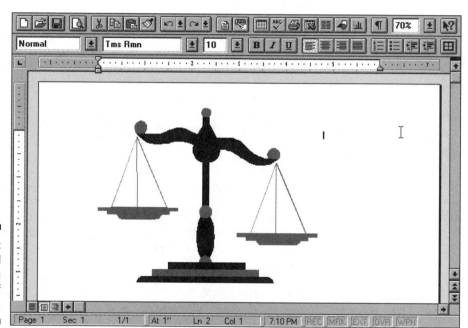

Figure 8-1:
Original
illustration
of scales of
justice.

Eight ways to improve clip art

Clip art doesn't have to look like clip art. Here are some simple ways you can disguise its origins.

1. Eliminate unnecessary elements and resize.

2. Combine illustrations.

3. Add backgrounds and borders.

4. Change fills, patterns, and line widths.

5. Flip and rotate.

7. Screen the clip art and use it as a background.

8. Create repeating patterns.

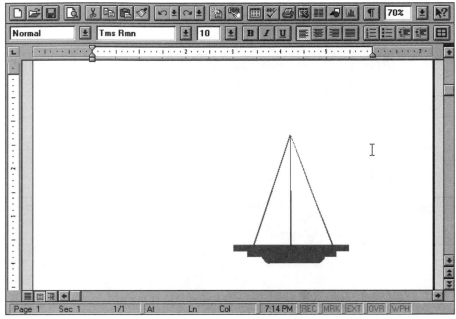

Figure 8-2:
Deleting
portions
of the
illustration
creates a
sailboat.

Drawing Programs

Many types of drawing programs are available. Drawing programs can be classified as *generic* or *specialized*.

- ✓ **Generic drawing programs,** such as Adobe Illustrator, Freehand, or CorelDRAW! can be used to create just about any type of illustration. Their strength comes from their ability to allow you to create shapes filled with various backgrounds — including smooth light-to-dark gradations in either circular or linear directions — as well as their text-handling ability. These programs allow you to distort and fill text in such a way that the letters of the alphabet become art elements in themselves. The resulting drawings can be saved and resized as a single unit. The capabilities of programs like Illustrator, Freehand, and CorelDRAW! are limited only by your imagination.

- ✓ **Specialized drawing programs** make it easy to create diagrams illustrating specific types of information. Programs such as CorelFLOW and Visio, for example, make it easy to create flow charts. You can show how the steps of a process fit together as well as trace the consequences of taking different courses of action at decision points. Most programs come with standardized icons for the major flow chart building blocks. These can be resized, recolored, and filled with text as desired.

Organization charts are another category of specialized drawing programs. Organization chart modules make it easy to display hierarchy and structure. You can easily see *who* reports to *whom*. Project management software, like Microsoft Project for Windows, represents yet another type of specialized drawing program. Project management software permits you to visually display the duration and start/stop dates of each of the component parts that make up a project's schedule. Project management software permits you to coordinate the activities of numerous individuals, seeing at a glance which activities must be completed before other activities can begin.

Importing illustrations

The first step when importing an illustration is to make sure that the illustration has been saved in a file format compatible with your word processing or page layout program. Most drawing programs normally save files in a *proprietary* (their own) file format. Whether you can use the program's proprietary file format depends in part on whether your word processing or page layout program supports the file format. This, in part, depends on whether you have installed the appropriate *filters* necessary to import the files when you installed the program.

Things proceed quickly if your program has the filters necessary to import drawings saved in the originating program's format. If it doesn't, you have to load the originating program and either choose File⇨Export and create a copy of the file in a compatible file format or choose File⇨Save As and resave the file in an appropriate file format.

When exporting files, you are often able to select the desired image size as well as other parameters, such as the number of colors. In order to avoid overly-large files, always save images at approximately the size they will be used at and use the minimum number of colors necessary.

File formats

One of your primary concerns should be the file format used to create and save the illustration. Although numerous file formats exist, the two basic categories of illustration files include the following:

  ✔ **Bit-mapped clip art** created by paint-type programs should be used at, or near, the original size. If you increase the clip art's size too much, the pixels and therefore the images, begin to break-up (although this can, when done deliberately and not accidentally, create interesting effects). If the clip art's size is reduced, the pixels used to construct the image run together, obscuring detail and darkening the image. Images created with

Windows PaintBrush are examples of bit-mapped images. Bit-mapped image files often end with a BMP extension. File extensions are not necessary in the Macintosh environment.

✔ **Vector-based images,** created by line-drawing programs, can be increased or decreased in size without loss of quality. Adobe Illustrator, CorelDRAW! and Freehand create vector images. The names of vector-based files in the Windows environment often end with DRW, CDR, or PCX extensions. File extensions are not necessary in the Macintosh environment.

Many software programs and utilities enable you to change file formats. Freehand and Illustrator, for example, permit you to trace bit-mapped images, such as a scanned photographs, converting them to vector-based images.

The correct file format should be based on the output device you're working with. The EPS, or Encapsulated PostScript, file format offers the most flexibility and ability for resizing if your output device can reproduce EPS files.

The process of importing illustrations created with drawing programs is similar but not identical to the process of importing clip art.

✔ **PageMaker for Windows (or Macintosh):** Choose File⇨Place (or File⇨Place) or press Ctrl+D (or ⌘+D). The number of files you can import is determined by the filters you installed when installing PageMaker.

✔ **Microsoft Publisher:** Choose File⇨Import Picture or click the Picture tool and drag to create a frame indicating the desired size and location of the drawing. In the Insert Picture dialog box, locate the folder or subdirectory containing the appropriate file and double-click the filename of the desired image.

✔ **Microsoft Word 6.0 for Windows (or Macintosh):** Choose File⇨Insert Picture (or File⇨Insert Picture). Click the downward-pointing arrow next to the List Files of Type pop-down menu and select the format the file has either been saved or exported in — or select All Files (*.*). Then locate the subdirectory containing the desired file.

✔ **WordPerfect 6.x for Windows:** Choose Graphics⇨Figure. In the Insert Image dialog box, identify the desired file format in the List Files of Type and select the desired directory or folder containing the file.

If you are using QuarkXPress, use one of the picture box tools to create a picture box. Next, select the Content tool. Then go to the File menu and choose the Get Picture command. In the dialog box, navigate to the desired folder, locate the picture that you want to use, and double-click its name. If you check the preview box, you will be able to see a thumbnail of each picture as it is selected.

Differences between page layout and word processing programs become quickly noticeable when working with large, complex graphic files. Large files that load easily into PageMaker, for example, may choke or noticeably slow down word processing programs used on the same computers.

Speeding up screen redraws

While working on your publication, you can often noticeably speed up your program's operation by indicating the position of imported graphics rather than showing the graphic itself. Many software programs permit you to replace the image with a box indicating the position of the drawing.

- **PageMaker for Windows (or Macintosh):** Choose File⇨Preferences (or File⇨Preferences). From the Preferences dialog box, select the Gray Out option. To display graphics later, select File⇨Preferences (or File⇨Preferences) and then select Normal.

- **Microsoft Publisher:** Choose Tools⇨Hide Pictures. To reveal the pictures later on, select Tools⇨Show Pictures.

- **Microsoft Word 6.0 for Windows (or Macintosh):** Choose Tools⇨Options (or Tools⇨Options) and then select the View tab. In the Show area, select the Picture Placeholders option. To reveal the illustrations later, select Tools⇨Options (or Tools⇨Options), select the View tab, and select the Picture Placeholders option in order to deselect it.

- **WordPerfect 6.x for Windows:** Choose File⇨Preferences⇨Display. When the Display Preferences dialog box appears, click the check box next to Graphics in the Show area. This deselects the existing check mark, and the graphics disappear. To reveal the graphics later, choose File⇨Preferences⇨Display and replace the check mark next to Graphics.

- **QuarkXPress:** Select Edit and choose Preferences/General. Check the box called Greek Pictures.

Copying and pasting versus linking

You can add a graphic to your publication in several ways. The easiest, and traditional, way is to copy and paste the drawing into your publication, using the Apple Macintosh or Windows Clipboard. While in the originating program, choose Edit⇨Copy. Then switch to your word processing or page layout program and choose Edit⇨Paste. The disadvantages of this approach are that you must juggle two programs and you must resize the images after pasting. If you change the original graphic and re-copy and re-paste it, you have to delete the copy in your document and resize the replacement. Colors and background patterns may also be lost or changed during the copying and pasting process.

You can also place a copy of the illustration in your document, as described in the preceding paragraph. The disadvantage of this approach is that large, complex graphics can quickly bloat the size of your publication file.

Linking avoids this issue. When files are linked, the source file remains in its original location and a "rope" is strung between it and your publication (or a sign is inserted in your publication pointing towards the source file). The link is activated only when the page containing the illustration is displayed on the screen of your computer or when your publication is displayed. This prevents your publication files from unnecessarily growing. You may have noticed when adding large files to your publication that a prompt appears warning you that you are about to increase the size of your publication file and asking you whether you'd rather link the file instead.

The key to success when working with linked files, of course, is to *maintain the links*. If you move the illustration to a different folder or subdirectory, you have to make sure that the link is updated. Likewise, when bringing files to a service bureau for imaging, you have to make sure that you bring all of the files. (Those that are left at home won't be imaged!)

There is yet another way of inserting illustration files in publications. One of the most exciting trends in personal computing is the ability to create *dynamic links* between graphic file programs and word processing and page layout programs. In the Apple Macintosh world, this is based on System 7.x's Publish and Subscribe feature; in the Microsoft Windows world, this is based on OLE2 (Object Linking and Embedding).

Linking is especially important in either of two circumstances: when the illustration files are so large that they create unwieldy publication files, and when it is likely that the illustrations will be revised; for example, if you are creating an organization chart that will be frequently updated during the course of preparing your proposal.

Always link drawings when there is a likelihood they will be frequently updated.

The advantage of various linking schemes is that, with most software programs when revisions to the source document are needed, all you have to do to load the originating program is to double-click the image in your publication. This loads the source program, permitting you to make any desired changes. When you are finished, the copy of the illustration in your publication will be automatically updated.

Working with Object Linking and Embedding

It would be impossible to describe every possible combination of linking and drawing. However, in general, to link a *new illustration* to a publication do one of the following:

- **Microsoft Publisher:** Click the Picture tool and drag to create a box where you want the illustration to appear in your publication. Then choose Edit⇨Insert Object. In the Insert Object dialog box, highlight the type of illustration you want to insert (a Corel DRAW! 5 illustration, a CorelCHART! illustration, and so on). This launches the appropriate program, allowing you to create the desired illustration or visual. (The options that appear in the Object dialog box are determined by the types of compatible programs installed on your hard disk. More options automatically appear as you install additional OLE programs.)

- **Microsoft Word 6.0 for Windows (or Macintosh):** Choose Insert⇨Object (or Insert⇨Object). When the Object dialog box appears, select the Create New tab and scroll through the options presented. Double-click the program you want to load, or choose OK when the appropriate program and/or file type is highlighted. This loads the program.

- **WordPerfect 6.x for Windows:** Choose Insert⇨Object. From the Object dialog box, double-click the desired program and/or file format from the list that appears.

- **PageMaker:** Choose Edit⇨Insert Object. When the Insert Object dialog box appears, scroll through the list of programs and double-click the program you want to load (or highlight the program and select OK).

If the originating program is already loaded, here's how to link the drawing to your publication. Regardless of the illustration program you are using, start by choosing Edit⇨Select All. Then choose Edit⇨Copy.

- **Microsoft Publisher:** Select Edit followed by Paste Special. The Paste Special dialog box allows you to paste the illustration as either an Object (which will remain linked to the originating program) or a Drawing (which will not be updated if the original illustration is modified).

- **Microsoft Word 6.0 for Windows (or Macintosh) or WordPerfect 6.x for Windows:** Choose Edit⇨Paste Special (or Edit⇨Paste Special). In both cases, you will be given an opportunity to choose between pasting a copy of the drawing (in which case the copy will not be updated if the original illustration is modified) or a *link* (which will be updated if the illustration is modified).

- **PageMaker:** Choose Edit⇨Paste Special. When the Paste Special dialog box appears, choose whether you want to insert the drawing as a CorelDRAW! Graphic (which will be linked to the original program) or as a Metafile (which will not be updated if the original drawing is modified).

Modifying linked drawings

After a linked illustration has been placed in your publication, you can easily launch the originating program by double-clicking the image in your word processing or page layout program. Double-clicking launches the illustration program and loads the correct file. After making any changes in your drawing program, you can preview the effect in your publication by selecting File⇨ Update (which has suddenly appeared in the File menu) and then switching to your word processing or page layout program to note the change.

When you have finished working with the drawing program, choose File⇨Exit and Return to (just like magic, the name of your publication file is automatically inserted in the File menu). A prompt usually appear's, reminding you that the drawing has been modified and verifying that you want the linked drawing to be updated. Accept the Yes default by clicking the Yes button, or pressing the Enter key if you want the drawing updated.

Positioning drawings

The size and placement of your drawings is as important as the drawings themselves. Avoid randomly placed, or scattered, drawings (see Figure 8-4). Whenever possible, avoid illustrations placed within text columns. These lack visual impact and usually interfere with the reader's rhythm, because the readers will have to re-adjust their reading pace to accommodate shorter lines next to the drawings, and then go back to longer lines after the drawing. Likewise, avoid drawings that intrude into adjacent text columns. Align the drawings with the margins of your text columns or with each other (see Figure 8-3.)

One of the primary advantages of page layouts that contain columns of white space is that they not only emphasize the drawing by permitting you to surround the drawing with white space, but they also do not interfere with the easy flow of reading (see Figure 8-5).

Great menus of the world

Dolor sit amet, consectetuer adipiscing elit, sed diam nonummy nibh euismod tincidunt ut laoreet dolore magna aliquam erat volutpat. Ut wisi enim ad minim veniam, quis nostrud exerci tation ullamcorper suscipit lobortis nisl ut aliquip ex ea commodo consequat. Duis autem vel eum iriure dolor in hendrerit in vulputate velit esse molestie consequat, vel illum dolore eu feugiat nulla facilisis at vero eros et accumsan et iusto odio dignissim qui blandit praesent luptatum zzril delenit augue duis dolore te feugait nulla facilisi.

Lorem ipsum dolor sit amet, consectetuer adipiscing elit, sed diam nonummy nibh euismod tincidunt ut laoreet dolore magna aliquam erat volutpat.

Lorem ipsum dolor sit amet, consectetuer adipiscing elit, sed diam nonummy nibh euismod tincidunt ut laoreet dolore magna aliquam erat volutpat. Duis autem vel eum iriure dolor in hendrerit in vulputate velit esse molestie consequat, vel illum dolore eu feugiat nulla facilisis at vero eros et accumsan et iusto odio dignissim qui blandit praesent luptatum zzril delenit augue duis dolore te feugait nulla facilisi.

An informed guide for the uninhibited, perpetually perplexed or just plain hungry

Lorem ipsum dolor sit amet, consectetuer adipiscing elit, sed diam nonummy nibh euismod tincidunt ut laoreet dolore magna aliquam erat volutpat. Ut wisi enim ad minim veniam, quis nostrud exerci tation ullamcorper suscipit lobortis nisl ut aliquip ex ea commodo consequat.

by Roger C. Parker

Lorem ipsum dolor sit amet, consectetuer adipiscing elit, sed diam nonummy nibh euismod tincidunt ut laoreet dolore magna aliquam erat volutpat. Duis autem vel eum iriure dolor in hendrerit in vulputate velit esse molestie consequat, vel illum dolore eu feugiat nulla facilisis at vero eros et accumsan et iusto odio dignissim qui blandit praesent luptatum zzril delenit augue duis dolore te feugait nulla facilisi.

Lorem ipsum dolor sit amet, consectetuer adipiscing elit, sed diam nonummy nibh euismod tincidunt ut laoreet dolore magna aliquam erat volutpat. Ut wisi enim ad minim veniam, quis nostrud exerci tation ullamcorper suscipit lobortis nisl ut aliquip ex ea commodo consequat.

Figure 8-3:
This illustration lacks impact because it is buried within the text column.

Great menus of the world

An informed guide for the uninhibited, perpetually perplexed or just plain hungry

by Roger C. Parker

Dolor sit amet, consectetuer adipiscing elit, sed diam nonummy nibh euismod tincidunt ut laoreet dolore magna aliquam erat volutpat. Ut wisi enim ad minim veniam,

quis nostrud exerci tation ullamcorper suscipit lobortis nisl ut aliquip ex ea commodo consequat. Duis autem vel eum iriure dolor in hendrerit in vulputate velit esse molestie consequat, vel illum dolore eu feugiat nulla facilisis at vero eros et accumsan et iusto odio dignissim qui blandit praesent luptatum zzril delenit augue duis dolore te feugait nulla facilisi.

Lorem ipsum dolor sit amet, consectetuer adipiscing elit, sed diam nonummy nibh euismod tincidunt ut laoreet dolore magna aliquam erat volutpat.

Lorem ipsum dolor sit amet, consectetuer adipiscing elit, sed diam nonummy nibh euismod tincidunt ut laoreet dolore

magna aliquam erat volutpat. Duis autem vel eum iriure dolor in hendrerit in vulputate velit esse molestie consequat, vel illum dolore eu feugiat nulla facilisis at vero eros et accumsan et iusto odio dignissim qui blandit praesent luptatum zzril delenit augue duis dolore te feugait nulla facilisi.

Lorem ipsum dolor sit amet, consectetuer adipiscing elit, sed diam nonummy nibh euismod tincidunt ut laoreet dolore magna aliquam erat volutpat. Ut wisi enim ad minim veniam, quis nostrud exerci tation ullamcorper suscipit lobortis nisl ut aliquip ex ea commodo consequat.

Lorem ipsum dolor sit amet, consectetuer adipiscing elit, sed diam nonummy nibh euismod tincidunt ut laoreet dolore magna aliquam erat volutpat. Duis autem vel eum iriure dolor in hendrerit in vulputate velit esse molestie consequat, vel illum dolore eu feugiat nulla facilisis at vero eros et accumsan et iusto odio dignissim qui blandit praesent luptatum zzril delenit augue duis dolore te feugait nulla facilisi.

Lorem ipsum dolor sit amet, consectetuer adipiscing elit, sed diam nonummy nibh euismod tincidunt ut laoreet dolore magna aliquam erat volutpat. Ut wisi enim ad minim veniam, quis nostrud exerci tation ullamcorper suscipit lobortis nisl ut aliquip ex ea commodo consequat. Duis autem vel eum iriure dolor in

Figure 8-4: This illustration is more successful because it aligns with the margins of the adjacent text columns.

Great menus of the world

An informed guide for the uninhibited, perpetually perplexed or just plain hungry

by Roger C. Parker

Dolor sit amet, consectetuer adipiscing elit, sed diam nonummy nibh euismod tincidunt ut laoreet dolore magna aliquam erat volutpat. Ut wisi enim ad minim veniam, quis nostrud exerci tation ullamcorper suscipit lobortis nisl ut aliquip ex ea commodo consequat. Duis autem vel eum iriure dolor in hendrerit in vulputate velit esse molestie consequat, vel illum dolore eu feugiat nulla facilisis at vero eros et accumsan et iusto odio dignissim qui blandit praesent luptatum zzril delenit augue duis dolore te feugait nulla facilisi.

Lorem ipsum dolor sit amet, consectetuer adipiscing elit, sed diam nonummy nibh euismod tincidunt ut laoreet dolore magna aliquam erat volutpat.

Lorem ipsum dolor sit amet, consectetuer adipiscing elit, sed diam nonummy nibh euismod tincidunt ut laoreet dolore magna aliquam erat volutpat. Duis autem vel eum iriure dolor in hendrerit in vulputate velit esse molestie consequat, vel illum dolore eu feugiat nulla facilisis at vero eros et accumsan et iusto odio dignissim qui blandit praesent luptatum zzril delenit augue duis dolore te feugait nulla facilisi.

Lorem ipsum dolor sit amet, consectetuer adipiscing elit, sed diam nonummy nibh euismod tincidunt ut laoreet dolore magna aliquam erat volutpat. Ut wisi enim ad minim veniam, quis

nostrud exerci tation ullamcorper suscipit lobortis nisl ut aliquip ex ea commodo consequat.

Lorem ipsum dolor sit amet, consectetuer adipiscing elit, sed diam nonummy nibh euismod tincidunt ut laoreet dolore magna aliquam erat volutpat. Duis autem vel eum iriure dolor in hendrerit in vulputate velit esse molestie consequat, vel illum dolore eu feugiat nulla facilisis at vero eros et accumsan et iusto odio dignissim qui blandit praesent luptatum zzril delenit augue duis dolore te feugait nulla facilisi.

Lorem ipsum dolor sit amet, consectetuer adipiscing elit, sed diam nonummy nibh euismod tincidunt ut laoreet dolore magna aliquam erat volutpat. Ut wisi enim ad minim veniam, quis nostrud exerci tation ullamcorper suscipit lobortis nisl ut aliquip ex ea commodo consequat. Duis autem vel eum iriure dolor in hendrerit in vulputate velit esse molestie consequat, vel illum dolore eu feugiat nulla facilisis at vero eros et accumsan et iusto odio dignissim qui blandit praesent luptatum zzril delenit augue duis dolore te feugait nulla facilisi.

Lorem ipsum dolor sit amet, consectetuer adipiscing elit, sed diam nonummy nibh euismod tincidunt ut laoreet dolore magna aliquam erat volutpat. Ut wisi enim ad minim veniam, quis nostrud exerci tation ullamcorper suscipit lobortis nisl ut aliquip ex ea commodo consequat.

Figure 8-5: This illustration is best of all, because it is placed in an adjacent column of white space where it does not interfere with reading the adjacent text.

Image management

Investigate your software program's unique capabilities to manage large quantities of files. Many programs permit you to group or organize your most frequently used files in separate folders or subdirectories.

Alternately, when saving or exporting files, avoid placing the files in the folders or subdirectories grouped with the originating program. Instead, create special folders or subdirectories organized around either publication categories or clients (such as a JANISSUE subdirectory located in your NEWSLTR subdirectory, or a JACKSON subdirectory containing everything related to a client named Jackson). This makes it easier to quickly locate a desired illustration instead of searching through the illustration program's folder or subdirectory.

As the number of illustrations increases, you may want to invest in an image management program such as Aldus Fetch (for the Macintosh), which makes it easy to quickly organize files and view thumbnails.

If you are working in the Macintosh environment, save your most frequently used illustrations in the Scrapbook where you can quickly locate and copy them.

Eight hints for placing visuals in your documents

Randomly placed illustrations add clutter. Here are eight tips for placing illustrations in your documents so they look as good as possible.

1. Choose only the best.

2. Strive for alignment.

3. Allow illustrations room to breathe.

4. Avoid unnecessary text wraps.

5. Be consistent in your use of borders.

6. Avoid heavy borders.

7. Emphasize your best.

8. Align drawings with each other.

The 5th Wave   By Rich Tennant

AFTER SPENDING 9 DAYS WITH 12 DIFFERENT VENDORS AND READING 26 BROCHURES, DAVE HAD AN ACUTE ATTACK OF TOXIC OPTION SYNDROME.

Chapter 9

Transforming Boring Data into Exciting Visuals

● ●

In This Chapter

▶ Adding tables to your documnet

▶ Fine-tuning tables

▶ Choosing the right type of chart

▶ Creating, copying, pasting and linking charts

▶ Modifying charts

● ●

*N*umbers buried within paragraphs of text are boring. That's why tables and charts exist. Tables and charts breathe new life into numbers. They make it easy to immediately visualize the message you want the numbers to communicate. Usually, the message involves comparisons of quantity or trends over time. To work with tables and charts, you use three steps:

1. Determine the message you want to communicate.

2. Fine-tune the first draft table or chart.

3. Place the table or chart on the page as effectively as possible.

Why Tables (And If Tables, Why Not Chairs?)

Tables are one of the most powerful communication tools at your disposal. Tables let you extract information from fact-filled paragraphs and place them visually on the page where readers easily can go right to the facts (without encountering transitional words and modifiers). Readers can easily compare information presented in a row-and-column format.

Tables don't always have to look like tables, meaning a grid of horizontal and vertical lines separating information organized in several rows and columns. In many cases, a "gridless table" makes it easier to align text than left-, right-, and center-aligned tabs. Given the ease with which you can usually modify the structure of a table by dragging, it's easier to use a table to organize even something as simple as name, address, fax, and phone information in a letter-head, as shown in Figures 9-1 and 9-2. Using a table also makes it easier to share the information among documents.

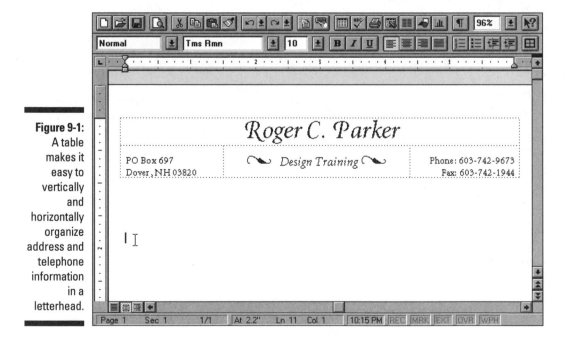

Figure 9-1: A table makes it easy to vertically and horizontally organize address and telephone information in a letterhead.

Roger C. Parker

PO Box 697
Dover, NH 03820

Design Training

Phone: 603-742-9673
Fax: 603-742-1944

Figure 9-2:
Completed
letterhead
showing
properly
aligned
elements
without
table
gridlines.

Adding and formatting tables

Today's word processing and page layout programs make it easy to add tables. In most cases, the tables are created within the program.

- ✔ **PageMaker for Windows (or Macintosh):** Creating tables is a two-step process. You create the table using the separate Table Editor application, and then you place it into your publication.

- ✔ **QuarkXPress:** Choose Style⇨Tabs and define tab stops. If you need to create complex tables, you may want to use the Tableworks PlusXTension.

- ✔ **Microsoft Publisher:** Select the Table tool and drag to create the box where the table will appear in your publication. In the Create Table dialog box, enter the desired number of rows and columns, or click the up/down arrows to indicate the desired number of rows and columns. You can also immediately determine the appearance of the table by scrolling through the formatting options available in the Table Format scroll box. Notice that the various formatting options appear in the Preview window. When you have chosen an option, double-click the name of the formatting option or choose OK when the name is highlighted.

- ✔ **Microsoft Word 6.0 for Windows (or Macintosh):** Choose Table⇨Insert Table (or Table⇨Insert Table). In the Insert Table dialog box, enter the number of rows and columns you want or click the up/down arrows. Then click the AutoFormat box and scroll through the list of formatting options. When the option you want appears in the Preview window, double-click the name of the Format or choose OK while the name is selected.

- ✔ **WordPerfect 6.x for Windows:** Choose Table⇨Create. When the Create Table dialog box appears, indicate the desired number of rows and columns. If you are working with the PowerBar visible, you can simply drag on the table icon to create a table containing the desired number of rows and columns. After the table has been added to your publication, choose Table⇨Lines/Fill and choose the desired borders and backgrounds.

Fine-tuning tables

The appearance of your tables is influenced by the following elements:

- ✔ The way you separate *cells,* or the information placed at the intersections of rows and columns.

✔ The *typeface*, *type size,* and *type style* used in the table. Ideally, there should be noticeable typographic contrast between the information used to identify the content of rows and columns compared to the information contained in the rows and columns.

✔ The *text alignment* of row and column headers as well as the text alignment of the information in individual cells. Often, different alignment will be used for the row and column headers (or titles) and the information within the rows and columns.

✔ *Spacing.* This element is critical in tables. Avoid text that is crammed next to adjacent gridlines or text that extends too close to text in the next column.

As with illustrations, avoid tables buried within text columns. When possible, align the table with the margins of adjacent text columns. Surround tables with white space so that they clearly stand out.

When possible, try to fit tables on a single page. Be especially on the look-out for tables that break over two pages. If tables must break across two pages, make sure that column headers appear at the top of the table on both pages. You may have to place tables inside a frame to keep them together on one page.

Always use your software program's page preview or thumbnail feature to make sure that tables have not inadvertently broken across two pages.

Choosing and Creating the Right Type of Chart

Each type of chart displays data in a different way. Knowing the interpretation you want readers to gain from your chart is the first step in choosing the right type of chart. Next, you must create the chart using either a dedicated charting program or the charting module that may be built into your word processing program.

Types of charts

Several basic types of charts exist as well as many variations. Each type excels at efficiently displaying data in a different way. Figures 9-3 through 9-8 show some chart types, and following are among the most important:

✔ **Pie charts** show how parts relate to a whole. If numbers indicating quantity, called *labels,* are included, the numbers can relate either values or percentages.

✔ **Vertical bar charts** make it easy for readers to compare data that changes over time.

✔ **Horizontal bar charts** display comparisons that do not involve time (or when the x-axis labels are too long).

✔ **Line charts** effectively display trends.

✔ **Area charts** display trends, contributions, and cumulative totals.

✔ **Scatter charts** display the distribution of data through time.

✔ **Group maps** display position and relative size. You can use this type of chart to display the responses on a quadrant displaying four quadrants.

✔ **High-low charts** display a range of values, such as stock prices during specified times. You can usually add tick marks to each range to indicate the opening and closing prices.

✔ **Radar charts, or spider plots,** display the distribution of data, such as survey responses, over multiple criteria.

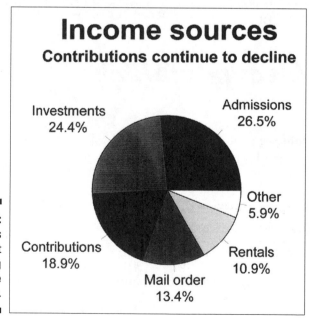

Figure 9-3:
Pie charts
excel at
displaying
part-whole
relationships.

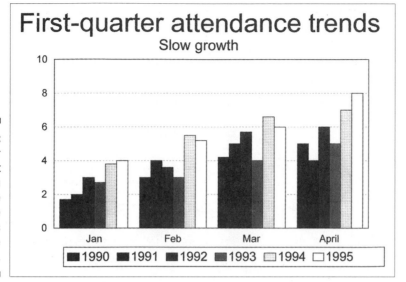

Figure 9-4:
Vertical bar
charts let
you
compare
one or more
data series
that change
over time.

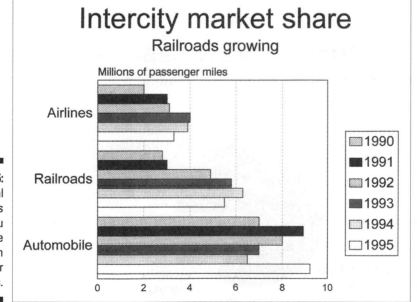

Figure 9-5:
Horizontal
bar charts
enable you
to compare
data with
longer
labels.

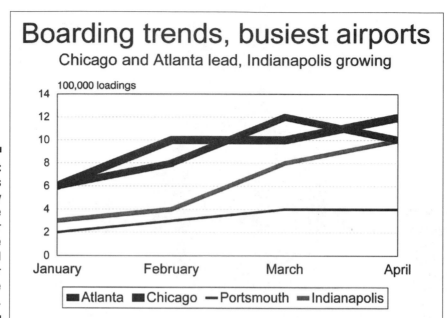

Figure 9-6:
Line charts display trends. Note that thicker lines can be used to add emphasis or indicate size relationships.

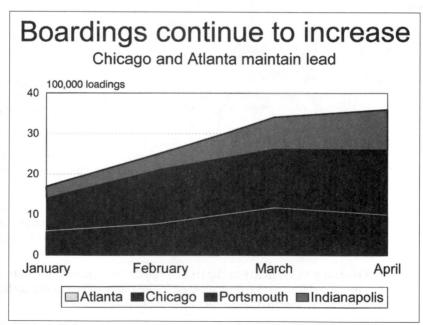

Figure 9-7:
Area charts simulta-neously display trends, contributions, and cumulative totals.

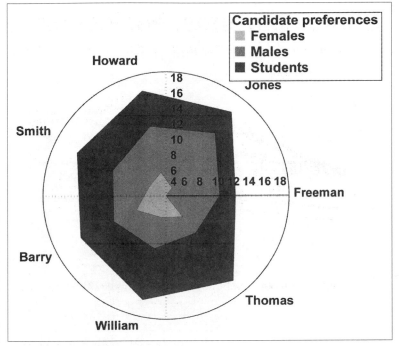

Figure 9-8:
Radar charts display the distribution of data over multiple criteria.

Modifying charts

You can modify the basic chart types in several ways. These modifications let you organize the data displayed in your charts as well as emphasize the desired interpretation of information. Here are some sample modifications for vertical bar charts:

- **Stacked vertical bar charts** let you to display both the contributions of individual elements as well as the comparative totals of each quarter's sales. See Figure 9-9.

- **100% stacked bar charts** similar to pie charts in that they emphasize relative contributions. You can compare how divisional sales contributed to the total sales of each quarter — consideration for the total sales. See Figure 9-10.

- **Overlapped vertical bar charts** emphasize the relationship between closely related items. Bars located in the back of the chart may be hidden by bars located in front of them. See Figure 9-11.

- **Three-dimensional effects** can be used to add depth to each of the preceding variations. You can usually vary the depth of the individual bars as well as the thickness of the chart. See Figure 9-12.

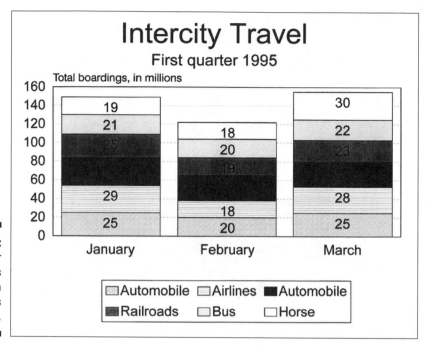

Figure 9-9:
Stacked bar charts display both contributions and totals.

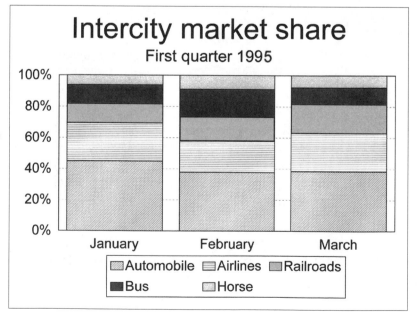

Figure 9-10:
100% stacked vertical bar charts make side-by-side comparisons of contributions possible.

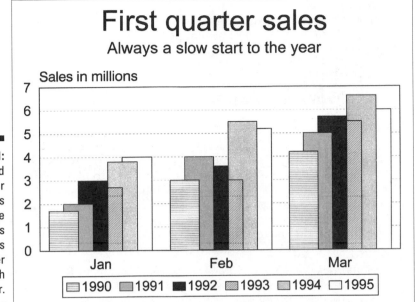

Figure 9-11:
Overlapped
vertical bar
charts
group the
data series
elements
together
for each
quarter.

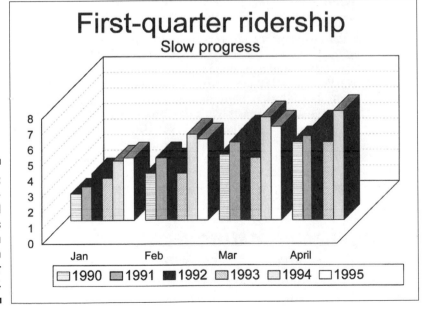

Figure 9-12:
Three-
dimensional
options
enable you
to add depth
to your
chart.

Use three-dimensional effects with care. The depth of a three-dimensional chart might be interpreted as a third dimension. Three-dimensional pie charts often distort the data by making the bottom appear larger and more important than appropriate.

Where do charts come from?

There are three major sources of charts. These include the charting modules that come with your word processing software program, stand-alone charting programs, and charts created with other programs.

- The major word processing programs come with *built-in charting modules*. Although somewhat limited in capability compared to the most sophisticated stand-alone applications, built-in applications make up for whatever limitations they have by their low cost (they're free), their ease of use, and the ease with which you can add charts to your publication.

- Numerous *stand-alone charting programs* are available for both the Apple Macintosh and Windows environments. AldusChart is available in the Apple Macintosh environment; Adobe Illustrator makes it easy to create charts using clip-art as fills for bar and column charts; DeltaGraph offers extensive capabilities in both the Macintosh and Windows platform; and Harvard Graphics recently introduced Harvard ChartXL, which offers numerous statistical and technical capabilities.

- You can also import charts created with *spreadsheet and presentation programs*. Spreadsheet programs such as Microsoft Excel offer extensive charting capabilities, as do presentation programs such as Microsoft PowerPoint and Harvard Graphics. As Object Linking and Embedding become more and more common, use of spreadsheet and presentation programs to create charts will undoubtedly grow.

Creating charts is old news to anyone who has worked with a spreadsheet program such as Microsoft Excel. You first enter data in cells that appear in a worksheet or data sheet (fancy terms for spreadsheet) and then you select the type of chart desired from a gallery of options.

Copying and pasting versus linking

Several parallels are apparent between illustrations and charts. In both cases, you can either copy and paste a chart or link it to the originating software program.

If you copy and paste a chart, it becomes a *static* element and cannot be easily revised or fine-tuned. If changes need to be made, the chart has to be deleted and then re-created, re-copied, re-pasted, and re-sized. And in the Macintosh environment, colors are sometimes replaced by gray-scale patterns.

If you *link* the chart by using the OLE2 Paste Special feature, all you have to do if changes are needed is double-click the chart in your publication. This reloads the program you created the chart in, enabling you to make any necessary changes. When you exit and return from the charting program, the chart in your publication is updated and does require repositioning or resizing. If you're using a Macintosh, you can use the Publish and Subscribe feature, which allows for automatic updating of modified illustrations and charts.

Fine-Tuning Charts

Minor modifications in the appearance of a chart can often pay big dividends in the communicating power of your chart and also make a major improvement in the appearance of your publication. Charts rarely emerge perfectly the first time around. Here are some of the ways you can fine-tune charts so that their message and appearance are more appropriate to your publication.

Anatomy of a chart

A knowledge of chart anatomy will help you choose the appropriate options.

- **Legend:** Helps readers relate colors or gray-scale patterns to text identifying the information displayed in a chart. You can usually move the legend by clicking it and dragging it to another location or resizing it.

- **Labels:** Indicate either the exact numeric quantities or the percentages represented by bar chart length or the size of pie chart slices.

- **Frame:** Consists of the background and border behind and around a chart. Frames help emphasize a chart by highlighting it against the page.

- **Gridlines:** Lines that provide a visual frame of reference for quantities as well as help separate data categories.

- **Tick marks:** Indicate minor intervals between gridlines.

- **X-axis and y-axis (in vertical bar charts):** In most cases, the horizontal axis, or x-axis, displays time intervals (First Quarter, Second Quarter, Third Quarter, and so on). The vertical axis, or y-axis, usually displays quantities.

Improving the appearance and communicating power of your charts

Often the first step involved in improving the appearance of a chart is to choose a different typeface — one compatible with the other text elements in your publication. The next step is to check the default type size and type style and make sure it is appropriate for the size that the chart will be after you place it in your publication. Often the typeface used is too small if you resize the chart after you place it in your publication.

Here are three ways to improve pie charts:

✔ Draw attention to an important slice in a pie chart by cutting it and pulling it away from the chart.

✔ Reduce the number of slices. Avoid pie charts with six or more slices. Consolidate the smaller slices into a "miscellaneous" slice. You can then use a second pie chart or a 100% stacked bar chart to display the data that comprises the "miscellaneous" slice, as shown in Figure 9-13.

✔ Instead of including data labels in your charts, consider placing data in an adjacent table, as shown in Figure 9-14. This way the chart can display the comparison or trend as clearly as possible, and readers who want details can refer to the data in the table.

Figure 9-13: A pie chart with an adjacent stacked bar chart is preferable to a pie chart with more than six slices.

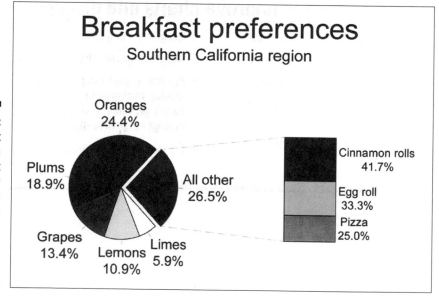

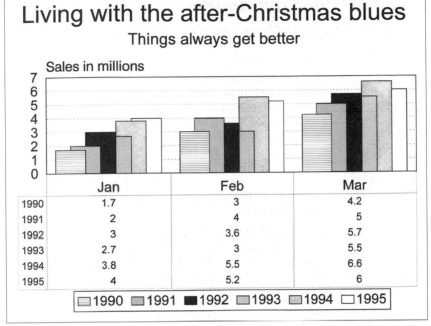

Living with the after-Christmas blues

Things always get better

Sales in millions

	Jan	Feb	Mar
1990	1.7	3	4.2
1991	2	4	5
1992	3	3.6	5.7
1993	2.7	3	5.5
1994	3.8	5.5	6.6
1995	4	5.2	6

▤1990 ▦1991 ■1992 ▨1993 ▥1994 ☐1995

Figure 9-14:
A table adjacent to a chart offers both visual interpretation plus details.

Ten ways to improve charts and graphs

1. Choose the right type of chart or graph.

2. Use a minimum number of chart elements.

3. Use data labels only when necessary.

4. Eliminate distracting borders and backgrounds.

5. Simplify x-axis and y-axis information.

6. Tilt x-axis information.

7. Avoid overusing 3-D charts.

8. Avoid complicated hatch patterns.

9. Provide a goal range. (A goal range is a shaded background added to a bar chart, which provides a visual indication of the desired range of responses or quantity.)

10. Provide a title and caption.

Placing charts in publications

The same considerations used for placing illustrations should be used for placing charts.

- **Avoid burying charts in text columns:** Charts look best when surrounded by white space. Charts placed within text columns create short lines that disturb the reader's rhythm and are often characterized by irregular word spacing and excessive hyphenation.

- **Avoid "floating" charts:** Align charts with each other and the margins of adjacent text columns.

- **When possible, surround charts with *white space:*** A small chart surrounded by white space often communicates better than a larger chart surrounded by text. Always provide plenty of breathing room between a chart and adjacent text.

Always remember to check the type size of the legend and any data labels used in charts. Make sure that the type is as easy to read as adjacent text.

Remember that when you resize a chart, you are also resizing the text. Although you would probably never knowingly use 6- or 7-point text in a publication, you may end up inadvertently doing so if you reduce the size of a chart.

Part IV
Adding Color and Getting It Printed

The 5th Wave   By Rich Tennant

In this part...

Part IV, "Adding Color and Getting It Printed," introduces a note of sobriety. You see that color is a two-edged sword. Although color can enhance your message, it can also obscure your message. This part shows you the advantages of high-resolution output and how to avoid expensive mistakes when outputting your publication at a service bureau and dealing with print shops.

Chapter 10
Working with Color

*W*e live in a color world. Color is everywhere around us; we even *dream* in color. But color isn't always an asset to our publications. To succeed, color must perform a necessary function; otherwise it just gets in the way of our message.

One of the difficulties involved in successfully working with color is the difference between what you see on-screen and how color appears when printed. Often, effects that look great on-screen simply add clutter and expense, making your message harder to understand while increasing printing costs.

It is also difficult to discuss color without getting technical; color, perhaps more than any other aspect of desktop publishing, involves a complicated mixture of both perceptual as well as technological considerations. Today's desktop publishing hardware and software have capabilities once restricted to yesterday's $100,000-plus systems, but that doesn't mean you *have* to put these capabilities to work.

Most of all, never use color as a crutch to compensate for poor design. The mark of a well-designed two-color (or more) publication is that its message would clearly emerge in black and white — perhaps with less impact, but it would still understandable.

Developing Realistic Expectations for Color

Color possesses tremendous communicating *power*. Perhaps the best way to understand the power of color is to prepare two sets of handouts before your next presentation. Prepare one set in black and white and the other in color. Before your presentation begins, place them in the middle of the table where your audience is sitting. Watch which pile disappears first. During the presentation, correlate audience comments and enthusiasm with those who have received the color handouts and those who had to settle for the black-and-white versions. You'll notice the color copies were picked up first and that most of the objections come from those who had to settle for the black-and-white handouts.

Color sells! Can you imagine going to a supermarket and finding the shelves lined with black-and-white packaging? How would you know which brands to choose? How would you like going to a bookstore or newsstand and finding that all the color book and magazine covers replaced by black-and-white versions? You'd probably be so bored you wouldn't buy anything.

Appropriate uses for color

Here are some of the best ways to use color in your publications:

✓ Use color to add *selective emphasis* to your message. Set key words (like *Warning*) in red or reversed against a red background. Place key paragraphs against a yellow background. Spreadsheet "totals" can be placed against a colored background, or you can use red ink to indicate negative numbers — a technique guaranteed to catch the eye of bankers and accountants.

✓ Color can help you *organize information*. Rather than using a grid of horizontal and vertical rules to organize a table, use colored backgrounds to help carry the reader's eyes across rows or up and down columns. Use light tint areas — perhaps 10% to 30% of the full color — behind sidebars, or short articles and features. This technique separates the extracts from the adjacent articles. Likewise, a headline for a short text paragraph and a series of small photographs and captions placed against a colored background clearly indicate that this section is a separate topic, not part of an adjacent article. You can also use colored backgrounds to separate advertisements from adjacent editorial material.

✓ Color helps you *organize your document*. You can code the various parts of your publication by adding colored symbols placed within the pages or by using colored bars along the edges of the pages.

- You can use color to add impact to *business graphics*. Pie charts and bar graphs printed in color have far more impact than the same visuals reproduced with chart elements indicated by shades of gray, parallel diagonal lines and/or varying cross-hatch patterns.

- Use color to communicate *newness*: you can color code each issue of your newsletter, using a different accent color for each issue.

- Most important, use color to communicate *emotion*. Bright colors — such as reds, oranges, and sky blues — communicate energy or optimism, while darker colors — such as grays, navy blues, and maroons — communicate conservatism and/or wealth. Other colors reflect a "back to nature" environmental consciousness or holiday/seasonal/patriotic atmospheres. Where would Halloween be without black and orange?

Inappropriate uses of color

To succeed, color must serve a function and be concentrated. Publications that make the most effective use of color use color in a few large areas rather than scatter it around the page in small areas.

- Color is wasted when dissipated. For example, color works well when set in a *large, heavy sans serif typeface*, such as a publication title or a newsletter nameplate. Color also works well when used as the *background* for a large, heavy sans serif typeface. But color is wasted when it is used as the background for small, colored text or when used for subheads set in the bold italics version of the typeface used for body copy — especially if the subheads are set in the same size as the body copy. In general, text set in color is significantly harder to read than text set in black, unless it is made larger and bolder. Likewise, headlines set in color are usually harder to read than headlines set in black. Small serif typefaces set in color are usually very difficult to read.

- Color works well when used for *large graphic elements*, such as large graphic accents, reversed areas behind logos, or large text elements. Likewise, color is lost when used for thin lines like vertical downrules, two- or three-line initial caps, or end-of-story symbols. Small areas of color simply increase printing costs and add clutter.

Table 10-1 summarizes some appropriate and inappropriate ways to employ color in your publications.

Table 10-1	Using Color Effectively	
Element	**Appropriate**	**Inappropriate**
Behind text	Large, bold sans serif typefaces (36 points or reversed areas larger) reversed out of 100% colored backgrounds	Several small text elements on a page containing serif type (12 point, for example), set in black or reversed out of small colored sections
Text	Large, simple messages set in a bold sans serif type (publication titles or headings 18 points or larger)	Subheads set in the same serif typeface as body copy, but using bold italics set in color; serif page numbers and end-of-story symbols
Photographs	Duotones of natural or inanimate objects when a second color is used with black to enhance some of the tonal values in a photograph	Pictures of people or food in a second color without black
Illustrations	Colors in a series of drawings to indicate progress or sequence	Color added simply to brighten a page
Backgrounds	Color behind an entire page for photographs, charts, or text to gain emphasis against a white background (the paper color)	Small serif type set against tinted (or shaded) colored backgrounds, especially when preparing artwork on a 300 dot-per-inch laser printer

Choosing the Right Colors

When you choose colors, be guided by the ease with which the colors can be noticed and the emotional responses they evoke. Color's impact is as much a function of the surface it's printed on as the ink used to reproduce it; desktop publishers must take into account the differences between the way colors appear on-screen and the way the colors appear when printed. Each color carries with it emotional responses that you must consider.

Working with the color wheel

The color wheel is a key to working successfully with color because it helps you understand color relationships and create harmonious color schemes (see Figure 10-1).

- **Warm colors** range from yellow-green to red. These colors evoke warm, emotional responses, perhaps related to primitive recognition of the reds, oranges, and golds of fire, sunshine, and autumn leaves. Warm colors make objects appear larger and closer to the reader. Warm colors are aggressive and attention-getting.

- **Cool colors** range from green to violet. These colors are associated with the blues and greens of water, sky, and nature. Cool colors appear to recede from the viewer. Cool colors have a calming effect and can look clean and crisp.

- **Complementary colors** are those that lie directly opposite each other on the color wheel. These colors attract the most attention when used in close proximity. Choose two complementary colors when you want to add excitement and visual tension to your publication.

- **Analogous colors** are close to each other on the color wheel, such as blues and purples, or reds and oranges. These colors can work with each other instead of competing against each other.

One of the most useful software programs you can purchase is called ColorUp, available from Letraset, Inc., Paramus, New Jersey. ColorUp contains an on-screen tutorial that describes the various colors as well as colors that combine well. ColorUp contains a pallette chooser that helps you select colors that work together.

Screen colors versus printed colors

The reason for the often major difference between what you see on-screen and what appears after your publication is printed is due to the way colors are produced. Color on your computer screen is *additive* color. Red, green, and blue light beams are projected onto the front of your monitor where they combine to form other colors. Equal amounts of red, green, and blue create white; the absence of red, green, and blue create black.

Color in printed publications, however, is created by *subtractive* color. Different colors are created by the paper and ink absorbing different amounts of red, green, and blue. Black results when all the colors are absorbed; white results when none of the colors is absorbed.

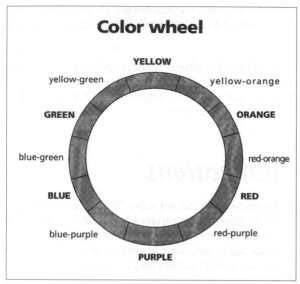

Color wheel

YELLOW

yellow-green   yellow-orange

GREEN   ORANGE

blue-green   red-orange

BLUE   RED

blue-purple   red-purple

PURPLE

Figure 10-1:
Choosing a color for the nameplate and graphic accents of the newsletter by using the Color Library feature.

To eliminate the difference between monitor and printed publication, numerous color-coding schemes have been developed. Instead of worrying about the appearance of color on-screen, desktop publishers can pick colors by entering the numbers of desired colors from printed sample books. The problem here is that the printed color sample books are rarely accurate: paper and printing variations can affect accuracy, and colors change as the books age or get exposed to light.

The Pantone Matching System, or PMS™ system, is one of the most widely used color systems supported by numerous hardware manufacturers and software publishers. Pantone sample books are sold at most book stores and art supply stores. To specify a Pantone color in a software program that supports the Pantone Matching System, choose the desired color from the sample book and enter its number in the appropriate color dialog box in your software program.

Factors influencing the appearance of colors

Most colors appear in the context of other colors: the other colors can be the color of the paper a publication is printed on as well as the color of the light where your publication is being read. Color printed on an ivory or gray paper will look different than the same color printed on a pure white paper.

The reflectivity of the paper your publication will be printed on also determines the appearance of color: notice that separate color sample books are available for coated (glossy) or uncoated paper stocks.

White, black, and gray should also be considered colors. Some colors look brighter when placed adjacent to a black or gray background than when viewed by themselves.

Finally, the saturation of the color affects its perception. Colors that look strong and vivid when printed at 100% strength often turn weak when tinted to 20% or 30%. Reds turn pink and blues wash out. Bright yellows and greens become almost unpleasant to look at when tinted.

Printing Color Publications

You can print publications in color in four ways. The easiest alternatives are to use a color printer in your office or to prepare black-and-white camera-ready artwork and instruct your commercial printer where you want to add color. The other approaches include using your computer to prepare separations for spot or process colors, if the software program you're using offers these capabilities.

Adding color in the office and using traditional techniques

The costs of color printers continue to drop. Today you can buy high-resolution color inkjet and laser printers for less than the cost of yesterday's black-and-white printers. For less than five hundred dollars, several vendors can sell you a color ink-jet printer that can greatly enhance the quality of your print communications.

It's important to note that color office printers, no matter how fast they operate, should not be considered replacements for color printing. Even the fastest color printer operates too slowly for creating more than a few copies of your memo or newsletter. You're definitely *not* going to print 500 copies of your newsletter on a color office printer; the supply costs and time involved would be prohibitive. (Plus, most color printers are not designed for two-sided printing, and only a few can hand the 11 by 17-inch sheets of paper that will be folded to form four $8^1/_2$-by-11-inch pages.)

What you *can* do, however, is prepare color masters that you can take to a color copy center to have color copies made on high-speed copiers. Although something is likely to be lost in the translation (such as color fidelity or color coverage), you're likely to save time and money over the costs of preparing originals on your printer.

Don't confuse your office ink-jet printer with a color copier or printing press. Respect its limitations in the context of the revolutionary low price you paid for it, and don't expect it to turn out hundreds of color newsletters a day.

If you're using this technique, choose and apply desired colors with your software program, printing frequently to check that the colors on the screen approximate the colors that emerge from your ink-jet or thermal wax printer (they probably won't). Printers differ in their capability to prepare output that corresponds to the Pantone Matching System.

Another traditional technique is to prepare black-and-white artwork and indicate on a tissue overlay locations where you want the printer (the *human* printer) to add color (or colors). Your printer, when he or she prepares the negatives for the printing press, will prepare separate negatives for each of the additional desired colors.

Note that the preceding two techniques describe the *only* ways you can add color to documents created with low-end page layout programs and word processing programs.

When you prepare black-and-white artwork for your printer to apply color to, be sure not to apply color by using your software program (don't set red headlines in red). Your black-and-white laser printer typically reproduces colors in shades of gray instead of the strong black needed for optimum reproduction. As a result, instead of areas of a bright blue, you'll end up with a lighter, or *tinted,* blue.

Preparing separations for spot color and process color

Most dedicated page layout programs, such as Corel Publisher, QuarkXPress, and PageMaker (but not Microsoft Publisher), allow you to prepare separations. When you print separations, what you're doing is printing a separate output layer for each of the colors used on a page.

The two ways you can prepare separations correspond to the two ways that dedicated page layout programs can handle color. The simplest is *spot* color. Use spot color when you want to add a single color to your document. You apply spot colors with your software, so that part of the page that you want to print in a separate color appears in a separate color on your computer's monitor. This color can be an ink color you choose by selecting from your software's color palette or it can be a Pantone color you select by number, from the Pantone sample book. Note that this color does not have to be reproduced full-strength; it can be a tint of the color, such as 30%. It can also be a graduated fill, such a full-strength going to white.

Process colors are created by mixing the four basic ink colors (cyan, yellow, magenta, and black) on a page. Colors are first separated and then an individual layer of paper is output for the layers representing cyan, yellow, magenta, and black.

Adding spot colors to your publication

Here's how you prepare to add spot color with PageMaker. Start by adding the desired spot color to your software program's color palette:

1. **Choose Element⇨Define Colors.**

2. **Click on the New button.**

3. **Select the Spot option.**

4. **Click on the downward pointing arrow next to the Libraries list menu.**

5. **Scroll through the list of available color libraries. If you are using the Pantone system, select the appropriate sample book depending on whether you are printing your publication on coated or uncoated stock. The Pantone library appears (see Figure 10-2).**

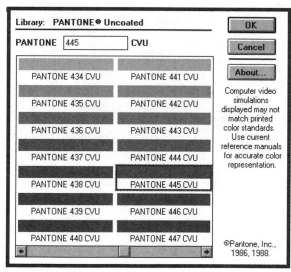

Figure 10-2:
The Pantone
Library

6. **Navigate through the samples provided, using the horizontal scroll bar. When you locate the desired color, click on it, followed by OK. You can now add the color to PageMaker's Color Palette under the Pantone number or name it something like Roger Border. Click on OK.**

Prepare your page, adding the border and desired backgrounds you want in a second color as well as the text and graphics you want to appear in color. To apply color to them, click on the object you want to appear in color, open the Element menu, and select Fill and Line (or Fill and Line if you want to adjust both at once and apply Roger Border from the Color palette).

Avoid using too many spot colors in a publication. In most cases, one — possibly two — spot colors will be enough to brighten and add character to a publication. Additional spot colors often visually clutter a publication. Instead of additional colors, consider using tinting or shading the original spot color.

Printing spot color separations

Here's how you print spot color separations for a blue background and horizontal rules:

1. **Choose File⇨Print. The Print dialog box appears.**

2. **Select Color. The Color dialog box appears (see Figure 10-3).**

Figure 10-3:
Choosing to print spot color separations in the Color dialog box.

Color		
○ Composite	☐ Allow PCL halftoning	**Print**
● Color/Grayscale		Cancel
○ Print colors in black		Document
● Separations		Setup...
Print Ink		Options
Process Black	Print all inks	
x Blue		Color
Green	Print no inks	
x PANTONE 425 CVU	All to process	Reset
Red		
☒ Print this ink		

3. **Select Separations.**

4. **Click on check box next to Print no inks.**

5. **Double-click on Process Black plus the color you have chosen.**

6. **Choose Print.**

As shown in Figure 10-4, two sheets of paper should emerge from your printer: one containing text and graphics to be printed in black, the other containing the text and graphics that should appear in the second color. Figure 10-5 shows the complete layout.

Continued on page 6

Figure 10-4:
Layers for
newsletter
front cover.

When you print Spot color separations, a separate page emerges for each of the spot colors you have indicated in your publication. Spot color separations are typically used when a publication contains a second, or second and third colors, simply used to highlight, or draw attention to, selected areas of a page, such as warnings set in red or a newsletter title reversed out of a blue background.

The alternative to spot color is to prepare *process* color separations. This is the approach used at the cutting edge of desktop publishing (called pre-press) — typically when scanned color photographs edited with PhotoShop or complex illustrations created with Illustrator or FreeHand are included in your publication. When you prepare separations for process colors, four separate layers — or pieces of artwork — emerge for each page of your document. These correspond to cyan, magenta, yellow and black — the four ink colors that, when mixed together in the proper amounts, can be used to create any other color.

National
Association of
Deep Thinkers
December 1994

Student Procrastination

101 excuses for late assignments

By: Perplexed N. Peoria

Dolor sit amet, consectetuer adipiscing elit, sed diam nonummy nibh euismod tin cidunt ut laoreet dolore magna aliquam erat volutpat. Ut wisi enim ad minim ullamcorper suscipit lobortis nisl ut aliquip ex ea commodo consequat.

Equat, vel illum dolore eu feugiat nulla facilisis at vero eros et accumsanatum zzril delenit augue duis dolore te nulla facilisi.

Excuses involving pets
Lorem ipsum dolor sit amet, consectetuer adipiscing elit, sed diam nonummy nibh euismod aliquam erat volutpat.

Lorem ipsum dolor sit amet, consectetuer adipiscing elit, sed diam nonummy nibh euismod tincidunt ut laoreet dolore magna aliquam erat volutpat.

Transportation excuses
Dolor sit amet, consectetuer adipiscing elit, sed diam nonummy nibh euismod tincidunt ut laoreet dolore magna aliquam erat volutpat. Ut wisi enim ad minim veniam, quis nostrud exerci tation ullamcorper suscipit lobortis nisl ut aliquip ex ea commodo consequat.

Parents
Duis autem vel eum iriure dolor in hendrerit in vulputate velit esse molestie consequat, vel illum dolore eu feugiat nulla facilisis at vero eros et accumsan et iusto odio dignissim qui blandit praesent luptatum zzril delenit augue duis dolore te feugait nulla facilisi.

Inside
Election of officers postponed.
2

New cold virus offers promise.
3

Getting ready for final exams
3

Convention postponed
4

Part-time employment
Lorem ipsum dolor sit amet, consectetuer adipiscing elit, sed diam nonummy nibh euismod tincidunt ut laoreet dolore magna aliquam erat volutpat.

Lorem ipsum dolor sit amet, consectetuer adipiscing elit, sed diam nonummy nibh euismod tincidunt ut laoreet dolore magna aliquam erat volutpat. Duis autem vel eum iriure dolor in hendrerit in vulputate velit esse molestie consequat, vel illum dolore

Continued on page 6

Flu outbreaks and final exams

Dolor sit amet, consectetuer adipiscing elit, sed diam nonummy nibh euismod tincidunt ut laoreet dolore magna aliquam erat volutpat. Ut wisi enim ad minim veniam, quis nostrud exerci tation ullamcorper suscipit lobortis nisl ut aliquip ex ea commodo consequat.

Season approaches
Duis autem vel eum iriure dolor in hendrerit in vulputate velit esse molestie consequat, vel illum dolore eu feugiat nulla facilisis at vero eros et accumsan et iusto odio dignissim qui blandit praesent luptatum zzril delenit augue duis dolore te feugait nulla facilisi.

Lorem ipsum dolor sit amet, consectetuer adipiscing elit, sed diam nonummy nibh euismod tincidunt ut laoreet dolore magna aliquam erat volutpat.

Figure 10-5:
Finished newsletter as it will appear after it arrives from your print shop with nameplate and graphic accents in a second color.

Adding and printing process color separations

PageMaker or QuarkXPress can separate scanned color photographs and other imported four-color graphics, saving you the time and costs involved when you have your commercial printer do it. Notice that you don't have to do anything in PageMaker or QuarkXPress to create process colors: the ready-to-separate-into-process-colors information is contained in the imported files with scanned color images or Freehand, Illustrator, or PhotoShop files.

Here's how to create separations for process colors with PageMaker:

1. **Choose File⇨Print.**

2. **Select Colors.**

3. **Select Separations. Verify that asterisks appear next to Process Cyan, Process Magenta, Process Yellow, and Process Black.**

4. **Choose Print. Four pages will emerge from your printer, one for each of the process colors. These separations will be identified along one edge of the page.**

Note that PageMaker and QuarkXPress allow you to print *both* process and spot color separations at the same time. This option allows you optimum reproduction of scanned images and complex illustrations as well as the most accurate printing of second or third colors used for borders, backgrounds, and headlines.

Chapter 11

How to Save Money
When Working with Color

- -

In This Chapter

▶ Making the most of black and white

▶ Getting color results on a black and white budget

▶ Marketing concerns when using pre-printed color paper

▶ Pre-printing your own second color text and accents

▶ Possible problems you may encounter

- -

*C*olor sells, but color also costs. The purpose of this chapter is to encourage you to use color as cost-effectively as possible. Often, the best way to do this is to start by examining black-and-white options. Before you make the move to color, you should convince yourself that you really *need* color and that you have pushed black-and-white to its limits.

Then, depending on the number of copies needed for your project, you should take a close look at the pre-printed color papers available from several vendors. These papers contain color frames — or doughnuts — that you fill in using your black-and-white ink-jet or laser printer. If you need only 100 brochures and newsletters, this approach could save you a lot of money.

The final step in the cost-effective use of color involves pre-printing repeating elements — such as your firm's logo and accent colors — for several issues of your newsletter or more copies of your brochure than you immediately need. Then, when you go to press, because the second color has already been printed, your print job is a single-color job — even though your customers and prospects will receive a color publication.

Making the Most of Black and White

Many designers are rediscovering the power of black and white. As high-resolution laser printers and imagesetters have improved in quality, it has become possible to use black and white more creatively. Black and white can be especially powerful when used with coated, or glossy, paper stocks. Quality printing on coated papers allows subtle variations in gray shades to emerge with startling impact.

Reverses and screens

The starting point for maximizing your use of single-color printing is to emphasize the importance of massing, or concentrating, areas of black and areas of gray with areas of white. Consider the example shown in Figure 11-1.

A similar technique involves using a few large, screened letters or graphic accents on a page. Initial caps could be set in a heavy, sans serif typeface, or all the text on a page could be placed against a single, oversize letter or number (assuming the letter or number had some significance). The success of this technique, of course, depends on restraint. The effect is diluted to the extent the technique is overused.

Another approach is to bleed a screened background to the edges of a page, as shown in Figure 11-2. This creates white "windows" that can highlight charts, scanned photographs, or short text blocks. Figure 11-3 shows a variation of this effect.

These techniques can be creatively employed. Working with illustration programs that enable you to layer graphic elements, you can create interesting effects by placing large type on various backgrounds — such as a portion of a letter that appears against white being set in black, while the portion against a black background appears in white. Or light gray letters can appear against dark gray backgrounds, and vice versa.

Once you have purchased and mastered a drawing program such as Adobe Illustrator or Freehand, you'll be able to experiment with various techniques for orchestrating contrasting grays against each other.

Alternatives to black

Paper does not always have to be white and ink does not always have to be black! Single-color printing can actually become very flexible when you con-

Major changes
ahead for health care providers

Dolor sit amet, consectetuer adipiscing elit, sed diam nonummy nibh euismod tincidunt ut laoreet dolore magna aliquam erat volutpat. Ut wisi enim ad minim veniam, quis nostrud exerci tation. Duis autem vel eum iriure dolor in hendrerit in vulputate velit esse molestie consequat, vel illum dolore eu feugiat nulla facilisis at vero eros et accumsan et iusto odio qui blandit praesent luptatum zzril delenit augue duis dolore te feugait nulla facilisi.

Lorem ipsum dolor sit amet, consectetuer adipiscing elit, sed diam nonummy nibh euismod tincidunt ut laoreet dolore magna aliquam erat volutpat.

Lorem ipsum dolor sit amet, consectetuer adipiscing elit, sed diam nonummy nibh euismod tincidunt ut laoreet dolore magna aliquam erat volutpat. Duis autem vel eum iriure dolor in hendrerit in vulputate velit esse molestie consequat, vel illum dolore eu feugiat nulla facilisis at vero eros et accumsan et iusto odio dignissim qui blandit praesent luptatum zzril delenit augue duis dolore te feugait nulla facilisi.

Lorem ipsum dolor sit amet, consectetuer adipiscing elit, sed diam nonummy nibh euismod tincidunt ut laoreet dolore magna aliquam erat volutpat. Ut wisi enim ad minim veniam, quis nostrud exerci tation ullamcorper suscipit lobortis nisl ut aliquip ex ea commodo consequat.

Figure 11-1:
Pages with large contrasting areas of black, white, and gray can attract attention even with single-color printing.

sider variations on black ink and white paper. Endless combinations of colors can be printed on lightly tinted cream, ivory, or lightly tinted colored papers. There is great latitude for creative experimenting, as long as you pay attention to maintaining the foreground/background contrast needed for easy reading. Choose dark, rich colors for inks, and choose papers tinted with complementary colors.

Confidence

Dolor sit amet, consectetuer adipiscing elit, sed diam nonummy nibh euismod tincidunt ut laoreet dolore magna aliquam erat volutpat. Ut wisi enim ad minim veniam, quis nostrud exerci tation ullamcorper suscipit lobortis nisl ut aliquip ex ea commodo consequat. Duis autem vel eum iriure dolor in hendrerit in vulputate velit esse molestie consequat, vel illum dolore eu feugiat nulla facilisis at vero eros et accumsan et iusto odio dignissim qui blandit praesent luptatum zzril delenit augue duis dolore te feugait nulla facilisi.

Lorem ipsum dolor sit amet, consectetuer adipiscing elit, sed diam nonummy nibh euismod tincidunt ut laoreet dolore magna aliquam erat volutpat.

Lorem ipsum dolor sit amet, consectetuer adipiscing elit, sed diam nonummy nibh euismod tincidunt ut laoreet dolore magna aliquam erat volutpat. Duis autem vel eum iriure dolor in hendrerit in vulputate velit esse mo-

A word about pets

lestie consequat, vel illum dolore eu feugiat nulla facilisis at vero eros et accumsan et iusto odio dignissim qui blandit praesent luptatum zzril delenit augue duis dolore te feugait nulla facilisi.

Lorem ipsum dolor sit amet, consectetuer adipiscing elit, sed diam nonummy nibh euismod tincidunt ut laoreet dolore magna aliquam erat volutpat. Ut wisi enim ad minim veniam, quis nostrud exerci tation ullamcorper suscipit lobortis nisl ut aliquip ex ea commodo consequat.

Lorem ipsum dolor sit amet, consectetuer adipiscing elit, sed diam nonummy nibh euismod tincidunt ut laoreet dolore magna aliquam erat volutpat. Duis autem vel eum iriure dolor in hendrerit in vulputate velit esse molestie consequat, vel illum dolore eu feugiat nulla facilisis at vero eros et accumsan.

Ryan's Petland
4401 Strip Mall Boulevard
Suburban Sprawl, NH 03820
603-222-5555

Welcome to Ryan's Petland

Figure 11-2: Screened backgrounds bled to the edges of a page can create "windows" for photographs or text.

Buy with confidence

Dolor sit amet, consectetuer adipiscing elit, sed diam nonummy nibh euismod tincidunt ut laoreet dolore magna aliquam erat volutpat. Ut wisi enim ad minim veniam, quis nostrud exerci tation ullamcorper suscipit lobortis nisl ut aliquip ex ea commodo consequat. Duis autem vel eum iriure dolor in hendrerit in vulputate velit esse molestie consequat, vel illum dolore eu feugiat nulla facilisis at vero eros et accumsan et iusto odio dignissim qui blandit praesent luptatum zzril delenit augue duis dolore te feugait nulla facilisi.

Lorem ipsum dolor sit amet, consectetuer adipiscing elit, sed diam nonummy nibh euismod tincidunt ut laoreet dolore magna aliquam erat volutpat.

Lorem ipsum dolor sit amet, consectetuer adipiscing elit, sed diam nonummy nibh euismod tincidunt ut laoreet dolore magna aliquam erat volutpat. Duis autem vel eum iriure dolor in hendrerit in vulputate velit esse molestie consequat, vel illum dolore eu feugiat nulla facilisis at vero eros et ac-

A word about pets...

cumsan et iusto odio dignissim qui blandit praesent luptatum zzril delenit augue duis dolore te feugait nulla facilisi.

Lorem ipsum dolor sit amet, consectetuer adipiscing elit, sed diam nonummy nibh euismod tincidunt ut laoreet dolore magna aliquam erat volutpat. Ut wisi enim ad minim veniam, quis nostrud exerci tation ullamcorper suscipit lobortis nisl ut aliquip ex ea commodo consequat.

Lorem ipsum dolor sit amet, consectetuer adipiscing elit, sed diam nonummy nibh euismod tincidunt ut laoreet dolore magna aliquam erat volutpat. Duis autem vel eum iriure dolor in hendrerit in vulputate velit esse molestie consequat, vel illum dolore eu feugiat nulla facilisis at vero eros et accumsan et iusto odio dignissim qui blandit praesent luptatum zzril delenit augue duis dolore te feugait nulla facilisi.

Lorem ipsum dolor sit amet, consectetuer adipiscing elit, sed diam nonummy nibh euismod tincidunt ut laoreet dolore magna aliquam erat volutpat. Ut wisi enim ad minim veniam, quis nostrud exerci tation ullamcorper suscipit

Ryan's Petland
4401 Strip Mall Boulevard
Suburban Sprawl, NH 03820
603-222-5555

Welcome to Ryan's Petland

Figure 11-3: A white panel adjacent to panels with reversed and screened backgrounds attracts attention because of its whiteness.

Additional creative opportunities occur when you use screened backgrounds in combination with text and photographs reproduced full-strength. Text can be printed at 100% and lightly tinted screens can be used behind text elements or as fills for letters. You gain further creative opportunities by using radial (light to dark from the center of an object) or linear (light to dark from the top, bottom, or diagonals) methods.

Recycled papers, often characterized by a built-in texture, offer additional opportunities for creative experimentation.

Pre-Printed Color Paper

During the past few years, several paper vendors have begun offering *doughnuts* that consist of pre-printed color accents. Designs employing both single colors and multiple colors are available. These designs can be considered frames that you complete by adding your specific text, illustrations, and photographs with your black-and-white ink-jet or laser printer.

One of the important contributions these pre-printed colored papers make is the way they make it affordable to create a corporate identity based on color, even if you need only a relatively small number of copies. The same designs (in terms of the colors used and the placement of the colors) are available in multiple formats. These designs are typically offered as letterheads, envelopes, brochures, business cards, postcards, and reply cards. In many cases, matching presentation folders, large (9-by-12 folders, for example) envelopes, greeting cards, thank you notes, and overhead transparency frames are also available.

These pre-printed color backgrounds permit you to establish a colorful visual identity for your firm on a black-and-white budget. To use them, you either print directly on the colored paper by feeding it through your laser printer, or you make a white master and feed the colored papers through your office photocopier.

The range of product offerings is huge and constantly growing. A great deal of creativity has been used to create brochure formats. Most colored papers for brochures have been printed on heavy, quality stock. In order to simplify folding, the fold lines have been scored. Equally important, several formats include perforated address/phone number index cards. Other formats include perforated coupons and pull-off reply panels for customers to return to you (with their check!).

The scoring for the folds and the die-cutting for index cards and reply cards emphasize the economies of scale made possible by pre-printed color papers. If you went to your local printer and asked him or her to print 100 brochures with a perforated index card or reply panel, you'd faint after you got the price quote. The hardest part about printing is setting up the presses; it doesn't cost much more to print 1,000 copies of a brochure than to print 100. So you'd end up paying a lot of money for just the few brochures you actually needed.

But by printing your message in black on pre-printed color paper, you can achieve tremendous savings because others around the country are sharing the cost of purchasing the high-quality papers, printing the colors, and die-cutting the perforated pull-off reply panels.

Using pre-printed colored papers

It is extremely easy to use these pre-printed colored papers, depending on the design you have chosen.

- With many designs, it doesn't matter where you place the text. Designs in this category consist of colored screened backgrounds, often graduated patterns. Sometimes, graduated fills are combined with colored header and footer rules and high-impact colored graphic accents along the edges of the page.

- Other designs, such as the brochures and covers for the first pages of proposals and reports, provide heavy ink coverage over most of the page, but provide windows of white space where you should place the title of your brochure or proposal.

If you take care using these formats, others will be hard-pressed to know that a brochure or report was printed in quantities of 50 or 100 using an inkjet or laser printer.

Several designs include software templates that indicate (on the screen of your computer) where to place titles and columns of text. Templates are available for the major word processing and page layout programs.

Quantity and price considerations

Do you dare use off-the-shelf colored background papers?

At first, you may worry that prospects and clients would recognize the source of your corporate identity. However, that worry assumes that your clients and prospects read the same desktop publishing magazines or receive the same direct-mail catalogs as you.

At one time, that worry may have been valid. Now, however, there is such a selection of pre-printed color materials available that it is unlikely your clients and prospects will be able to say "A-hah!" and identify the source of your letterhead and envelopes.

There's also an inverse psychology at work. As a client, I tend to respect vendors who spend their money carefully; I'm not interested in supporting someone else's ego trip. If I recognize a colored paper stock, I appreciate the vendor for being concerned enough about quality to use color, as well as also concerned about saving money in order to avoid graphic overkill.

Let's face it: the message and the care with which something has been placed on a page is more important than the source of the paper it's printed on!

Are pre-printed colored papers for you?

The underlying assumption behind pre-printed colored papers is that everyone has a limited universe of really important people — and that time is often just as limited. When considering the use of pre-printed colored papers, take a close look at the quantities you will be producing.

If you're a consultant preparing an important proposal and brochure for a few important clients, it certainly makes sense to print individual copies of the brochures and proposals on colored paper stocks. But if you're preparing several hundred letterheads or brochures, you may find it cheaper to use fewer colors and conventional printing techniques.

Learning from pre-printed color papers

Even if you decide not to use pre-printed color papers, you can learn a lot about design by studying the catalogs that advertise colored papers.

Your creativity is likely to be stimulated by looking at the various designs offered, taking note of the colors used and the placement of the colors. The catalogs can teach you a lot about the power of graduated fill patterns combined with strong accent colors. You can also see the importance of framing windows of white space with bright colors or detailed fill patterns.

Observation is one of the keys to strengthening your design skills. The more you observe, the better a designer you'll be.

Pre-printing second and third colors

One of the most important ways you can reduce printing costs, especially if you're printing a series of brochures or newsletters, is to limit your use of second, or accent, colors to a few consistent locations. You then can pre-print several months' worth of paper containing the second color and store it until you need it.

When you print the individual brochures or newsletters, your print job is a single-color print job, because the accent color has already been printed. Figures 11-4 through 11-6 outline the process. You thus greatly reduce your cost.

Printing is an excellent example of an economy-of-scale business. You pay less if you purchase a large quantity of paper and print it all with a second color than if you buy the paper in several smaller lots and print each brochure or issue of your newsletter as a two-color job.

In addition to purchasing paper at bulk, quantity discounts gained by purchasing the paper ahead of time helps you avoid the possibility of your favorite paper not being available when you need it.

Suggested applications

Here are some possible applications of pre-printed second colors:

- Part of the title of your newsletter can be pre-printed in a second color. Your firm's logo can also be printed in color on the front page. In addition, you can add a pair of second-color accent bars to frame the table of contents that will always appear in the same position on the front page of each issue of your newsletter.

- On the inside pages of your newsletter, you can repeat the title in color at the top of each page. You can also add colored header and footer rules as well as a colored and screened box (used to draw attention to important upcoming events) that will always be placed in the same location in each issue.

- You can unify a series of brochures by pre-printing a background color on the front page of your brochures and repeating your firm's logo in color on each page.

Parker's Strategic Investment Quarterly

Implications of proposed interest rate increases frighten investors

June 15, 1995

Dolor sit amet, consectetuer adipiscing elit, sed diam nonummy nibh euismod tincidunt ut laoreet dolore magna aliquam erat volutpat. Ut wisi enim ad minim veniam, quis nostrud exerci tation ullamcorper suscipit lobortis nisl ut aliquip ex ea commodo consequat.

Duis autem vel eum iriure dolor in hendrerit in vulputate velit esse molestie consequat, vel illum dolore eu feugiat nulla facilisis at vero eros et accumsan et iusto odio dignissim qui blandit praesent luptatum zzril delenit augue duis dolore te feugait nulla facilisi.

London's reaction
Lorem ipsum dolor sit amet, consectetuer adipiscing elit, sed diam nonummy nibh euismod tincidunt ut laoreet dolore magna aliquam erat volutpat.

Lorem ipsum dolor sit amet, consectetuer adipiscing elit, sed diam nonummy nibh euismod tincidunt ut laoreet dolore magna aliquam erat volutpat. Duis autem vel eum iriure dolor in hendrerit in vulputate velit esse molestie consequat, vel illum dolore eu feugiat nulla facilisis at vero eros et accumsan et iusto odio dignissim qui blandit praesent luptatum zzril delenit augue duis dolore te feugait nulla facilisi.

Lorem ipsum dolor sit amet, consectetuer adipiscing elit, sed diam nonummy nibh euismod tincidunt ut

laoreet dolore magna aliquam erat volutpat. Ut wisi enim ad minim veniam, quis nostrud exerci tation ullamcorper suscipit lobortis nisl ut aliquip ex ea commodo consequat.

Paris reactions
Lorem ipsum dolor sit amet, consectetuer adipiscing elit, sed diam nonummy nibh euismod tincidunt ut laoreet dolore magna aliquam erat volutpat. Duis autem vel eum iriure dolor in hendrerit in vulputate velit esse molestie consequat, vel illum dolore eu feugiat nulla facilisis at vero eros et accumsan et iusto odio dignissim qui blandit praesent luptatum zzril delenit augue duis dolore te feugait nulla facilisi.

Lorem ipsum dolor sit amet, consectetuer adipiscing elit, sed diam nonummy nibh euismod tincidunt ut laoreet dolore magna aliquam erat volutpat.

Tokyo's reaction muted
Ut wisi enim ad minim veniam, quis nostrud exerci tation ullamcorper suscipit lobortis nisl ut aliquip ex ea commodo consequat.

Duis autem vel eum iriure dolor in hendrerit in vulputate velit esse molestie consequat, vel illum dolore eu feugiat nulla hendrerit in vulputate velit esse molestie consequat, facilisis at vero eros et accumsan et iusto odio dignissim qui blandit praesent

luptatum zzril delenit augue duis dolore te feugait nulla facilisi.

Ottawa praises move
Lorem ipsum dolor sit amet, consectetuer adipiscing elit, sed diam nonummy nibh euismod tincidunt ut laoreet dolore magna aliquam erat volutpat. Ut wisi enim ad minim veniam, quis nostrud exerci tation

Continued on page 2

Late breaking news

Ut wisi enim ad minim veniam, quis nostrud exerci tation ullam.

Corper suscipit lobortis nisl ut aliquip ex ea commodo consequat.

Ut wisi enim ad minim veniam, quis nostrud exerci tation.

Ullamcorper suscipit lobortis nisl ut aliquip ex ea commodo.

Figure 11-4:
Two-color newsletter as it will print with colored title set against a tinted background and screened panel for late-breaking features.

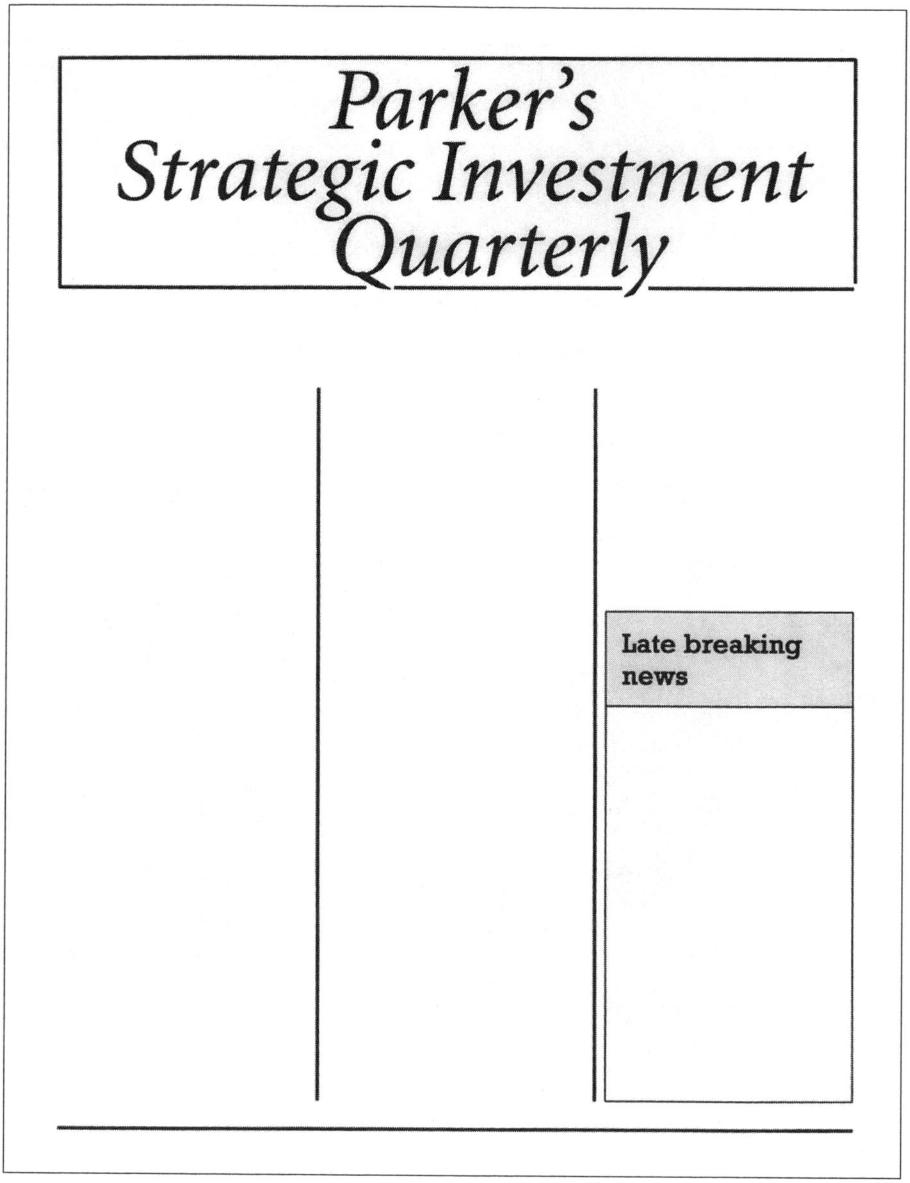

Parker's Strategic Investment Quarterly

Late breaking news

Figure 11-5:
Start by
pre-printing
several
months
worth of
sheets with
second
color
elements,
including
title, graphic
accents,
and shaded
background
for each
issue's
feature.

Implications of proposed interest rate increases frighten investors

June 15, 1995

Dolor sit amet, consectetuer adipiscing elit, sed diam nonummy nibh euismod tincidunt ut laoreet dolore magna aliquam erat volutpat. Ut wisi enim ad minim veniam, quis nostrud exerci tation ullamcorper suscipit lobortis nisl ut aliquip ex ea commodo consequat.

Duis autem vel eum iriure dolor in hendrerit in vulputate velit esse molestie consequat, vel illum dolore eu feugiat nulla facilisis at vero eros et accumsan et iusto odio dignissim qui blandit praesent luptatum zzril delenit augue duis dolore te feugait nulla facilisi.

London's reaction
Lorem ipsum dolor sit amet, consectetuer adipiscing elit, sed diam nonummy nibh euismod tincidunt ut laoreet dolore magna aliquam erat volutpat.

Lorem ipsum dolor sit amet, consectetuer adipiscing elit, sed diam nonummy nibh euismod tincidunt ut laoreet dolore magna aliquam erat volutpat. Duis autem vel eum iriure dolor in hendrerit in vulputate velit esse molestie consequat, vel illum dolore eu feugiat nulla facilisis at vero eros et accumsan et iusto odio dignissim qui blandit praesent luptatum zzril delenit augue duis dolore te feugait nulla facilisi.

Lorem ipsum dolor sit amet, consectetuer adipiscing elit, sed diam nonummy nibh euismod tincidunt ut

laoreet dolore magna aliquam erat volutpat. Ut wisi enim ad minim veniam, quis nostrud exerci tation ullamcorper suscipit lobortis nisl ut aliquip ex ea commodo consequat.

Paris reactions
Lorem ipsum dolor sit amet, consectetuer adipiscing elit, sed diam nonummy nibh euismod tincidunt ut laoreet dolore magna aliquam erat volutpat. Duis autem vel eum iriure dolor in hendrerit in vulputate velit esse molestie consequat, vel illum dolore eu feugiat nulla facilisis at vero eros et accumsan et iusto odio dignissim qui blandit praesent luptatum zzril delenit augue duis dolore te feugait nulla facilisi.

Lorem ipsum dolor sit amet, consectetuer adipiscing elit, sed diam nonummy nibh euismod tincidunt ut laoreet dolore magna aliquam erat volutpat.

Tokyo's reaction muted
Ut wisi enim ad minim veniam, quis nostrud exerci tation ullamcorper suscipit lobortis nisl ut aliquip ex ea commodo consequat.

Duis autem vel eum iriure dolor in hendrerit in vulputate velit esse molestie consequat, vel illum dolore eu feugiat nulla hendrerit in vulputate velit esse molestie consequat, facilisis at vero eros et accumsan et iusto odio dignissim qui blandit praesent

luptatum zzril delenit augue duis dolore te feugait nulla facilisi.

Ottawa praises move
Lorem ipsum dolor sit amet, consectetuer adipiscing elit, sed diam nonummy nibh euismod tincidunt ut volutpat. Ut wisi enim ad minim veniam, quis nostrud exerci tation

Continued on page 2

Ut wisi enim ad minim veniam, quis nostrud exerci tation ullam.

Corper suscipit lobortis nisl ut aliquip ex ea commodo consequat.

Ut wisi enim ad minim veniam, quis nostrud exerci tation.

Ullamcorper suscipit lobortis nisl ut aliquip ex ea commodo.

Figure 11-6:
Each issue then becomes a single-color printing job, limited to only issue-specific information.

Storage and other technical considerations

Here are some things to watch out for when pre-printing second colors:

✔ Before committing to a large print run of a second color, make sure that your firm or association is going to use the pre-printed colored sheets and that a new art director isn't going to come along and re-design the logo!

✔ Make sure that you store the paper in an appropriate location, free from dust and safe from damage. The dimensions of the paper may change slightly, and the paper may slightly change color, depending on differences in humidity between the day the second color was printed and the day your newsletter or brochure is printed.

✔ Printers often charge for storage. Find out in advance whether your printer is going to charge for storing the pre-printed pages and how much you'll be charged. Find out who's responsible in case the sprinkler system accidentally goes off!

Part V
Putting It All Together

"It says,' Seth- Please see us about your idea to wrap newsletter text around company logo. Production!'"

In this part...

Part V, "Putting It All Together," looks at ways to build constant improvement into your design career as well as into individual classes of products. This part discusses the importance of creating a "family look" for all of the print communications your firm produces. This part contains numerous "before and after" examples that will help you review many of the tips and techniques previously described.

Chapter 12

Working with Service Bureaus and Print Shops

. . . .

In This Chapter

▶ Evaluating high-resolution office printers

▶ Questions to ask service bureaus

▶ Preparing and submitting files to service bureaus

▶ Choosing papers for printing

▶ Soliciting bids from print shops

▶ Quality control for printed projects

▶ Dealing with printing hassles

. . . .

*W*hat are you going to do now that your project is finished? There's still a long journey between well-designed, carefully crafted pages on the screen of your computer and printed copies in the hands of your prospects and customers.

The final stages involve a lot of legwork and, unfortunately, a certain amount of trial-and-error experimentation. If you enjoy dealing with your computer, you may find dealing with printers and service bureaus a more taxing enterprise; the people you'll deal with may be more frustrating than your software. Yet your project must be imaged — camera-ready artwork must be produced — and a print shop needs to duplicate it in the quantities you want.

You can never open communications with service bureaus and printers early enough. But first you should ask yourself, "Do I need high to deal with a service bureau?"

High-Resolution Laser Printers

The desktop publishing revolution was fueled, in great part, by 300 dot-per-inch laser printers. For almost a decade, 300 dots-per-inch was the norm. Thousands of books, brochures, and newsletters were printed using artwork prepared on 300 dot-per-inch laser printers.

What 300 dot-per-inch laser printers lack in ultimate quality they make up for in cost and convenience. So what if the type appeared slightly thicker than you wanted, and curved letters exhibited an obvious stair-stepping appearance — the results were certainly better than what was available from dot-matrix or daisywheel printers.

When higher resolution was required — after proofing on "Old Reliable" — files could always be sent to outside service bureaus for resolution on 1,270; 2,540; or even 3,600 dots-per-inch printers. This treatment yields much sharper, crisper letters, smoother background fills, and immeasurably better-looking photographs.

Now, however, the distinction between office laser printers and service bureaus is beginning to blur.

High-resolution, tabloid-sized laser printers

Until recently, laser printers capable of producing high-quality artwork were prohibitively expensive — beyond the reach of the casual user or small, self-funded graphic design studio. Laser printers capable of outputting tabloid-sized pages — necessary if you want to include text or visual elements bled to page edges and the registration marks necessary for printers to line up each page on their presses — typically cost between $7,000 and $10,000.

If you want to print proofs of 8$\frac{1}{2}$-by-11-inch pages containing bleeds on a PostScript laser printer limited to 8$\frac{1}{2}$-by-11-inch pages, print them at 95 percent actual size.

Now, however, a new breed of high-resolution office laser printers has emerged. These printers offer 600, 900, and 1,200 dot-per-inch resolution. In addition, they can handle tabloid-sized (11-by-17-inch) and, in some cases, slightly larger paper stocks. The capability to print on large papers permits you to print registration marks, two-page spreads, and bleeds on tabloid-sized pages.

More important, the costs of these new-generation printers is actually *less* (in some cases, by a factor of two) than the first 300 dot-per-inch, 8 1/2-by-11-inch printers. More important, these new units often print significantly faster than their predecessor because they include Level 2 PostScript and sufficient memory to print pages containing numerous fonts and complex graphics. These printers often can be used for both the Macintosh and Windows environments. And they operate faster because they often contain — or you can add — hard disks that speed printing by eliminating the need to download fonts.

High-resolution office laser printers

Does it make sense for you to consider a high-resolution office laser printer? Factors to consider include quality expectations, the type of projects you prepare, the number of camera-ready pages you prepare each month, and convenience. Take a look at these issues:

- ✔ **Convenience:** It's certainly nice to be able to produce camera-ready artwork in your office. No longer will you have to travel cross-town or send files by modem. Revisions are certainly easier, too. If you notice a typo at the last minute, you can quickly print out a replacement page.

- ✔ **Font hassles:** High-resolution office laser printers eliminate the possibility of font incompatibilities. Font incompatibilities are usually the cause of the difference between what you see on the screen of your computer and what you get back from the service bureau.

- ✔ **Quality:** The quality of 600; 1,200; and 1,800 dot-per-inch inch laser printers is usually noticeably better than what you're used to getting out of your 300 dot-per-inch laser printer. Type is thinner and curved surfaces are smoother. Screened backgrounds are smoother and photographs look better. The only way you can really tell if the quality is acceptable, however, is by outputting a sample on the printer you're considering and comparing it to the same file after it has been produced by a service bureau on a high-resolution image setter. If you're going to print a lot of photographs, a certain amount of experimentation may be necessary in order to decide how light or dark the images should be.

- ✔ **Cost factors:** The cost-effectiveness of high-resolution laser printers depends on how much artwork you produce each month. It certainly doesn't pay to purchase a unit costing between $3,000 and $4,000 if you're going to output only a four-page newsletter every two months. But, in high-volume applications, a high-resolution laser printer can quickly pay for itself. You'll have to balance the per-page costs (including travel and courier services) with the lease and supply costs of your own printer.

It's nice to know that these alternatives exist, however. I know of one author — no naming names, of course, except he has a beard and lives in Dover, New Hampshire — who produced a 300-page book that *couldn't be imaged by the publisher's service bureau!* The entire project would have been dead meat if it were not for the presence of a high-resolution laser printer at my, er, the author's office. The book contained numerous photographs and typeface specimens, and not one reader or reviewer commented negatively on the quality of the artwork!

Perhaps the best reason for investing in a high-resolution, large-format office laser printer is to avoid the issues raised in the next section!

Locating and Dealing with Service Bureaus

Service bureaus are firms that, in essence, own expensive toys and rent you time on them on a per-page basis. They provide the personnel needed to image your files at high-resolution.

In this electronic age, service bureaus can be local or far away. I know of people who routinely send their files hundreds, even thousands, of miles away for imaging and return by overnight courier services.

It's an imperfect science, however, and you can never begin working too early with a service bureau. In most cases, it probably is best if you deal on a face-to-face basis with service bureaus, at least in the beginning.

Initial contact with service bureaus

The first step is to locate a service bureau. Some are usually listed in the Yellow Pages of your local telephone book. Some are affiliated with printers. If in doubt, call a local design firm or pick up your local computer-user newsletter. If you are using a dedicated page layout program such as PageMaker or QuarkXPress, call the company. Many software companies maintain lists of authorized service bureaus and may be able to recommend someone in your area.

You should ask several questions on your first visit to a service bureau. Bring a pad of paper along and jot down responses (or make photocopies of the Service Bureau checklist provided in this chapter). You should ask the following questions:

✔ **What type of imagesetter do you use?** This is vital. When you start a project, even if you are going to proof your documents on a DogMatic 300 ink-jet printer, you should target the imagesetter that will be used to produce final camera-ready artwork. (More on this later.) You should probably ask for the current version of the imagesetter's printer driver to install on your computer.

✔ **Do you prefer program data files or Encapsulated PostScript Files?** Service bureaus differ in their preferences, and sometimes they don't have any preferences. In brief: Encapsulated PostScript Files eliminate the possibility of font incompatibilities. The problem is when there's usually some last-minute problem, because Encapsulated PostScript Files cannot be opened and revised at the service bureau. What you provide is what you get, and if you have inadvertently left "Print Registration Marks" unchecked, they won't be there when you receive your camera-ready artwork. See the sidebar if you're unsure how to prepare an Encapsulated PostScript File.

✔ **Are you happy working with Windows files?** Although the size of the installed base of computers running Microsoft Windows is approximately ten times that of the Apple Macintosh environment, most service bureaus are more comfortable working with Macintosh files. This is especially true if their traditional clientele has been limited to professional graphic design firms. In many cases, service bureaus convert Windows files to Macintosh files, which introduces opportunities for lots of strange things to happen.

✔ **How do you like to receive files?** Does the firm prefer files to be submitted on diskette or by modem? More important, what make and model of removable storage media can they work with? If your files are going to contain scanned images and complex illustrations, you probably should submit them on a Syquest removable hard disk rather than on a dozen floppy diskettes.

✔ **What's your usual turnaround?** Most service bureaus offer rush service, but what is considered normal? Overnight, 24 hours, or 48 hours? (Sounds like a good name for a movie!)

✔ **How do you charge?** By the page or by the hour? Remember that pages containing scanned images and complex illustrations take longer to image than do simple pages of text. What about mistakes? Who pays (usually you) and how much if files fail to print, or if everything comes out in Courier? Are pages containing separations charged at the regular rate? You should also find out how much they charge for trouble-shooting and repairing program data files (opening up a PageMaker file and correcting a typographic error noticed at the last minute, for example).

✔ **Who are some of your clients?** Service bureaus, unlike lawyers who specialize in bankruptcies, are usually willing to provide the names and phone numbers of satisfied clients. Find out people to contact and call them.

> ✔ **What typefaces do you have available?** Most service bureaus can provide you with either a typeface specimen book, or a list of available typefaces organized by vendor as well as name of typeface. (*Hint:* Make sure Expert sets are available if you use them; otherwise, you may be required to provide the printer fonts — for a one-time use only, of course).

Most important of all, try to find out how much experience they have had working with your particular software program and the length of document you typically produce. Try to find out if they deal with clients like you. A service bureau serving large book publishers may be unable to devote much time and attention to your four-page newsletter.

It's never a good idea to pay for someone else's learning curve. Don't be a guinea pig and become a service bureau's first Windows user! Search around until you find a service bureau experienced in imaging Windows files.

Proofing your work and submitting files to service bureaus

When you proof files destined for high-resolution imagesetting, be sure that you do not change the printer targeted in the Page Setup window. Remember that the size of your publication is based on the limitations of the targeted printer. Line endings and page breaks will likely change if you choose a different printer. Most software programs prompt you before they change the target printer.

You can submit files to a service bureau in two ways: program data files or Encapsulated PostScript Files. These are files you print to diskette.

Preparing Encapsulated Postscript Files

Although every program is slightly different, the *basic* procedure for preparing an Encapsulated PostScript File is as follows:

1. Select the Apple LaserWriter driver.

2. Click on the Options button.

3. When the Options dialog box appears, click on the radio button next to Encapsulated PostScript File. (It may also be called "Print to Disk.")

4. Name the file.

At this point, software programs differ and the going gets rough. Each program offers you slightly different options. The only options that some programs (like WordPerfect 6.x for Windows) offers is the ability to name the file your publication will be printed to. PageMaker, on the other hand, offers numerous alternatives. Check your software program's documentation and be prepared for some experimenting until you get the procedure down pat.

When you submit files to a service bureau, make sure that you submit all necessary files. This is especially important if you are submitting program data files. It is vital that you submit all the printer fonts needed to print your document as well as all linked graphic files.

- **Failure to provide printer fonts** (unless the service bureau already has them) means that your beautiful words will be imaged in Courier.

- **Failure to provide custom kerning and tracking files** means that line-endings and page breaks may change.

- **Failure to provide linked graphic files** means that carefully created illustrations and scanned images will be replaced by gray boxes or boxes with large Xs through them. Either that possibility, or low-resolution (72 dots-per-inch on the Macintosh) screen images will replace high-resolution scans.

Make sure that you have provided everything necessary:

- Fonts used in your publication
- All necessary font kerning files
- All the files containing scanned images and illustrations
- All your program data files

You should provide printer fonts for each style variation used in your publication, such as Times Italic, Times Bold, and Times Bold Italic, as well as Times Roman, and so on.

If you are submitting Encapsulated PostScript Files, you have to make sure that the files are prepared exactly right. Any problems that occur when you submit Encapsulated PostScript Files to a service bureau are your fault and you'll likely have to pay for your mistakes.

Potential problem areas include the following:

- You may have failed to include printer's *registration marks* (if desired).

- While proofing your document, to save time (and toner) you may have elected not to print graphics. If you save your file to diskette while the Omit TIFF files option is checked, the images won't be present.

- If you failed to check the Include downloadable fonts option, your file will print with low-resolution screen representations of the fonts.

- *Separations* won't be imaged unless you place a check-mark next to the For Separations option.

✔ If you had previously proofed your publication by printing *thumbnails* — up to 16 reduced-sized images on each page — and didn't disable this feature, instead of 8½ by 11-inch pages, your pages will be approximately an 1¼ by 1½ inches!

✔ If you were *proofing pages at reduced size*, unless you return the percentage of enlargement or reduction to 100%, you'll receive odd-sized pages.

✔ If you were tiling images (printing an 11-by-17-inch publication on 8½-by-11-inch pages by printing out sections of the larger page and joining them together) you must disable the tiling feature or you won't receive the large page as a single piece of artwork.

✔ If you last *proofed a single page or a range of pages*, and you fail to reset pages to all, you'll receive only the single page, or range of pages, last printed. (This item applies only to PageMaker.)

Make sure that you have checked the proper options when printing to disk.

✔ Have you reset the enlargement/reduction ratio to 100%?

✔ Did you disable the Thumbnail printing option?

✔ Have you indicated the proper way to print colors?

✔ Are the appropriate options checked for printing graphics and scanned images?

✔ Did you check the option: "Include downloadable fonts"?

✔ Have you indicated how you want color separations to be printed?

✔ Have you indicated custom screen angles and lines per inch (if you want these features)?

✔ Have you indicated whether you want to receive mirror images or negatives, according to your printer's instructions?

✔ Did you disable the tiling feature (if you were proofing large pages on an office laser printer)?

✔ Did you reset the page range to all?

Always provide your service bureau with an actual-sized hard copy proof of your project. This will help them immediately identify problems, such as missing fonts or scanned images. If the service bureau is preparing color separations and you do not have access to a color printer, use a tissue overlay with color applied with felt tip markers to indicate where color should appear.

Working with Print Shops

You can never begin working with commercial printers soon enough. Your first concern will be to locate an affordable printer who can do you job at the appropriate quality level. This task isn't as easy as it may first seem; a certain amount of legwork is in order.

At the same time that you're gathering printing quotes, you should also be selecting the paper you want your project to be printed on. Ultimately, paper has as much to do with the success of your project as the colors you select. Unfortunately, it's difficult to choose a paper stock without the help of the printer who will be printing your publication, *so the problems addressed in the next two sections should be resolved simultaneously*. Otherwise, you may select a paper stock your printer can't get or doesn't like working with.

Gathering printing quotes

Print shops differ in the type of jobs they specialize in. Some printers specialize in low-quality, high-volume, low-cost work like restaurant menus and placemats, order forms, flyers for car washes, and other time-sensitive — but not especially quality-sensitive — jobs. Others specialize in low-volume, high-quality, "prestige" black-and-white or two-color work for high-paying clients. Still others specialize in high-volume, four-color work like brochures in quantities of 10,000 and up. None of the kinds of printers just mentioned may be appropriate for 2,500 copies of a two-color newsletter. Still others may print newspaper inserts for discount stores in quantities of 100,000.

Your first task is to *eliminate the extremes* and locate printers who want your business and want to set up a long-term relationship based on your particular combination of quality, quantity, and price. (Of the three, quality and quantity will ultimately prove more important to your satisfaction than price.)

After you have located several possibilities, you can narrow down your choices to the two or three you will ask to bid on most of your future work.

It's always a good idea to have more than one printer bid on your work. You may find great discrepancies in bids depending on how busy the print shop is and whether or not the necessary paper is in its warehouse.

It's important to start your search as soon as possible. In order to maintain some semblance of sanity, keep track of the following considerations with each printer. After you have visited the printers in person, you can do much of your future contact by phone or fax.

As you do when you visit service bureaus, look for non-verbal clues that may indicate the quality of the work and co-operation you're likely to receive from them. Are the premises clean? Is the phone politely answered? Are "portfolio quality" pieces on display in the waiting area? How long has the printer been in business? Who are some of its clients?

Pay particular attention to the size of the printing presses they have and whether they can print more than one color at a time. Find out how they want to receive your project: as camera-ready art, negatives, or electronic files? How much of their work involves desktop-published documents? Try to ascertain what type of projects they enjoy printing and in what quantities. (A printer specializing in telephone books probably won't want to do your business cards.)

When choosing a print shop, you should consider the following factors:

- Type of projects they specialize in
- Quality of samples displayed
- Page size they can handle
- Types of projects they typically produce
- Multi-color presses on premises
- Who they have as clients
- Whether they prefer camera-ready artwork, negatives, or electronic files
- Cleanlinessss
- Politeness
- Knowledge

Selecting paper

At the same time that you're checking out the printing terrain, you should also be learning more about paper. After all, it's impossible to accurately solicit printing quotes without knowing the paper your project will be printed on. Paper differs in terms of color, texture, and weight. Other important terms include opacity, ink-holding power, and brightness.

- **Color** refers to tint. There are few whites. White ranges from cool grays to warm ivories. Remember that the background of your pages influences how colors appear. Book stores specializing in graphic arts often stock books showing how various colors look when printed on different colored papers.

✔ **Surface texture** involves the content of your publication and the image you want to project. Photographs reproduce best on smooth textured papers, but the trade-off is that coated (or glossy) paper stocks may make serif text difficult to read. Strive for a balance between photo quality and feel (how the paper feels in your hand). Antique and vellum textures are noticeably rough, while satin and polished stocks are very smooth.

✔ **Weight** is measured in terms of 500 sheets. The size of the paper being weighed, however, differs depending on whether the paper is designed to be used for the insides of a book (text stock) or the cover of a book (cover stock).

✔ **Opacity** refers to the degree to which ink printed on one side shows through to the other side. Opacity is a function of the thickness of the paper and whether or not it is coated.

✔ **Ink-holding capabilities** differ among various types of paper. Coated papers increase printing costs because, being less absorbent than un-coated stocks, ink takes longer to dry.

✔ **Size** plays a role in colors, textures, and weights — which are not available in all sizes. You may find that the perfect paper is not available in a size that permits cost-effective printing.

The best way to become familiar with paper is to request the free swatch, or sample, books available from the major paper suppliers. Look in the Yellow Pages of your telephone book and check out the advertisements in publications like *Print* and *Communication Arts*.

Soliciting printing quotes

After you have selected the appropriate paper for your publication and have determined the color and quantity, it's time to start soliciting printing quotes. Keep in mind the numerous things that can go wrong, and plan for the worst-case scenario.

✔ Remember that, just as printers don't stock every paper available, paper suppliers often run out of stock. By working as far ahead of time as possible, your printer may be able to obtain a desired paper from another supplier or distributor without paying outrageous, last-minute shipping costs.

✔ Printers often can offer you a better deal if they can schedule your project in the down time between their regular clients. By finding out when your printer has extra time available, you may be able to greatly reduce your printing charges.

✔ Deadline Madness always costs more than scheduled work. If you wait until the last minute and discover a typographic error that must be corrected, you'll likely incur significant overtime charges — especially if your work is on the printing press and they can't do any other work until you correct your mistake. Last-minute work also results in higher shipping and postage costs.

Things will always go wrong. Allow time for last-minute problems by soliciting printing bids as far ahead of time as possible. Keep the following specifications in mind:

✔ Date that artwork is to be ready

✔ Quotation deadline

✔ Trim size

✔ Number of pages

✔ Folds

✔ Quantity required

✔ Paper manufacturer

✔ Paper name, weight, and surface

✔ Binding: stapled, saddle stitched, or glued

✔ Number of colors

✔ Bleeds

✔ Number of photographic halftones (if appropriate)

✔ Printed copies picked up or delivered

✔ Cost for first printing

✔ Cost for additional printings

✔ Cost for halftones (if appropriate)

✔ Cost for delivery (if appropriate)

✔ Overrun terms

✔ Payment terms

Most of the specifications you need to consider are self-explanatory. Only a few points may need elaboration at this point:

- **Trim size** refers to the physical size of the printed page.

- **Binding** refers to how the pages are attached to each other.

- **Continuous tones** refers to the traditional way of submitting black-and-white photographs that the printer converts to a pattern of dots and strips into the printing negatives.

- **Quantity** tends to creep up as a project nears print-date, and it's useful to have this information in hand. In many cases, it's useful to have the printer bid on a base amount say of, 2,500 or 5,000, as well as provide a cost for each additional 500 or 1,000 copies.

Before signing a contract with your printer, read the fine-print regarding over-runs. In many areas, the standard printer's contract allows the printer to deliver — and charge for — a certain additional percentage of the original press run. If the standard printing contract in your area allows the printer to print up to 15% more copies than you ask for, you'll be charged an additional 15%.

Avoid unpleasant surprises by finding out the terms in your area in advance, and negotiate accordingly. The original reason (read rational) for this practice was to allow for a certain number of copies to be below-standard — it takes a while for printing presses to get up to speed and achieve even print coverage.

The preceding stuff outlines some of the considerations involved in choosing paper and printing. Ideally, by submitting quotations well in advance of deadline, you can establish a working partnership with your printer. Once the printer becomes convinced of your sincerity, they may be able to suggest ways to save money, such as using an oversize paper and printing your publication two-up, that is, printing two copies at once and trimming them apart.

When you take your project to the printer, prepare actual-sized proofs of your project. Use tissue overlays to indicate where color should appear. Your proofs will help your printer.

Never assume anything. Always be as specific as possible when dealing with printers. Whenever possible, visit your printer while your job is running to make sure that it is turning out right. You'll be amazed at the problems that can be avoided by a last-minute press check. Midnight trips to printers located in distant suburbs (or even across the country) is one of the reasons Madison Avenue Art Directors are so well paid! Doesn't your project require as much tender loving care?

Evaluating your print shop performance

Immediately after you receive your printed publication, check it for quality. Check for even ink coverage and the quality of photographs. Check to see that colors appear in the correct location. Check that folds appear at the right locations and that the edges of the publication are neatly trimmed.

Later, check it for quantity and quality. Check to see that you have received the agreed-upon quantity. Rather than counting every piece, measure by *weight* or *thickness*.

Chapter 13

Creating and Enhancing a Corporate Identity

. . . .

In This Chapter

▶ What is an identity package?

▶ The advantages of a corporate identity

▶ The elements of a corporate identity

▶ Styles and templates

▶ Pre-printed versus on-the-fly letterheads

▶ How to create successful advertisements

▶ How to create successful brochures

. . . .

Do you, or your firm, have a corporate identity package? A corporate identity package refers to the conscious effort to create a unique "look" that unifies all of your print communications, from letterheads to annual reports.

A corporate identity saves money by creating a synergy among all of your print communications so that your advertisements share an obvious family resemblance to brochures and newsletters. Your firm's presence gains when all of your print communications share an immediately identifiable look.

The Elements of a Corporate Identity

A corporate identity package consists of two parts: electronic files (styles and templates) and a three-ring binder containing a written Corporate Style Guide plus sample documents. You should create the styles necessary to format *every element of page architecture* for every type of document you're likely to need. Styles maintain typographic consistency throughout all your print communications while templates save time by creating the framework into which you place the type and visuals needed for individual brochures, newsletters, or documentation.

Your style guide should always include finished sample documents so that others can quickly grasp an idea of what a document will look like when completed.

Creating styles

Styles are electronic files that contain retrievable formatting information. Most word processing and page layout programs let you include the following formatting information in styles:

- **Character formatting** attributes such as typeface, type size, type style, letter spacing, and case (normal, all caps, or small caps).

- **Paragraph formatting** attributes, such as alignment (flush-left/ragged-right, justified, and so on), hyphenation (including hyphenation zone and limiting the number of lines in a row that can be hyphenated), line spacing, tabs, paragraph spacing, paragraph borders, and background fills as well as codes to keep paragraphs intact (moved as a whole to the next column or page if they won't fit at the bottom of one column) or to lock a paragraph to the next paragraph (to keep subheads from becoming separated from the text they introduce).

The most flexible software programs enable you to create separate styles for character-level formatting and paragraph-level formatting. Having separate character and paragraph level styles allows you to easily choose a different typeface and/or type size or style for individual words or sentences within a paragraph. You can easily use 9-point sans serif run-ins in a paragraph where the remaining text is set in a 12-point serif typeface. When only one style of style is available, it will include both character and paragraph styles.

Most software programs permit you to create styles by example as well as to create the styles in advance. When you create styles by example, you first format the text, highlight it, and then save it as a style. In addition, most programs enable you to apply a set of styles to an existing document. This makes it easy for users on a network to share styles, maintaining document consistency.

Creating templates

Templates go one step beyond styles. Styles define character and paragraph formatting, but templates define entire documents. Templates include styles as well as page formatting information such as the following:

- Page size, margins, and number of pages
- Borders and the placement of page numbers
- The number and width of columns, column spacing and (when appropriate) the thickness of the vertical downrules between columns
- Repeating elements (such as newsletter nameplate, masthead, table of contents, or department headers)
- Non-printing guides that define placement of headlines, chapter opening information (such as chapter number and chapter title), column tops and bottoms, and so on

You can use the Save As command located in the File menu of most programs to save documents as templates. Saving a document as a template means that you can open it and make changes to it, but you must save it under a different filename.

One way you can work faster is to delete all non-essential templates from your word processing or page layout program's subdirectories. You can always re-install at a later date. This way, when you or another user selects Template, only those templates that support your firm's corporate identity will appear, making it faster and easier to select the right file.

Written style guide

The third element of a corporate identity program is to create (and distribute to everyone involved in producing print communications) a written Style Guide. This Style Guide should include the following information:

> ✔ A list of all of the templates used to create your firm's documents
>
> ✔ Instructions defining how each of the templates is to be used, describing the types of documents based on each template
>
> ✔ Samples of completed documents based on each of the templates
>
> ✔ Instructions describing how to share and load the templates and apply the styles as well as warnings limiting the user's ability to change or delete templates

The name of the template that each document is based on should be clearly written on each sample. All styles should be identified with callouts, as shown in Figure 13-1. That way, readers will know what's going to happen when they select a template and apply a style.

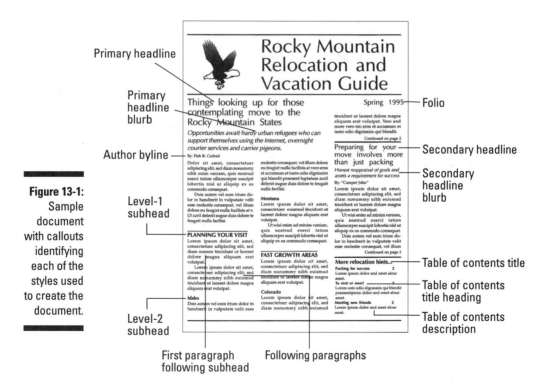

Figure 13-1: Sample document with callouts identifying each of the styles used to create the document.

Callouts pointing to the sample document: Primary headline, Primary headline blurb, Author byline, Level-1 subhead, Level-2 subhead, First paragraph following subhead, Following paragraphs, Folio, Secondary headline, Secondary headline blurb, Table of contents title, Table of contents title heading, Table of contents description

Components of a Corporate Identity Package

Every firm or association's corporate identity package includes a slightly different mixture of documents. In general, the following types of documents are included:

- Correspondence and business cards
- Memos and fax forms
- Advertisements
- Brochures
- Documentation and manuals
- Newsletters
- Press releases
- Price lists
- Proposals
- Qualification sheets

Correspondence

Letters, faxes, and memos form the lifeblood of most firms and associations. In most cases, letters, faxes, press releases, price lists, and qualification sheets are based on the same template. The primary differences will be the identifying heading as well as the forms that permit you to automatically add the correct date and identify the recipient, the subject of the communication, and those who are receiving copies.

Figures 13-2, 13-3, and 13-4 show how a variety of documents can be based on a similar design.

Business cards should reflect the same size and typographic relationships as found on correspondence, although the size of the logo and type sizes may have to be proportionately reduced to fit the smaller area.

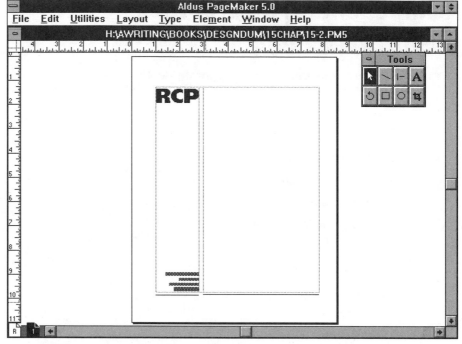

Figure 13-2:
The basic "empty" template organizes the firm's logo, address, and motto around a vertical spine .1 inches wide.

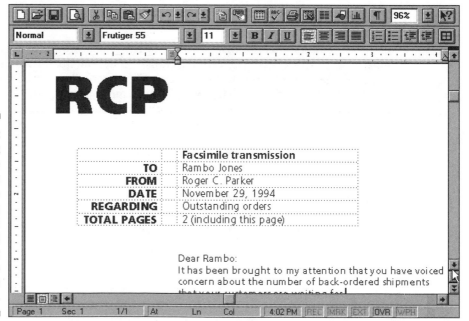

Figure 13-3:
The fax template includes a table straddling the vertical spine and containing cells to organize information.

RCP

PROPOSAL Lighting Rods and Fire Protection
DATE January 13, 1995
TO Executive search committee

Summary

Dolor sit amet, consectetuer adipiscing elit, sed diam nonummy nibh euismod tincidunt ut laoreet dolore magna aliquam erat volutpat. Ut wisi enim ad minim veniam, quis nostrud exerci tation . dolore eu feugiat nulla facilisis at vero eros et accumsan et iusto odio dignissim qui blandit praesent luptatum zzril delenit augue duis dolore te feugait nulla facilisi.

Background

Lorem ipsum dolor sit amet, consectetuer adipiscing elit, sed diam nonummy nibh euismod tincidunt ut laoreet dolore magna aliquam erat volutpat. Lorem ipsum dolor sit amet, consectetuer adipiscing elit, sed diam nonummy nibh euismod tincidunt ut laoreet dolore magna aliquam erat volutpat.

First recommendation — Duis autem vel eum iriure dolor in hendrerit in vulputate velit esse molestie consequat, vel illum dolore eu feugiat nulla facilisis at vero eros et accumsan et iusto odio dignissim qui blandit praesent luptatum zzril delenit augue duis dolore te feugait nulla facilisi.

Second recommendation — Lorem ipsum dolor sit amet, consectetuer adipiscing elit, sed diam nonummy nibh euismod tincidunt ut laoreet dolore magna aliquam erat volutpat. Ut wisi enim ad minim veniam, quis nostrud exerci tation ullamcorper suscipit lobortis nisl ut aliquip ex ea commodo consequat.

Roger C. Parker
PO Box 697
Dover, NH 03820
603-742-9673

Lorem ipsum dolor sit amet, consectetuer adipiscing elit, sed diam nonummy nibh euismod tincidunt ut laoreet dolore magna aliquam

Figure 13-4:
The proposal template reflects the same basic arrangement of header and footer information but uses subheads to break the text into manageable bite-sized chunks.

Ten ways to create a good-looking letterhead

1. Align elements along an invisible spine.

2. Use "invisible tables" to organize information in your letterhead.

3. Separate logo from address/phone information.

4. Place logos and address/phone/fax information in headers and footers.

5. Place logo and address information at lower left.

6. Use Watermarks to place visuals behind text.

7. Choose off-center placement for logo and address/phone/fax/E-mail information.

8. Experiment with contrasting typefaces, weights and styles.

9. Use True Small Caps and Old Style Figures.

10. Use abbreviations whenever possible.

Advertisements

Consistency is the key to success when running advertisements. Although the content of each of your ads is likely to change, success comes from a handling of white space, headlines, visuals, and text. One of the oldest "rules of thumbs" of advertising is that clients become bored with their advertising just when prospects are beginning to notice them. Don't be panicked into prematurely changing your format.

Pay most of your attention to headlines when creating advertisements and be guided by gravity. Headlines are the most important part of an advertisement. Your ad is likely to fail if readers can't easily locate and read the headline or make an easy transition from your headline to the supporting copy that follows. Although headlines located in the center, to the left, or at the bottom of an advertisement may appear "different," readership will inevitably fall.

White space around the headlines is one of the keys to creating effective advertisements. Advertisements with small headlines surrounded by white space will likely attract more attention than advertisements with headlines shoehorned into position, as Figures 13-5 and 13-6 illustrate.

Come to the Great Model Railroad Swap Meet
March 8, 1995

Dolor sit amet, consectetuer adipiscing elit, sed diam nonummy nibh euismod tincidunt ut laoreet dolore magna aliquam erat volutpat. Ut wisi enim ad minim veniam, quis nostrud exerci tation ullamcorper suscipit lobortis nisl ut aliquip ex ea commodo consequat. Duis autem vel eum iriure dolor in hendrerit in vulputate velit esse molestie consequat, vel illum dolore eu

feugiat nulla facilisis at vero eros et accumsan et iusto odio dignissim qui blandit praesent luptatum zzril delenit augue duis dolore te feugait nulla facilisi.

Lorem ipsum dolor sit amet, consectetuer adipiscing elit, sed diam nonummy nibh euismod tincidunt ut laoreet dolore magna aliquam erat volutpat.

Exposition Center
3504 33rd Avenue West
Montpelier, NH 03802

Figure 13-5:
Large, "shouting" headlines that fill every available inch lack impact.

Eight ways to create better-looking advertisements

1. Surround headlines with plenty of white space.

2. Include a coupon whenever possible.

3. Use consistent borders and white space in all ads.

4. Use a consistent placement of text and visuals in all ads.

5. Use consistent typography in all of your ads.

6. Always include a caption with visuals.

7. Always place the logo and address/phone/fax information in the same location.

8. Don't be afraid to edit!

Model Railroad Swap Meet

Dolor sit amet, consectetuer adipiscing elit, sed diam nonummy nibh euismod tincidunt ut laoreet dolore magna aliquam erat volutpat. Ut wisi enim ad minim veniam, quis nostrud exerci tation ullamcorper suscipit lobortis nisl ut aliquip ex ea commodo consequat. Duis autem vel eum iriure dolor in hendrerit in vulputate velit esse molestie consequat, vel illum dolore eu feugiat nulla facilisis at vero eros et accumsan et iusto odio dignissim qui blandit praesent luptatum zzril delenit augue duis dolore te feugait nulla facilisi.

Lorem ipsum dolor sit amet, consectetuer adipiscing elit, sed diam nonummy nibh euismod tincidunt ut laoreet dolore magna aliquam erat volutpat.

March 8, 1995
Exposition Center
3504 33rd Avenue West
Montpelier, NH 03802

Figure 13-6: Headlines surrounded by plenty of white space enhance readability.

Brochures

Brochures are needed for just about every type of business. Even if they repeat information contained in Qualification Sheets or Case History Sheets, brochures are valuable because of their perceived higher value—they are typically printed in color on a higher-quality paper.

Two primary challenges are involved in successful brochures: one involves the placement of information on the front and back panels, and the other challenge involves the need to build a consistent amount of white space into every panel. The front panel must

✔ Establish the appropriate mood for the brochure. Is the tone of the brochure intended to be quiet or explosive?

✔ Set the brochure apart from others. The brochure must fit in with the rest of the firm or association's corporate identity, yet be unique.

✔ Promise the reader a benefit for reading the inside information.

✔ End with a clearly-identified call to action. It must be easy for the reader to respond to the brochure. This is why the back panel of many brochures contains either a summary of the points covered in the brochure or a large, easy-to-fill-in order form.

The front panel of a brochure should be as simple as possible. A large, shaded illustration can be used as the background for the headline on the front panel.

If the brochure is designed for display in a literature rack, the headline should be placed as close to the top of the brochure as possible so that it will not be hidden by other brochures placed in front of it.

One of the easiest ways to build unity into your brochures is to use a deep left-hand margin, emphasized by a vertical rule on each page. Headlines can be hung to the left of the vertical rule, interrupting the vertical rule where necessary. A consistent amount of white space should appear at the top and bottom of each panel. Another way to create consistency is to repeat the firm's logo at a small size along the bottom of each panel, as shown in Figure 13-7.

Figure 13-7:
A deep left-hand indent, hung headlines, a vertical rule and consistent logo placement help unify each of the pages of this three-panel brochure.

INSTALLATION

Dolor sit amet, consectetuer adipiscing elit, sed diam nonummy nibh euismod tincidunt ut laoreet dolore magna aliquam erat volutpat.

Ut wisi enim ad minim veniam, quis nostrud exerci tation ullamcorper suscipit lobortis nisl ut aliquip ex ea commodo consequat. Duis autem vel eum iriure dolor in hendrerit in vulputate velit esse molestie consequat, vel illum dolore eu feugiat.

SETUP

Nulla facilisis at vero eros et accumsan et iusto odio dignissim qui blandit praesent luptatum zzril delenit augue duis dolore te feugait nulla facilisi.

TRAINING

Lorem ipsum dolor sit amet, consectetuer adipiscing elit, sed diam nonummy nibh euismod tincidunt ut laoreet dolore magna aliquam erat volutpat.

Lorem ipsum dolor sit amet, consectetuer adipiscing elit, sed diam nonummy nibh euismod tincidunt ut

Dolor sit amet, consectetuer adipiscing elit, sed diam nonummy nibh euismod tincidunt ut laoreet dolore magna aliquam erat volutpat.

FINANCING

Ut wisi enim ad minim veniam, quis nostrud exerci tation ullamcorper suscipit lobortis nisl ut aliquip ex ea commodo consequat. Duis autem vel eum iriure dolor in hendrerit in vulputate velit esse molestie consequat, vel illum dolore eu feugiat.

Nulla facilisis at vero eros et accumsan et iusto odio dignissim qui blandit praesent luptatum zzril delenit augue duis dolore te feugait nulla facilisi.

COMMITMENT

Lorem ipsum dolor sit amet, consectetuer adipiscing elit, sed diam nonummy nibh euismod tincidunt ut laoreet dolore magna aliquam erat volutpat.

Desktop Consultants
4403 East Arlington Farm Way
Arlington Falls, NH 03880
603-772-0981

HOW TO BUY YOUR FIRST DESKTOP PUBLISHING SYSTEM

Dolor sit amet, consectetuer adipiscing elit, sed diam nonummy nibh euismod tincidunt ut laoreet dolore magna aliquam erat volutpat.

Ut wisi enim ad minim veniam, quis nostrud exerci tation ullamcorper suscipit lobortis nisl ut aliquip ex ea commodo consequat. Duis autem vel eum iriure dolor in hendrerit in vulputate velit esse molestie consequat, vel illum dolore eu feugiat.

Nulla facilisis at vero eros et accumsan et iusto odio dignissim qui blandit praesent luptatum zzril delenit augue duis dolore te feugait nulla facilisi.

DESKTOP CONSULTANTS   DESKTOP CONSULTANTS   DESKTOP CONSULTANTS

Newsletters

Newsletters are so important that this book has a *Newsletters For Dummies* insert. This insert contains a case study describing the steps involved in creating a successful newsletter.

Not only does *Newsletters For Dummies* describe the steps involved in creating a newsletter, but it also provides a handy review of this book by reinforcing many of the ideas I've introduced.

Long documents

The key to effective long documents, such as proposals and reports, is a clearly visible information hierarchy. One of the easiest ways to create a visible information hierarchy is to introduce proposals and reports with an Executive Summary that introduces the structure of the document that follows.

Four elements affect the success of long documents:

- **Headers and footers:** Keep readers informed of their progress through the document. Headers and footers also help quickly locate desired information.

- **Subhead hierarchy:** Each subhead level must appear typographically distinct.

- **Visuals:** Must not interfere with the reader's progress through the document. Whenever possible, avoid text wraps by placing charts and tables next to text columns rather than inside text columns.

- **Easy reading:** Choose the proper relationship between typeface, type size, line length, and line spacing.

Six ideas for improving long documents

1. Break long documents into short sections.

2. Use a deep indent.

3. Surround headers and footers with white space.

4. Use distinct typographic contrast for each subhead level.

5. Use uppercase type with care.

6. Use color whenever possible.

Part VI
Ten Tens: One Hundred Design Tips

The 5th Wave
By Rich Tennant

"These kidnappers are clever, Lieutenant. Look at this ransom note, the use of 4-color graphics to highlight the victims photograph. And the fonts! They must be creating their own-must be over 35 typefaces here...."

In this part...

*P*art VI, "Ten Tens: One Hundred Design Tips," reviews many of the important ideas previously described and introduces other ideas that didn't comfortably fit within the individual chapters. This section is always one of my favorites, and it's the section I write first.

Chapter 14

Ten Questions to Ask Before You Begin a Project

. . . .

Start by asking yourself the same questions that newpaper reporters ask: Who? What? When? Where? and Why? Success comes to the extent that you analyze your readers, your message, and the competitive environment in which your publication will appear.

When is it due in my reader's hands?

Start by considering the date your project must appear in your reader's hands. The amount of time available should influence the complexity of your designs. When time is short, choose as simple a layout as possible. Avoid designs that require fancy illustrations or new software features unless you have time to master the learning curves and prepare the files. Never try to simultaneously learn a new program and use it!

Who are my readers?

Analyze your readers. Who are they? How old are they? What are their expectations? Remember the obvious: older readers appreciate larger type sizes, for example.

How motivated are my readers?

If readers are interested in your message, they'll be less demanding and more willing to put up with design shortcomings than if they are casual readers.

Where will readers encounter my publication?

Will readers encounter your message surrounded by other messages, as in a newspaper, or will your message occupy their entire visual frame of reference? Will they be reading at home, on an airplane, or sitting at a desk in an office?

What is the image I want to project?

What non-verbal clues do you want to provide? Do you want to appear daring or conservative, affordable or expensive, "public" or withdrawn? By identifying the message you want to project, you can make the typeface, border, color, and paper choices that will best reinforce your message.

What text and graphics elements must my publication accommodate?

What is the precise mix of text and graphics? Will your publication consist of a few long stories or a mixture of long and short features. How long is the typical paragraph? Will there be many headlines and subheads? How about visuals? Do you have to plan for photographs, illustrations, charts, graphs, and tables? What repeating elements must be included — your firm's logo, affiliations, or corporate ownership marks? A mystery containing page after page of text requires an entirely different design than a publication composed of a complex mix of photographs, alerts, hints, and warnings.

How can I make my reader's job easier?

Become your reader's advocate. Simplify your designs and eliminate unnecessary text and visual elements. Choose the right type size and line spacing based on the length of the lines (or width of your columns). Eliminate unnecessary distractions, such as awkward word and letter spacing or excessive hyphenation. Avoid unnecessary distractions, such as dot leaders in lists or a publication masthead. Make relationships obvious by using white space to separate or connect.

What limitations must be accommodated?

Available hardware resources should influence the sophistication of your designs. Avoid scanned photographs, graduated backgrounds, and typefaces with thin strokes if you are preparing camera-ready artwork on a 300 dot-per-inch laser printer.

Don't incorporate special graphic effects, such as bleeds (where text or visuals extend to the edge of the page), if you are preparing artwork for an $8^1/_2$ by 11 document on your laser printer. Most laser printers are unable to print to the edge of the page.

Likewise, don't incorporate color into your designs unless you are certain you can afford color printing. To avoid disappointment, always consult with your print shop before getting too involved with a project.

What kind of paper will my project be printed on?

Your choice of paper and typefaces should be influenced by the type of paper your project will be printed on. Avoid bright colors and small, intricate typefaces containing thin strokes if your publication is going to be printed on a glossy paper stock. The reflectance of the paper might make it difficult to read your message. Likewise, thin typefaces are apt to be lost if you're printing on a porous, textured, or recycled paper. Again, check with your paper supplier before progressing very far in your work.

What functions can I delegate?

Train yourself to delegate routine tasks to others. Consider yourself a mentor and strive to improve the desktop publishing and design abilities of your coworkers. The more you delegate, the more you'll have time to improve your design skills and fine-tuning your projects.

Chapter 15

The Ten Most Important Parts of a Page

• •

*E*very page is different, yet most are built using the same materials. Your success as a designer depends on how you handle the following ten elements.

Margins

Margins are the space between the top, bottom, and side edges of a page and adjacent columns of text. By using margins of varying depth, you can build additional white space into your pages. Often, the first step to becoming a better designer is to experiment with asymmetrical margins, creating pages with more space to the left of the text than the right.

Grid

A *grid* consists of a network of non-printing horizontal and vertical lines. (These lines appear on your computer screen but not the printed publication.) Grids determine the placement of text and visuals. Each page of your document should be based on the same grid, even though the placement of text columns can vary from page to page (see Chapter 5). Simple documents that contain relatively few text elements can be based on a simple one- or two-column grid. Choose five-, six-, or seven-column grids if your documents contain a variety of text and graphic elements of varying importance.

Headers and footers

You can use headers and footers to remind readers of information such as page number, publication title, chapter title, section title, and (most important) the author's name.

Headers can also contribute to document unity by building a consistent amount of white space into the top and bottom of each page. You can add graphic accents, such as horizontal rules, can be added to headers and footers to create visual boundaries that unify and define each page.

Headlines and titles

Headlines are the most important text element on each page. Headlines serve as the primary entry point for readers. Readers skimming through a document are unlikely to begin reading the body copy unless they are attracted by the headline. Good headline typography makes it easy for readers to quickly grasp the importance of the text that follows. Poor headline typography discourages readers, making it unlikely that readers will read the text that follows.

Subheads

Subheads are the next most important text element on a page. Subheads break long, intimidating columns of text into easy-to-digest bite-sized chunks. Subheads also build white space and visual variety into your text columns. Always include lots of subheads. Each subhead offers you an opportunity to attract another "skimmer" into taking the time to read your text. Subheads also permit you to organize and reinforce the important points contained within the text.

Pull quotes

Pull quotes are short phrases that summarize important points described in the text columns. They are often voiced in the first-person. Pull quotes should be set larger than body copy and subheads but smaller than headlines. Pull quotes let readers quickly see "What's going on?" in the adjacent text column. If the pull quote is well written, the reader will be encouraged to read more.

Visuals

All words and no play make for boring reading. Whenever possible, try to replace text with the appropriate visuals. Visuals communicate at a glance. Photographs communicate "you are there!" detail far better than words. Illustrations, such as cut-away drawings or maps, inform better than words. Clip art can create atmosphere or ambiance. Charts and graphs translate numbers into relationships and trends that readers can grasp at a glance. Tables organize and simplify detailed information, such as product model numbers and specifications. Organization charts communicate hierarchy and responsibility. Timelines communicate before, during, and/or after time relationships. Flow charts communicate sequence.

Captions

Always add captions to explain the significance of adjacent visuals. Studies have shown that, after headlines, captions are the second best read part of a page. Readers turn to captions because they appear short and, thus, appear easy to read. Provide captions that tell a story and sell the adjacent text.

White space

White space is not "wasted space." *Hang this on your boss or client's door!* White space is an inexpensive emphasis and organization tool. White space creates contrast that attracts the reader's eyes. White space around a headline, for example, attracts the reader's eyes to the headline. Use white space to communicate relationships. Large amounts of white space separate elements; small amounts of white space connect elements. For example, use more white space above subheads than between the subheads and the text they introduce. Use white space to indicate the end of one article and the beginning of the next.

Graphic accents

Today's page layout and word processing programs offer an enticing assortment of graphic accents, including lines, borders, and backgrounds. Use them with discretion. Use them functionally rather than decoratively. Too many graphic accents create unnecessary clutter, which projects a disorganized, unprofessional image.

Use horizontal lines at the top and bottom of a page to frame the page and use them within text columns as a separation device. Use shaded backgrounds with care. Although the shaded backgrounds may attract attention, they often make text harder to read by reducing the foreground/background contrast needed for easy word recognition and reading. Only use vertical downrules between text columns when they're necessary to prevent readers from reading across the columns.

Chapter 16
Ten Essential Typefaces

● ●

*T*he best way to avoid arguments is to avoid discussing politics, religion …
and type. The path to eternal damnation (and broken friendships) is paved
with good intentions. Yet I would be remiss if I didn't include some personal
favorites — some legitimate (real as opposed to 600 fonts for $69.95) typefaces
you can safely make a commitment to, typefaces incorporating the artistic
integrity and flexibility necessary to serve you well for many years, typefaces
that will (with perhaps one exception) never go out of style.

Here, in order of specialized usage, are my ten "must have" typeface recommen-
dations. As they say on the Op Ed page, "The opinions expressed are my own
and do not reflect…."

Helvetica Condensed

> # PANOSE
> # abekmoqst
>
> The best way to evaluate type is to compare it at a variety of sizes.
> Large sizes, i.e. 48 point and larger, reveal how the type will look
> when used for headlines and titles. But you should also set a
> sample paragraph of text in 11-point type, so you can see how the
> type will look when used in body copy.

Helvetica Condensed, or one of its sans serif equivalents, is the first "new"
typeface anyone serious about improving their design abilities should immediately consider adding to their typographic toolbox. Adobe's Helvetica Condensed package includes Helvetica Condensed Black and Helvetica Condensed
Light. Used for headlines and subheads, Helvetica Condensed Black creates a
strong visual contrast with just about any serif typeface you're likely to use for
body copy.

As described in Chapter 5, Helvetica Condensed Black is "bolder" than Helvetica Bold, yet takes up less space without sacrificing legibility. Because it is more condensed, a three-line headline often becomes a stronger two-line headline when set in Helvetica Condensed Black. Helvetica Condensed also works well for tables and forms.

If your laser printer shipped with Univers, however, substitute the Univers Condensed package. And if you're using the Arial TrueType fonts, which ships with Microsoft Windows, choose Monotype's Arial Condensed package.

Charter

PANOSE

abekmoqst

The best way to evaluate type is to compare it at a variety of sizes. Large sizes, i.e. 48 point and larger, reveal how the type will look when used for headlines and titles. But you should also set a sample paragraph of text in 11-point type, so you can see how the type will look when used in body copy.

If you're looking for an ideal "correspondence" font — one that will make your letters and faxes stand out from the rest without standing on their heads and attracting undue attention to themselves — choose Charter. Charter was designed by Matthew Carter to compensate for the limitations of 300 dot-per-inch output. Originally available only from Bitstream, Charter is now licensed by the International Typographic Corporation and available from other venders. Charter is a "strong" serif font.

Charter's strength comes from its sharply defined serifs and its relatively even stroke weight: no "thin" strokes are apt to get lost, or drop out, when reproduced by a laser printer or office copier.

A side-by-side comparison of a paragraph printed using Charter to the same paragraph set using the ubiquitous Times Roman illustrates the added strength Charter can bring to your page.

Monotype Amassis

PANOSE
abekmoqst

The best way to evaluate type is to compare it at a variety of sizes. Large sizes, i.e. 48 point and larger, reveal how the type will look when used for headlines and titles. But you should also set a sample paragraph of text in 11-point type, so you can see how the type will look when used in body copy.

Choose Monotype Amassis if you send a lot of faxes or are looking for a sans serif correspondence typeface that projects professionalism and strength. Amassis is a "humanist" slab serif typeface. What this means is that the letters are shaped like those written by a human, but the letters are of relatively even thickness and the serifs are pronounced and horizontal.

The result is an easy-to-read typeface that looks "serious" without looking "sterile." An added benefit: Amassis is available in a variety of weights, from thin to thick, which makes it possible to add visual interest to your correspondence without introducing different typeface designs. Use the Roman (or regular) version for the text of your letter, but use the Heavy version for your firm's name and use the Light version for your address and phone number. The result will be an image of professionalism and restraint — plus your faxes will come through crystal clear.

The preceding typefaces are ideal for wide, single-column documents, such as letters and faxes, and the following three are better suited for narrow, multi-column documents, such as books and newsletters.

Monotype Baskerville

PANOSE
abekmoqst

The best way to evaluate type is to compare it at a variety of sizes. Large sizes, i.e. 48 point and larger, reveal how the type will look when used for headlines and titles. But you should also set a sample paragraph of text in 11-point type, so you can see how the type will look when used in body copy.

If you're producing a long document, such as a book, and want to project an image of orderly, nonflamboyant beauty, choose Monotype Baskerville. Monotype Baskerville is a typeface your readers can look at all day without tiring of it. Each letter is beautifully proportioned and unlikely to be confused with any other. Monotype Baskerville is a timeless classic that is a variation of a design that has been successfully used for books for hundreds of years.

An added bonus: Monotype Baskerville is available with a complete set of True Small Caps and Old Style Figures. Monotype Baskerville also ships with a semi-bold weight that will allow you to emphasize titles and proper nouns without "shouting" at the reader.

Adobe Minion

PANOSE
abekmoqst

The best way to evaluate type is to compare it at a variety of sizes. Large sizes, i.e. 48 point and larger, reveal how the type will look when used for headlines and titles. But you should also set a sample paragraph of text in 11-point type, so you can see how the type will look when used in body copy.

Adobe Minion is a digital adaptation of Garamond, another typeface that has stood the test of time. Adobe Minion is a typeface designed for long text passages. You can read it all day "without noticing it," rather than feeling that the book is somehow very beautiful.

Adobe Minion is a complete package including semi-bold and extra-bold weights, True Small Caps, Old Style Figures, Swash letters for "signing" your faxes, and ornaments that can be used for end-of-story symbols. Many beautiful typefaces shout "look at me!" Adobe Minion says "pay attention to the words." You'll never outgrow this package.

Century Old Style

PANOSE

abekmoqst

The best way to evaluate type is to compare it at a variety of
sizes. Large sizes, i.e. 48 point and larger, reveal how the
type will look when used for headlines and titles. But you
should also set a sample **paragraph** of text in 11-point type,
so you can see how the type will look when used in body
copy.

Century Old Style is a twentieth-century "workhorse" publication font which
incorporates many of the characteristics that have contributed to the long life
of older designs. Century Old Style is an excellent choice for newsletters and
documentation. Century Old Style has a relatively high x-height, which helps it
look noticeably larger on a page than Times Roman, Baskerville, or Minion set
in the same size.

At small sizes, Century Old Style's generous proportions (the large openings in
the lowercase *a*'s and *e*'s) help make each letter easily identifiable. At large
sizes, the subtle changes in stroke thickness and the sharp serifs add visual
interest and project a "determined" or "chiseled" image. Just about every
typeface foundry offers a version of Century; Monotype's version is illustrated
at the beginning of this section. Most versions include semi- and extra-bold
versions as well as Old Style Figures and True Small Caps.

When compared to Baskerville, Minion, and Times Roman, Century projects a
somewhat more contemporary look.

Optima

PANOSE

abekmoqst

The best way to evaluate type is to compare it at a variety of
sizes. Large sizes, i.e. 48 point and larger, reveal how the
type will look when used for headlines and titles. But you
should also set a sample paragraph of text in 11-point type,
so you can see how the type will look when used in body
copy.

Optima is just about the only "nondenominational" sans serif typeface; it can be used for both headlines and extended passages of body copy. As described in Chapter 5, sans serif typefaces often work better for headlines than they do for body copy. Optima, designed by Herman Zapf, is the exception.

One of the reasons that Optima works so well for body copy is that the strokes making up the letters contain *stress* — not the stress associated with writing a book under deadline conditions (oops!), but smooth variations in thickness between the horizontal and vertical strokes of each letter.

Choose Optima if you're looking for a single typeface design that can be used for every category of every print communication your firm produces. Optima works equally well for correspondence, documentation, and newsletters.

Optima is available from the major typeface foundries (Bitstream calls it Humanist 777). In addition, some typeface foundries, such as URW, offer various weights of their version of Optima, enabling you to add extra weight to headlines.

Frutiger

PANOSE
abekmoqst

The best way to evaluate type is to compare it at a variety of sizes. Large sizes, i.e. 48 point and larger, reveal how the type will look when used for headlines and titles. But you should also set a sample paragraph of text in 11-point type, so you can see how the type will look when used in body copy.

Frutiger is a more specialized sans serif typeface. Frutiger is often called a "humanist" sans serif because the shapes of its letters are more similar to the shapes of serif typefaces than most other sans serif designs. Frutiger is available in a variety of weights, from Light to Extra Black. More importantly, a matching Condensed typeface package is available.

Choose Frutiger if you want to project a crisp, state-of-the-art contemporary image and are willing to take more care in choosing line spacing. Unlike most sans serif typefaces, which aren't very pleasing to read in large doses, you can set very readable body copy with Frutiger. And because Frutiger ships with a variety of weights, from Light to Extra Black, Frutiger is ideal for "layered" publications, such as *Wired!*, where some articles are set in a very heavy typeface next to others set in a very light typeface.

A matching Condensed typeface package is available for headlines, table headers, and forms. Frutiger was originally designed by Adrian Frutiger for the signage at the DeGaulle Airport in Paris — a tribute to its readability from long distances.

Futura

PANOSE

abekmoqst

The best way to evaluate type is to compare it at a variety of sizes. Large sizes, i.e. 48 point and larger, reveal how the type will look when used for headlines and titles. But you should also set a sample paragraph of text in 11-point type, so you can see how the type will look when used in body copy.

Futura is a multi-weight sans serif typeface available from numerous typeface foundries. Futura reflects simple, straightforward, almost geometric letter forms which, because of their austerity, create a pleasing contrast to just about any serif typeface. The complete Futura package includes numerous Condensed Heavy and Extra Heavy weights that can be used for high-impact headlines. Futura is often used in advertising typography, although its strong letters can be used to create high-impact newsletter headlines and subheads — especially when Condensed versions are chosen.

Compared to Helvetica, Futura projects a more in-your-face appearance. It has more character and doesn't blend into the background. Because of this, more care has to be used when matching it to adjacent serif body copy typefaces.

Tekton

PANOSE

abekmoqst

The best way to evaluate type is to compare it at a variety of sizes. Large sizes, i.e. 48 point and larger, reveal how the type will look when used for headlines and titles. But you should also set a sample paragraph of text in 11-point type, so you can see how the type will look when used in body copy.

It's possible to take things too seriously, which is why there's Adobe Tekton and Monotype's matching Blueprint. Tekton and Blueprint were designed to mimic an architect's clear, steady hand. Tekton and Blueprint are ideal for "annotating" documents and adding informal comments. You probably wouldn't want to use either typeface for headlines or body copy, but you certainly could use them for document identification (Fax or Invoice, for example) and callouts to drawings and charts.

Chapter 17

The Ten Most Common Desktop Publishing Design Blunders

• •

*A*s an editor of *Newsletter Design* and a judge in the Newsletter Clearing House's yearly newsletter design competition, I review thousands of desktop published newsletters each year. I've noticed that the same mistakes are made over and over again. These mistakes aren't limited to newsletters, of course. They're found everywhere, as you've probably noticed — or will notice after reading this book!

Long lines of small type, short lines of large type

The number one mistake is a failure to relate type size to line length. The wrong type size presents an immediate turn-off to readers. Long lines of small type present a gray, "this is going to require a lot of work!" appearance. They are also extremely difficult to read. Short lines of large type create equally hard-to-read documents. Excessive hyphenation often occurs when type is too large for line length (or column width).

As a rule of thumb, aim for lines containing approximately seven words, or between 30 and 50 characters per line. Avoid body copy containing fewer than 20 characters or more than 60 characters.

Inconsistent column layouts

The best-looking documents are constructed on a grid that remains consistent from page to page. Document unity is destroyed when some pages are based on a two-column grid facing others based on a three-column grid. Sometimes, part of a page is based on a two-column grid, while the remainder is based on a three-column grid!

Changing column structures make everyone work harder. It's harder to create a document when the columns are constantly changing, and it's harder for readers to constantly readjust their reading rhythm to accommodate changing column structures.

Narrow columns of justified text

Eek! Narrow columns of justified text, especially type sizes at the upper range of acceptability for the line length, are frequently characterized by awkward word spacing. Word spacing changes noticeably from line to line, creating ugly "holes" in the text and making it difficult for readers to establish a rhythm. Frequently, a line containing several short words — characterized by extremely tight word spacing — follows a line containing one or two long words — characterized by H — U — G — E gaps between words. The result is ugly, ugly, ugly.

Reserve the use of justified text to lines long enough to contain several word breaks so that word length doesn't unduly influence word spacing. Note that most programs allow you to specify minimum and maximum justification limits (see Chapter 7).

Default line spacing in headlines

Although you *sometimes* can get by with default line spacing, or leading, in body copy, default leading creates headlines with the lines set unnaturally far apart. Most page layout and word processing programs automatically set line spacing at 120% of the type size chosen. Although this might be okay when you work with 11-point type, when you work with 36-point type, the lines are set so far apart you can land a Boeing 747 between them.

Get in the habit of reducing line spacing for headlines. Or create headline style definitions with reduced line spacing.

Periods followed by two spaces

This design blunder is *everywhere!* I once received a letter from the Vice President of Academic Affairs at a prestigious art and design school containing two spaces after each period. Like all documents containing two spaces after each period, the letter had a bunch of "holes" in the text. It looked as if someone had shot at the letter.

Two spaces following periods is especially bad when they appear in justified text — especially short columns of justified text. In lines containing a few words, the spaces expand, becoming even more noticeable. Not only that, but sometimes the spaces line-up, creating rivers of white space that trail through the text columns.

If you can't break yourself (or your coworkers) from the habit of hitting the spacebar twice after each period, use your program's Find (or Search) and Replace feature to locate every instance of two spaces and replace them with a single space.

Small, floating initial caps

To succeed, initial caps must be significantly larger than the body copy they introduce; otherwise, they look accidental.

Initial caps must also clearly relate to the text they introduce. They should never float in splendid isolation, only parenthetically related to adjacent text. One of the best ways to relate initial caps to adjacent text is to make sure that the baseline of the initial cap (the invisible line the cap rests on) aligns with the baseline of one of the lines of text in the paragraph. In addition, wrap the text as tightly to the initial cap as possible. Finally, you might consider setting the first word or phrase in small caps. This creates a visual transition between the initial cap and the text.

Overpowering graphic accents

Rules, boxes, and screens should be used with restraint. Often, like children in a candy store, desktop publishers go hog-wild when they discover their software program's line drawing, border, and background tools. *Boxitis* occurs: pages are placed in boxed borders, the title of the publication is boxed, and vertical rules are added between columns. In addition, many text elements are reversed (set in white against a dark background), and other text elements are screened (set against a gray background). Clutter is the inevitable result of this graphic overkill.

There appears to be an unspoken hierarchy of graphic elements among newcomers to desktop publishers: when in doubt, box an item. When in double doubt, add a shadow box (make the right and bottom borders heavier). When in triple doubt, add a screened background! The fact that nobody wants to read the resulting text becomes secondary to the demonstration of desktop publishing virtuosity.

Headlines set in uppercase type

It's been said over and over again, but nobody seems to listen: avoid the use of uppercase headlines. Repeat after me: *Avoid the use of uppercase headlines!* Remember that communication between writer and reader is based on the reader's ability to recognize word shapes. This communication happens unconsciously. Words set in lowercase type have distinct shapes, created by the interplay between letters with ascenders (such as *l*'s, *t*'s and *b*'s), letters with descenders (*g*'s, *y*'s, and *p*'s) and letters without ascenders and descenders (*a*'s, *e*'s, *o*'s). Each word has a distinct shape that readers can quickly recognize.

Long captions set in small, italicized type

Captions are typically set in a smaller type size than adjacent body text. This causes problems when captions extend the full width of photographs spanning two or more columns. The inevitable result is a line of extremely hard-to-read text. To make the situation worse, captions are often set in italic. Even at normal text sizes, italicized text is harder to read than normal, or Roman, text (partly because the letters are closer together). So a bad situation becomes worse when an italicized caption extends the width of the photograph.

Failure to hyphenate

Hyphenation splits words that are too long to fit at the end of one line over two lines. Unless you're an experienced designer striving for a unique effect (see, every rule has its exception), body copy should always be hyphenated. Word spacing suffers when text is not hyphenated. Although most people hyphenate justified text, they often neglect to hyphenate flush-left/ragged-right text. When flush-left/ragged-right text is not hyphenated, there is too much of a difference between short and long lines. Short lines are too short; long lines are too long. Often, an extremely short line is sandwiched between two long lines. Or the constantly alternating line lengths create distracting shapes along the right margin of the column.

Chapter 18

Ten Ways to Improve Simple, Everyday Documents

• •

*S*top right there! There's no such thing as a "simple, everyday document." Every print communication you send out has a life of its own and lives on to reflect you until the day it's thrown away!

Accordingly, never turn off your design consciousness. Strive to improve the appearance and communicating power of everything you produce — even everyday projects like correspondence and faxes. Here are ten ways you can make even simple projects project a better impression.

Never underline

Take a hammer and disable your underlining key. *Only kidding!* At minimum, remove the underlining button from your Toolbar or Icon Bar. Underlining is bad news. Underlining is bad because it obscures the shapes of your words, and readers recognize words by their shape. Underlining is also ugly. Notice how the line intersects the descenders (portions of characters that extend below the baseline) or letters like *g, j, y,* and *p.* Alternatives to underlining include boldface, italic, and small caps.

Align text with pre-printed rules and logos

Align the left and right margins of your correspondence with pre-printed elements such as header or footer rules, logos, or address information. Letterheads project a "devil may care" attitude when the text area does not line up with text or graphic elements on your stationary. You'll be surprised at the major improvement that takes place when you line up text elements.

Adjust paragraph spacing

Avoid duplicate paragraph spacing. Use one and only one way to indicate new paragraphs. Do not both indent the first line of new paragraphs and add extra space between paragraphs. Do not press Enter or Return twice between paragraphs. If you are indenting the first line of new paragraphs, make sure you really want to use the standard, default, half-inch indent (a shallower indent is usually sufficient.) If you are adding extra space between paragraphs, paragraph spacing equal to $1^1/_2$ lines is usually enough to visually indicate a new paragraph without unnecessarily spacing text out on the page.

Use symbols whenever possible

Avoid spelling out words like copyright, percent, registered, and trademark. Replace them with the appropriate typeset symbols (©, %, ® and ™). In addition, when using fractions, see whether a pre-built fraction symbol isn't already available in the the font you're using. Typeset fractions, such as $1^1/_4$, $2^1/_2$ and $3^3/_4$ look a lot better than 1 1/4, 2 1/2 and 3 3/4. Many Expert fonts contain additional fractions. Finally, replace asterisks (*) with bullets (•), empty or filled ballot boxes (❑, ■) and daggers (†) in lists. Check out the symbols available in fonts like Adobe's Zapf Dingbats or Microsoft Wingdings.

Eliminate excess space in lists

Avoid pressing the spacebar between dollar signs and the numbers they introduce, or numbers and cents signs that follow. Likewise, eliminate space between numbers and percentage symbols. Dollars and cents signs, percentage symbols, and so on should appear right next to the numbers they introduce or follow.

When you create numbered or bulleted lists, use shallower indents than the defaults typically provide. Most word processing programs add unnecessary space between the bullet or number and the text that follows, creating distracting gaps.

Always use typeset punctuation

Nothing separates newcomers from experienced communicators like the proper use of typeset punctuation. The most obvious problem is the use of inch marks (") instead of the proper open (") and closed (") punctuation and foot marks (') instead of an apostrophe ('). Other giveaways include the use of two separate hyphens (--) instead of em dashes (—) to introduce parenthetical expressions and en dashes to indicate duration (–).

Use accented characters when necessary

Always use the proper accented characters when using Americanized foreign words. These characters help readers avoid confusing resume and résumé, expose and exposé, and so on.

Exercise typographic restraint

Avoid using novelty typefaces. Although these might initially attract attention, they are often hard to read in large doses. Likewise, if you are using 300 dot-per-inch inkjet or laser printers, avoid typefaces with tiny serifs and thin strokes (so called 'Modern' typefaces, such as Bodoni). Instead, choose a robust typeface designed for 300 dot-per-inch reproduction. These typefaces do not contain curved or diagonal surfaces or thin strokes. Examples include Adobe Stone Serif, Bitstream Charter, Monotype Amassis, and Lucida. Their ample proportions and sturdy design make a noticeable difference in your correspondence.

Review line endings

Make sure that no more than three lines in a row end in hyphens (two is a preferable maximum). Avoid hyphenating proper names. Avoid hyphenating compound words or words beginning or ending with em or en dashes. Make sure that dates and proper nouns aren't split over two lines — for example, *Roger C.* on one line and *Parker* on the next or *Sept. 26* at the end of one line and *1955* at the beginning of the next (and if you believe that's my birthday, there's this bridge in New York City I'd like to sell to you).

Be sure you really want to use justified alignment

Let the image you're trying to project influence your choice of text alignment. Only use justified text alignment, allowing your software to create lines of equal length by varying word spacing within the line, when appropriate. Often, justified text is used in routine correspondence out of habit rather than as a deliberate design intent. Instead of being impressed by your sophistication, the use of justified text in informal communications may lead your readers to feel you're trying to showcase your software's capabilities.

Chapter 19
Ten Ways to Use Color Effectively

* *

*T*wo-color printing works best when it is used consistently and with restraint. Color works best when it is concentrated in a few areas. Use color to organize and add selective emphasis. Here are some ways you can effectively put two-color printing to work in your publications.

Color nameplates and titles

You can brighten your newsletter and separate it from the others by placing its title against a colored background. All or part of the name can be reversed out of a colored panel. Or, if you are using a single word set in a large, bold, sans serif typeface, you can set the title in color. Avoid using colored ink for words set in a small, serif typeface because they tend to get "lost".

Logos and associated artwork

A single color element on a page can breath new life into a document. Blank pages with your logo preprinted in color unobtrusively along the top or bottom are often enough to brighten a long proposal or report. A color element does not have to be large to attract attention. In fact, if it is too large, it will probably distract readers from the adjacent text.

When you choose a color for a corporate identity, be sure that its emotional message is compatible with the atmosphere you want to project. Don't use deep purples or dark grays if you want to look inexpensive, for example.

Business graphics

Charts and graphs reproduced in black and white lack impact, especially when compared to the same charts reproduced in color. Black-and-white pie charts and bar graphs, which use various hatch patterns (such as diagonal lines) to separate the individual segments, rarely succeed. The same charts come alive when reproduced in color. Try setting the most important line in a line chart in color or using colored backgrounds in area charts.

You can also color code business graphics by using progressively brighter colors to indicate importance, perhaps setting "comparison" lines in a line chart in a tinted color and using the color full-strength for the most important line you're discussing.

Borders and frames around business graphics

You can add selective emphasis to business graphics, as well as unify your publication, by using a light, tinted second color background behind charts and diagrams and using the color full-strength to draw attention to the most important pie chart segment or line in a line graph. Just be sure to make lines printed in color heavier than the lines printed in black.

Coding different sections of a publication

Just as the Yellow Pages make it easy to immediately locate the business-to-business advertising, colored accents along the edges of the pages of different sections of your publications can subdivide long documents. If you are using a color inkjet printer, you can add colored identification accents to the headers and footers of your proposals and reports as you create them.

If you are having a long document printed, colored bleeds along the edges will make it easy for readers to locate the beginning, middle, and end of the document (or sections relating to experience, qualifications, and satisfied clients).

Adding selective emphasis to text

You can draw attention to warnings by including a red "danger" icon next to them. If you are preparing correspondence with a color inkjet printer, you can add color by placing text against a bright yellow background. The yellow box will draw your reader's eyes to the dominant paragraph without destroying legibility (black text against a yellow background is easy to read). If you are preparing proposals and reports with an inkjet printer, you can add colored panels behind summaries or introductory text.

Printing entire pages against a colored background

You can add impact to selected pages of your newsletter by printing the entire page against a colored background. This makes the entire page stand out as if it were printed on colored paper. If the page contains a photograph, illustration, or chart, omit the color behind the visual. The visual will "pop" off the page because its contents appear against a white background (assuming you're using a white paper).

Organize table elements

Rather than use a grid of horizontal and vertical lines to organize the rows and columns of a table, use colored backgrounds to emphasize either row or column headers. If you are using colored backgrounds to emphasize column headers, use the same column to emphasize the "totals" at the bottom of each column. This unifies the top and bottom of the table. You can also use two-color printing to add a light screened color behind every other row, or every five rows, to organize the information and carry the reader's eye horizontally along the row, rather than using a "prison cell" grid of black horizontal and vertical lines.

Emphasizing a single word in a headline or title

You can add impact to a title or headline by setting the most important word in color. Or you can set the most important word in black and use color for the lesser words. In either case, the contrast between the black and colored ink will help draw your reader's attention to "what's different." When you use this technique, avoid an even balance between black and colored ink. One or the other must dominate; otherwise, they'll cancel each other out.

Drawing attention to parts of a photograph

Today's desktop publishing software makes it easy to add sophisticated photographic effects that would previously have been prohibitively expensive. For example, you can add color to the most important elements of a black-and-white photograph, perhaps printing the important elements as a duotone (where highlight and shadow areas are printed in black ink and the middle tones are printed in a second color). This technique draws your reader's eye to the most important part of the photograph and provides the overall environment in which the important elements appear.

The 5th Wave — By Rich Tennant

"NOPE – I'D BETTER WAIT 'TIL ALL MY FONTS ARE WORKING. A HATE LETTER JUST DOESN'T WORK IN *Filigree Flowerbox Extended*."

Chapter 20
Ten Color Clichés and No-Nos

· ·

Many publications suffer because a second color is added out of habit rather than with definite purpose. Color works best when it serves a function. Color detracts from publications when it is used to "brighten up" otherwise dull publications. Often, this "brightening up" distracts readers, instead of strengthening the writer's message. Based on an analysis of hundreds of newsletters, here are ten areas where two-color printing often hinders publications.

Small graphic accents in color

Color works best when concentrated in large areas. Color distracts and weakens publications when scattered over a page. Examples include vertical downrules between columns in a second color. Used in this way, the second color serves no purpose and distracts the publication instead of enhancing it. If the rules are thin and dark, the color appears weak and the cost of printing the second color is wasted. If the rules are thick and/or bright, the downrules distract the reader's eyes away from the text in the columns. Likewise, thin borders around sidebars, tables of contents, mastheads, and pull quotes are often wasted when printed in a second color. The second color makes the borders harder to locate rather than easier to locate. A single bold horizontal bar at the top of each page or a reversed box behind a logo has far more impact than the same amount of ink scattered around the page.

Small initial caps in color

Another sure-fire way to show that you're a desktop publishing newcomer is to set initial caps in color, especially undersized ones. *Color cannot compensate for size!* If the initial cap is too small, setting it in color may make it appear even smaller. (Black type against white creates a stronger contrast than blue against white.) If the initial cap is large and a bright color is chosen, the bright color can makes the initial cap too prominent — so prominent, in fact, that it becomes difficult to concentrate on the text that follows.

When setting initial caps in color, remember that the color can destroy the unity between the initial cap and the portion of the word that follows. Initial caps should *introduce* words, not appear as separate entities.

Tinted backgrounds behind small type

Tinted, or screened, colored backgrounds are often placed behind short text blocks, such as sidebars, tables of contents, calendars of upcoming events, and mastheads containing publication information. Although the intent is to separate the text from the surrounding articles and attract attention to the text, often the reduced contrast between the text and the colored background make the text harder to read. This is especially true when text set in a small serif typeface is placed against a screened blue or green background.

Failure to increase weight or size of text printed in color

Colored text is harder to read than black text. This is *especially* true when subheads are set the same size as the body copy. Unless the subheads are set significantly larger, the subheads are likely to be harder to read than if they were set in black. To achieve desired emphasis, always combine colored subheads with another tool of emphasis. For example, set colored text in a slightly larger type size or make the colored text both larger and bolder. This is especially true when setting text against colored backgrounds or reversing text out of a colored background.

Colored end-of-story symbols

Pages containing numerous end-of-story symbols often look like an outbreak of measles has occurred. Instead of providing a restrained, dignified end-of-story announcement, the colored end-of-story symbols distract from the page. Likewise, bullets and asterisks in lists set in color are weakened distractions rather than attention-getters. Avoid the temptation to set page numbers appearing in a table of contents in a second color unless you also set the numbers in a larger, bolder type.

Photographs printed in a second color

Avoid printing black and white pictures, especially pictures of people, in a second, or *accent,* color. People look funny when printed in red, blue, or green. The only possible exceptions are duotones, a creative process that involves separating the photographs and printing the highlights and shadows in one color and the middle tones in a second color. This can add interest to the photograph without making the people look like they came from Mars.

Text with inadequate foreground/background contrast

Legibility requires significant foreground/background contrast. Always make sure that there is enough contrast between text and its background so that readers can make out individual letters. Be especially careful when printing colored text on background tints of the same color. Blue text placed against a light blue background is extremely difficult to read, as is red against a pink background or green against a light green background. Text is only legible in the presence of maximum tonal contrast.

Inappropriate cultural signals

Colors send out silent, non-verbal signals that appeal to the reader's emotions. Make sure that your color choices are appropriate for the message you want to communicate. Reds signal "losing money" to bankers and accountants, for example. Yellows signal "caution" and indicate "outdoors." Blues are restful, lavenders are "death," and dark grays are elegance. Interestingly enough, a local toy store selling collectibles uses a coding system that's all wrong: yellows indicate discontinued items available only in extremely limited quantities, greens indicate discontinued items, blues indicate last year's models and reds indicate this year's "plentiful" items. A more useful scheme might use red to indicate "almost out," yellow for "about to run out," blue for "low stock" and green for "readily available."

Publications printed entirely in a single color dark or bright color

Color works best when used to organize or add selective emphasis. Rarely do publications printed entirely in a single color ink work well. One of the reasons is that photographs rarely reproduce as well in second colors as they do in black and white. Another reason is that the use of a single color ink throughout a publication eliminates the "differentness" that permits color to organize or add emphasis. The only exception is publications printed in a very dark gray — almost approaching black (especially when used on an off-white paper). Deep, dark gray ink approaches the legibility of black but is less harsh than black, projecting an elegant impression.

Bright papers

Color doesn't only refer to ink; color also refers to the paper your project is printed on. Choose ink colors and paper colors at the same time. Identical inks can look totally different when printed on different colored papers. Avoid the use of bright colored papers. Bright backgrounds make it harder for your readers to make out individual letters. Choose subdued colors that complement, rather than compete with, the ink carrying your message.

Chapter 21

Ten Ways to Work More Efficiently

● ●

You cannot separate production efficiency from design excellence. The more efficiently you work, the more time you'll have to fine-tune your designs. Each time you reach for your mouse, open a menu, and scroll through the options, and then click on a command (instead of using a one-step keyboard shortcut), and each time you select formatting options located in four dialog boxes (instead of a choosing a single style), you're wasting energy and enthusiasm that you could just as easily use to improve your documents. It's not so much the time that's wasted as it is the physical and emotional energy that's being drained. Unnecessary mouse movement wears out your mouse and your wrists! Each mouse click and menu scroll drains water from the reservoir, replacing enthusiasm with fatigue.

By working as efficiently as possible, you'll gain the energy and enthusiasm to review your project one more time and, in doing so, you're likely to discover simple changes that spell the difference between "adequate" and "outstanding." Design success is in the details. Create the time and enthusiasm needed to fine-tune the details by doing routine tasks as efficiently as possible.

Master the shortcuts already present

You can never know everything about your favorite software programs. There's *always* room for improvement. I've been working with Microsoft Word for Windows for several years, for example, and it was only a few minutes ago that I tried an idea I ran across reading a computer magazine while standing in line at the check-out counter. (Since you asked, clicking on the "open file" button in the Standard Toolbar allows you to cycle one by one through the various open documents. This eliminates the need to reach for the mouse to open the Window menu and click on the name of the desired document.)

If you're working in the Microsoft Windows environment, investigate how your software program uses the right mouse button. With PageMaker, it's always been a lot easier to use the right mouse button to toggle between Actual Size and Fit in Window views than to open the Layout menu, select View, and choose Fit in Window or Actual Size. The latest Windows word processing and presentation programs go even further. Click on a text or graphic element with the right mouse button, and the appropriate menus immediately appear next to the object, allowing you to cut, copy, paste, or change various formatting attributes.

Use keyboard shortcuts whenever possible

You waste time and energy every time you remove your hands from the keyboard. It always takes a few seconds to return your right hand to the proper keyboard location — and there's always a chance that you'll place your hand one row off — so instead of writing *Liam Clancey* you write *:oam C;amceu* (who recently emigrated from Ireland to France). At the very least, this causes you to waste time with your spell checker.

Use styles to maintain consistency

Styles are necessities, not luxuries. Styles enable you to assign multiple formatting options with a single keystroke. Instead of scrolling through multiple font, paragraph, and border dialog boxes, you can assign names to multiple formatting options, such as Head1, Sub1, Body1, Body2, and so on. Each named style can define the subtlest nuances of formatting, including spacing above and spacing after, indents, word and letter spacing, hyphenation preferences, and so on.

More importantly, styles can be shared among documents. This makes it possible, for example, to create a coherent corporate identity throughout an organization, so that the text on everybody's correspondence lines up with the firm's pre-printed logo, and no text runs below the names of the Board of Directors printed at the bottom of the letterhead.

Create templates

Templates eliminate the need to reinvent the wheel every time you start a new project. Templates are files containing page layouts and styles that can be opened but not saved. A newsletter template, NEWSTEM, for example, typically contains the front-page nameplate and back-page mailing label information, headers, and footers for each page, plus the styles needed to format the text. Before you work on a new issue based on the template, you save the file with a different name, such as FEBNEWS or SEPTNEWS.

Create forms for frequently repeated information

You can use a form to add information to a document before you actually work on the document. The information then appears automatically in the proper location in the document. By using forms, you avoid retyping frequently repeated information, saving time and effort. Most word processing programs let you use forms to enter a recipient's name and address information in correspondence and fax cover sheets. In the future, forms will probably be used to create headers and footers as well as format newsletter headlines and stories.

Reuse tables and charts

The latest generation of Windows word processing programs let you save and easily reuse frequently used graphic elements. For example, you can save the formatted tables you use to add budgets or calendars to your letters or proposals. If you're working with PageMaker, you can save tables on the Pasteboard, beyond the image area of your documents.

Use OLE 2.0 and similar technologies

As hardware performance catches up to software performance, document-to-document copying and pasting will be replaced by various linking technologies. Consider what happens if you copy a chart from an Excel spreadsheet to an annual report. In the old days, if the chart needed to be revised, you'd have to delete the chart, load Excel, make the changes, and repeat the copy, paste, and resize process. The new way is much simpler. First you load Excel from within your word processing or page layout program by double-clicking on the chart. Then make the changes to your chart and close Excel. The chart will appear properly sized in the annual report; no further sizing or recoloring is required.

Use macros to automate frequently repeated tasks

Macros are files that can work more quickly and accurately than you. Macros let you replace complicated mouse and keystroke sequences, such as opening another program and searching for a special file, with a few keystrokes. You can use macros to copy style libraries among documents, reformat documents to accommodate different printing options, create tables of contents, update headers and footers, and simplify opening documents created with different word processing programs.

Copy "one of a kind" formatting with blotters and eyedroppers

The latest illustration, presentation, and word processing programs include an eyedropper-like feature that makes it easy to copy formatting attributes from one text or graphic object to another. This feature is useful when you're not likely to need access to the formatting attributes in the future.

Investigate add-in programs

Many small independent firms are creating software enhancements that "ride on the back of" the foundation programs offered by firms such as Adobe, and Quark. The best examples are Aldus Additions and Quark Extensions, although more are certain to appear for programs such as Adobe PhotoShop and word processing programs such as Microsoft Word.

The best way to become aware of program add-in's is to read the catalogs and product offerings included with your software packaging, pay attention to the mail that comes after you register, and pay attention to the advertisements in the back pages of the various desktop publishing and computer magazines.

Chapter 22

Ten Ways to Make Your Service Bureau and Print Shop Love You

• •

*A*lthough service bureaus and print shops are filled with a combination of high and low technology (such as computerized image setters on the one hand and mechanical, ink-splattered printing presses on the other), people form the heart of these vital components of your desktop publishing success. Here are some high-tech as well as "warm and fuzzy" ways you can become a valued customer whose work is enthusiastically embraced and carefully monitored rather than a customer whose work is simply tolerated between coffee breaks.

Avoid deadline madness

Deadlines have always been with us. There's never enough time to do the job right. Bosses and clients always wait until the last minute before deciding that literature needs to be prepared or documentation printed. And newsletter deadlines come up with startling regularity.

But just because *you* work under deadline conditions doesn't mean you have to share the misery with your suppliers! By soliciting printing quotes as far in advance as possible and by planning for "worst case" scenarios when establishing schedules for image setting and printing, you can build in the flexibility and breathing room necessary to accommodate the inevitable last-minute problems likely to occur.

Working in advance can save you money. By establishing a dialog with your printer well in advance of deadlines, the printer might be able to suggest a less expensive paper he has on hand rather than a similar paper that would have to be special ordered. If you know this far enough ahead of time, you could seek your client or supervisor's approval—and be a hero for saving everyone money!

Include a paper sample of every project

When soliciting bids, always try to include either a printed copy of an earlier version of your document or a tight layout along with sample paper stock. By providing your service bureau or print shop with as much information as possible, you create fewer opportunities for misunderstandings.

When you submit files to a service bureau, always send proofs printed on a laser printer. That way, if something goes wrong and Courtesan (a Parker-original typeface designed after a Hollywood madam) turns into Courier, the service bureau will at least *know* something is wrong and may even be able to locate the missing font without bothering you.

Likewise, provide the print shop with proofs of your document. If your document involves more than one color printing, provide color proofs — even if you just use colored markers to indicate where second and/or third colors are supposed to appear. You can use tissue overlays to indicate places where each additional color should appear. Color proofs avoid ambiguity. You can't hold print shops accountable for mistakes they're not aware of.

Include crop marks and registration marks

Whenever possible, include crop marks on camera-ready artwork. Crop marks help the printer maintain proper page alignment on the printing press.

Provide necessary fonts

Before submitting a file to a service bureau, make sure that they have the available fonts. Call or fax them a list of the fonts included in your project. Specify both the typeface foundry (such as Adobe, Bitstream, or Monotype) as well as the name of the typeface (such as Caslon or Garamond).

If the service bureau doesn't have the appropriate fonts, you can either submit your work as Encapsulated Postscript Files or provide copies of the fonts with the understanding that you are providing the printer fonts for one-time use only.

You can avoid a lot of potential problems by sticking to name-brand fonts. Avoid sending service bureaus projects created using off-brand or "699 fonts for $6.99" fonts. Stick to quality fonts from name-brand vendors.

Include linked graphic files

When scanned images or illustrations are linked rather than included in files created with a page layout program, make sure that you include the files when you submit your project to a service bureau; otherwise, your beautiful Free-hand illustration is likely to be replaced by a low resolution screen image or a gray box indicating the location where the illustration should have appeared.

Avoid "hidden" fonts

If you have extensively reformatted your document, especially if you have tried several typefaces, some "hidden" fonts may remain. There may be leftover spaces originally created with the discarded typeface. When this occurs, the image setter is likely to waste time searching for the font and informing the service bureau operator that a font is missing. Under certain conditions, line endings and page breaks might also change. These problems can be avoided by making the proper use of styles and by using the various utilities available to identify each of the fonts used in a project before it leaves your computer.

Avoid overly-large files

Compress your files by using File⇨Save As before submitting files to a service bureau and break large projects into component parts whenever possible. Like large urban police departments, large files are more prone to crashes and corruption than smaller, more manageable files.

Solicit at least three written printing bids

Always prepare and distribute at least three "request for bid" packages. These packages should include a sample of what the finished project should look like, identification of desired paper stock and weight, and the quantity to be delivered. Leave nothing to chance. Get everything in writing, including delivery deadlines, possible delivery and/or storage costs (if you are not going to immediately pick the project up at the print shop). Find out how long the bid is good for (print shops bid low when they're not busy).

You'll probably find considerable variation from print shop to print shop, even month to month variations.

Don't haggle over price

There's a thin line between prudence and extravagance. It's important that you always get at least three printing bids for each job, and it's important that you read the fine print of the print shop's quotation sheet (which usually allows them to over-print your order and commits you to paying for the overage). But don't be so price-conscious that you sacrifice service.

Don't expect superior service if you've forced your service bureau or print shop to match the price submitted by No-Name Printing in Yokohama. Your project simply won't receive the tender loving care it deserves if you're difficult to deal with or the service bureau or print shop is not making a fair and reasonable profit. By all means, don't overpay. But don't encourage your service bureau or print shop to cut quality because your job isn't profitable.

Pay cash whenever possible

Even after you've established credit with a service bureau or print shop, pay cash upon receipt. Not only will you often save money by paying upon delivery — many service bureaus and print shops offer a discount for immediate payment — you'll also be making it a bit better easier for the service bureau or print shop to meet their payroll. In return, your print shop or service bureau will work a bit harder for you on the next project, taking a little extra care, going the extra mile.

Show your appreciation

The Golden Rule provides a good framework for dealing with service bureaus and print shops. Always write a letter of appreciation when a service bureau or print shop does an especially good job on a project, comes in under-budget, or works extra hard on a weekend to save your tail. Just as you respond better to praise than threats, your service bureau and print shop will reward your appreciation with greater efforts down the road.

Don't depend on phone calls or verbal compliments. Verbal conversations can not be hung-up over the time clock or shown to prospective clients. Put your compliments in writing. It's more real.

Chapter 23
Ten Free Ways to Improve Your Design Skills

• •

*D*esktop publishing and design isn't completely technology-based. Craftsmanship and design success come from giving yourself the time needed to do the job right as well as the momentum provided by a high enthusiasm level. Here are ten "free" things you can do to improve your desktop publishing efficiency and design skills.

Prepare realistic schedules

Design is based on detail, and detail takes a lot of time. It is impossible to do good work under last-minute deadline conditions. Part of your role as a designer involves establishing realistic schedules for yourself and others. Work backward from the date your publication needs to be completed and prepare deadlines for each task. Build some slack into your schedule. Circulate copies of this schedule to everyone involved. Create a fuss when others fall behind in their responsibilities. After all, you'll be the one who is blamed if the annual report contains a typo!

Design with your computer turned off

Try beginning beginning work on a project using a pencil, paper, and eraser. Sit at a desk rather than at a computer. Your ideas will often flow faster if you work rapidly at reduced size using a pencil and paper than if you lock yourself to your computer. Computers are literal. You're apt to be frustrated by the time it takes to open and close menus, make typeface and type size choices, and so on. Don't add too much detail to your drawings. Let your ideas flow using the minimum "shorthand" necessary to remind you that "headline goes here," and "text columns go here."

After you isolate one or two possible solutions to your design problem, turn on your computer and convert your scribbled ideas to columns and grids.

Analyze and critique print communications everywhere

Train yourself to critically analyze the thousands of advertisements, press releases, business cards, billboards, newspaper headlines, and direct-mail solicitations you encounter each day. Ask yourself questions like: What were the challenges the designer faced? Did the designer choose the right solutions? How would I have done the job differently?

Create a *swipe file.* A swipe file is a file folder (which grows to a file drawer, which grows to a file cabinet, which grows to two file cabinets, which soon forces you to seek new housing arrangements) containing samples of good and bad design. (Often you can learn more from the bad samples than you do from the good samples.) Use stick-on notes to remind yourself why you saved the samples. Train yourself to identify ten right decisions and ten wrong decisions in each piece.

This disciplined self-instruction and analysis will do wonders for your design sensitivity and your ability to defend your decisions.

Loiter in bookstores

The next time you're in a bookstore, analyze the books and magazines on display. Train yourself to identify the design and typography techniques that contribute to easy-to-read books and magazines versus those that appear hard to read. Why is there always a "look" to design and architecture magazines? What are the components of that look? Does the look facilitate or hinder readability?

Redo old projects

No project should ever be considered completed. Try to put aside a little time each week to open your portfolio and take a fresh look at work you did six months, a year, or two years ago. How well does your work stand up to the test of time? What would you do differently if you had the project to do all over again? Occasionally, redo a project.

If you do a makeover on one of your previous projects, bring the before and after to your next job interview and show it to your potential client or boss. The fact that you're motivated enough to redo your own work will tell more about you than the actual work you've done.

Seek new challenges

Avoid stagnation, especially if your job is more production-oriented than creative-oriented. Stagnation leads to boredom, and boredom leads to sloppy design and poor workmanship. Seek new responsibilities. Push yourself to the outer limit of your comfort zone. You may find you're capable of much more than you think.

Solicit freelance and pro bono work

If your work is more production-oriented than you desire, solicit freelance work or do free work for local non-profit associations. Just about every non-profit organization requires brochures, newsletters, and business cards. You'll be doing good while improving your design skills. Experience is the best teacher. The only way you can become a more efficient desktop publisher and better designer is by doing a lot desktop publishing and design.

Keep up to date with the latest news

Subscribe to a variety of publications. Balance your reading between publications that are hardware- and software-oriented and those that are design- and communication-oriented. Balance your reading of *Aldus Magazine* and *Publish* with *Communication Arts, Print,* and *Art Director.* Don't overlook newsletters. Two of the best are *In-House Graphics* and *Communication Briefings.*

Attend demonstrations, meetings, seminars, and workshops

You've got to get out of the house more! Attend software demonstrations advertised in the local newspaper, computer user group meetings and — when the budget allows — seminars and workshops. You're likely to return from these group endeavors with a heightened sense of enthusiasm and design sensitivity. Interacting with other desktop publishers provides an opportunity to learn from their experiences as well as share your own successes. Always have samples of your best work along; who knows when you're going to meet your next "breakthrough" client or employer?

Investigate new media opportunities

Investigate the new hardware and software technologies that are appearing, such as presentation software and multimedia. The lessons you learn when mastering a new set of skills will permit you to return to your day-to-day jobs with enhanced enthusiasm.

Appendix A
Glossary

● ●

*O*ften the best way to master and review a new technology is to review its terminology. Here are brief definitions of frequently encountered desktop publishing and design terms.

Advancing colors: Colors such as red and yellow, located to the right of the color wheel, best used for text and graphic accents because they attract more attention than receding colors (blues and greens), which are located at the left of the color wheel.

Alternate characters: Many typeface designs include optional upper- or lower-case alphabet characters or numbers that can be used for creative applications. These include True Small Caps, stylized ampersands, letters with exaggerated design elements, and ornaments designed to separate paragraphs or indicate the end of stories. See *ampersands*, *swash characters*, *Old Style Figures*, and *True Small Caps*.

Ampersand: Stylish typeface character used in titles and logos in place of the word *and* (&). In some typefaces, the ampersand can be quite flamboyant. Indeed, some typeface designs consist entirely of ampersands.

Asymmetrical: Way of organizing text and graphic elements on a page creating unequal top/bottom or left/right balance. Typically used in modern and informal publications.

Auto leading: Allowing your software to determine the amount of space between lines of type instead of choosing a desired amount of line spacing based on the type

size, line length, and typeface design. You can greatly improve the appearance of headlines as well as body copy by carefully controlling line spacing. See *leading*.

Ballot boxes: Typographic symbols used in place of asterisks to introduce items in lists. May be empty (*outlined*) or filled (*solid*).

Bar: 1) Place where desktop publishers, designers, and design writers hang out and search for meaningful employment opportunities. 2) Thick horizontal or vertical rule used as a graphic accent, such as a border at the top of a page or within columns to separate text elements.

Baseline: The invisible line characters rest on.

Black: Typeface alternative containing characters created with extra-thick strokes, also called "bolder than bold." In addition to bold, most sans serif typefaces are available in Black and Extra Black (sometimes called Heavy and Extra Heavy).

Bleed: 1) What designers do when clients don't pay printing bills on time. 2) Graphic accent (such as a horizontal rule), text or visual that extends beyond the normal margins of a page to the page's physical edge, or *trim*. Bleeds increase printing costs but can be an extremely powerful design tool. See *trim*.

Blurb: Short descriptive text between a headline and an article elaborating on the headline and summarizing the text that follows.

Book faces: Typefaces designed primarily for use in body copy text, as contrasted to typefaces designed primarily for headlines and titles. See d*isplay faces.*

Border rules: Lines (created with your program's line-drawing tool) that allow you to define the top, bottom and, if you want, sides of your pages. You can border pages with lines of identical length and thickness, or you can use lines of different length and width at the top and bottom of each page to emphasize the live area of each page.

Bullet: Symbols used in lists instead of asterisks.

Byline: Line of text identifying the author or photographer. Often includes their credentials.

CD-ROM: Important hardware advancement that permits easy distribution and immediate access to large collections of computerized information, including type, photographs, large software programs, and interactive training. CD-ROMs are valuable because of their small size, light weight, and low duplication costs. For all practical purposes, CD-ROM's are playback-only devices, although the cost of CD-ROM recorders is coming down. See *removable storage media.*

Caption: Text identifying a photograph, illustration, or chart. After headlines, captions are the second best read text element on a page. Captions should summarize the importance of not only the visual but attract readers into the adjacent text.

Case: Typographic specification indicating whether text will appear in all capitals (uppercase), small letters (lowercase), or mixed upper- and lowercase type.

Cell: The space formed by the intersection of a row and column in a table.

Chunking: Breaking long documents into a series of shorter elements that can be read as desired.

Clip art: Previously created, out-of-the-box illustrations that you can use as is or modify by ungrouping, combining with other illustrations, and adding backgrounds and borders.

Color wheel: Diagram that shows the locations of the various colors and how they interact with each other. The color wheel is usually reduced to ten segments: clockwise, beginning with red (straddling 12:00 noon), and then orange, yellow, light green, darker green, green (straddling 6:00 p.m.), turquoise, blue, dark purple, and light purple. See *complementary colors.*

Complementary colors: Complementary colors appear directly opposite each other on the color wheel. Complementary colors create the greatest contrast; typically one is a dominant, or *advancing,* color and the other a quiet, or *receding,* color. See *color wheel, advancing color,* and *receding color.*

Condensed: Typographic term indicating typeface designs containing characters that have been redrawn to occupy less horizontal space. True condensed typefaces, in contrast to text that has been horizontally scaled (distorted by compressing) have been redrawn to preserve legibility by increasing the x-height of the type. This prevents the inner spaces of *a*'s and *e*'s from filling in. See *expanded.*

Continuous tone: A black-and-white photograph "right out of the darkroom" containing numerous gray tones that flow gradually into each other. See *halftone, LPI,* and *screen.*

Contrast: 1) Visual interest added to a page by alternating white space with areas of gray text and black headlines. 2) The direction and amount of differences between the thickest and thinnest strokes that make up a letter.

Copyfitting: Determining how many words will fit in a column inch, set in a given typeface at a given type size and line spacing. Copyfitting helps you determine how much space is needed to accommodate previously written text. Copyfitting from rough layouts helps you determine how many words must be written to fill the space available.

Corporate identity: The consistent image created by a firm or association's print communications, ranging from letterheads and business cards to brochures, newsletters, and documentation. The elements that make up a corporate identity include the consistent use of a limited number of typefaces, type sizes, colors, and logo. These elements typically appear in the same position and at the same size on each type of document.

Crop marks: Indicate how the image area should be placed on the printed page.

Cropping: Photographs usually include extraneous detail at the top, bottom, and sides. Cropping removes this unwanted information, allowing the most important message-bearing elements of the photograph to emerge with added clarity.

Deck: Text placed between a headline and the text it introduces that elaborates on the importance of the headline and relates it to the reader's self-interests. Decks permit shorter, larger headlines. Decks are usually set in a type size midway between the headline and the body copy. See *blurb.*

Descender: Portions of letters such as lowercase *g, y,* and *p* extending below the baseline (the invisible line type rests on).

Dingbat: Typographic symbols used to introduce lists and to signify the end of stories.

Discretionary hyphen: Typographic code that allows you to predetermine where a word will be hyphenated. If the word does not need to be hyphenated, the hyphen does not appear. Discretionary hyphens appear and disappear automatically as text is added or deleted.

Display type: Typefaces designed to be used for headlines and/or at large size. Often, display typefaces attract attention but are unreadable when more than a few words are encountered at small size. Some typeface families contain fonts that have been redrawn to look good at large size.

Downrules: Vertical rules added between columns to prevent readers from reading across the space between columns (Called the *gutter*).

Drop cap: Initial cap cut into the paragraph it introduces. Drop caps work best when they are at least three lines tall.

Duotone: Using two colors to print a photograph. The photograph is first separated into tonal ranges. One ink is used to reproduce the shadows and highlights, and a second ink is used to reproduce the middle tones.

Ellipses: Single typographic character consisting of three closely spaced periods used to indicate omitted text.

Emboss: Three-dimensional effect created with an illustration program that allows text to look like it is raised from the background.

Em dash: Typographic punctuation mark used in preference to two hyphens to introduce parenthetical expressions.

Em space: Space equal in size to the square of the type size, or, approximately, the width of the uppercase M in the typeface and type size being used. One or two em spaces are the proper indent for the first line of paragraphs.

En dash: Typeset punctuation used to indicate duration (June – July, for example). An en dash is longer than a hyphen and shorter than an em dash.

Expanded: Typeface designs that have been redrawn instead of distorted by stretching. Expanded typefaces are ideal for short, high-impact titles and headlines. See *condensed.*

Eyebrow: Short text element above a headline introducing the headline. See *kicker.*

Eyedropper: Time-saving feature found on many of the latest drawing, presentation and word-processing software programs. The Eyedropper feature, found with different names, makes it easy to share formatting attributes (typeface, type size, color, line thickness, fill pattern, and so on). Use of the Eyedropper tool makes it unnecessary to create and name a style for objects whose formatting attributes will be copied only once or twice. See *style.*

Fills: Backgrounds created by using cross-hatch patterns, imported bitmapped graphics, or transitions from one color to another.

Filter: Creative effects applied with an illustration program to selectively emphasize or de-emphasize all or portions of a photograph. Filters can be used to sharpen or blur images or apply special effects.

Flip: Repositioning a text or graphic object end for end. Objects can be flipped horizontally or vertically.

Folio: Publication information, such as the issue number and date, appearing on the front page of a newsletter. Also includes page numbers on inside pages.

Font: Originally, one size and style of a single typeface design. Because type is now scaled to size as needed, a font refers to one variation of a typeface design, such as Roman (or *regular*), bold, or italic.

Font Manager: Software applications that make it easy to add or temporarily remove typeface designs from your system's operating system, speeding operation and reducing memory requirements. Font managers don't erase or remove the files from your hard disk but simply remove them from active use, reducing the possibility of system crashes. Examples include Fifth Generation System's Suitcase for the Macintosh and Ares FontMinder for Windows.

Font manipulation programs: Software applications that enable you to modify existing typeface designs or create new designs. Font manipulation programs enable you to add, remove, or connect serifs; horizontally stretch or compress type; add or remove space to either side of the type; raise or lower the x-height; or create a logo that can be added to a document with a single keystroke. See *logo* and *x-height*.

Footer: Information and graphic elements automatically repeated at the bottom of each page. Page numbers and horizontal rules are typically placed in footers. See *header*.

Forced justification: Justification option found on many page layout and word processing programs that evenly spaces letters across a column. Useful for creating publication titles and department headings. Not to be used for normal body paragraphs.

Formatting: Altering the appearance of text, a graphic accent, or a visual by changing its formatting attributes. Formatting attributes for text include typeface, type size, line spacing, and color. Formatting attributes for a graphic object include line thickness and color or fill color and pattern. Formatting attributes for a visual include size, color, and the presence or absence of a border. See *fill* and *pattern*.

Forms: Documents containing text and horizontal lines designed to be filled in by others at a later date.

Frame: Container, frequently used in word processing programs, that allows text or visuals to be moved and locked to a specific position on a page or locked to adjacent text. Containers allow headlines to span more than one text column and allow pull quotes to be positioned between columns. Containers also enable you to add borders and captions to visuals. These borders and captions remain with the visuals if the frame is moved.

Frieze: Design term referring to horizontal alignment of photographs arranged side by side, usually along the top or bottom of a page. When a page contains numerous small photographs, a frieze is often preferable to a haphazard placement on the page, which can project a disorganized appearance.

Golden Mean: Visually balanced height to width ratio, roughly 3 to 5, found widely in nature and throughout design history, characteristic of "pleasing" page layouts (page size and text area) and photographs.

Gradient: Background fill created with illustration and presentation programs characterized by a smooth transition from one color to another, or from one color to white or black. The direction of the transition can be top to bottom, bottom to top, side to side, diagonally, or from the title to the edges of a 35mm slide or overhead transparency. Text can also be filled with gradient screens. See *radial screen*.

Greeked: Typographic and page layout technique involving the use of nonsense-text instead of real words. Because you're not apt to try to read the Latin text, you're more likely to concentrate on the overall appearance of the text on the page.

Grid: The underlying framework or structure of a document. The grids appears on-screen as a series of non-printing rules and define column placement.

Gridlines: Horizontal and vertical lines used to organize tables and separate rows and columns. Gridlines can also be used to organize charts. Horizontal gridlines provide a scale, or frame of reference, for quantities; vertical gridlines indicate intervals.

Grouping: Software feature found in illustration and presentation programs that lets you to create a single object out of one or more text or graphic objects so that you can move and resize them as a single unit. Most programs with a grouping feature also include an ungrouping feature that allows you to later disassemble the object.

Gutter: Horizontal space between columns. Also the space between the right margin of a left page and the left margin of the right page. See *downrules*.

Halftone: Screen, or texture, applied to a photograph allowing it to be printed as a series of lines or dots. See *continuous tone, LPI,* and *screen*.

Hanging indent: Page layout device where the first line extends to the left of the lines that follow. Usually used in bulleted or numbered lists so that the first line and the lines that follow it are aligned, allowing the bullets or numbers to be surrounded by white space.

Hanging punctuation: Punctuation, typically opening quotation marks, placed in the margin to the left of the text it introduces. Hanging punctuation in the margins adjacent to the text allows the first letter after the quotation mark to align with the first letters in the lines that follow. When setting justified text, commas, periods, and closed quotation marks can be placed to the right of the right-hand margin of the text column, maintaining the alignment of the last letters in each line.

Hard space: Important typographic code that prevents words from splitting if they are too long to fit at the end of a line.

Header: Text and graphic elements, such as border rules, automatically placed at the top of each page. Header information typically includes chapter number and title or author's name. Different information usually appears on the right and left pages. See *footer*.

Heavy: Sans serif typeface designs characterized by strokes thicker than bold. In some typefaces, Heavy typefaces are referred to as Black.

Hue: The distinguishing characteristics between colors as identified by name (red, blue, or green, as contrasted to their brightness or saturation).

Hypertext: Enables you to jump to a different page in the same document or to a different document altogether by double-clicking a word or graphic. Characteristic of multimedia programs.

Hyphenation Zone: Typographic term referring to the space that a word must span if the word will be hyphenated, or split over two lines. By adjusting the hyphenation zone, you can determine how many words will be hyphenated. Reducing the width of the hyphenation zone increases the number of hyphenated words; increasing the hyphenation zone reduces the number of hyphenated words.

Icon: Graphic element used in place of something else, typically words or commands.

Image manipulation program: Software program designed specifically to modify scanned photographs by changing their tonal range, colors, and adding special effects such as embossing, blurs, and textures.

Imagesetter: Term used to describe high-resolution output devices found at a service bureau. These devices create camera-ready artwork at 1,270 or 2,564 dot-per-inch resolution. See *resolution* and *service bureau.*

Indents: Paragraphs where the lines do not extend the full width of a column. Text can be indented from the left, right, or both the left and right. Often used for lists and extended quotations.

Infographic: Information translated into visuals combining elements of illustrations and charts.

Initial cap: Oversize letter often used to introduce the first paragraph of a story but sometimes used to break up long text columns. Initial caps can be dropped or raised. See *drop cap* and *raised cap.*

Inline: 1) Where your kindergarten teacher made you stand on the way to recess or the school bus. 2) Graphics locked to text paragraphs so that the graphic moves as preceding text is edited or deleted.

Italic: Typeface designs that have been redrawn at an angle (in contrast to oblique designs, which have been simply slanted). Italic should be used instead of — but never with — underlining to emphasize words or titles within a text passage. See *oblique.*

Jumpline: Phrase directing reader to another page where the current story is continued.

Justified: Text characterized by lines of equal length, which a software program achieves by varying letter and word spacing within each line. In justified text, the last letters in each line are aligned with the last letters in the lines before and after it. See *rag.*

Justification limits: Important commands found in most word processing and page layout programs that enable you to define the minimum and maximum variation in word spacing that can be applied to line up the last letters of each line. The justification limits of most software programs are too generous, allowing lines with a few long words to exhibit large gaps between words, and word spacing in lines containing a few short words to be unnaturally compressed.

Kerning: Increasing or decreasing spacing between specified pairs of letters. Certain combinations of upper- and lowercase letters look awkward next to each other, especially at large, or headline, size. Typical letter combinations include an uppercase Y next to a lowercase *a* or an uppercase W next to an lowercase *a.*

Kerning pair: Although most typeface designs ship with pre-adjusted spacing between certain pairs of letters, many programs enable you to fine-tune the spacing for special pairs of letters at certain sizes. These programs create kerning pair files that your software references when placing text on the page.

Keyboard shortcuts: Software feature that lets you access frequently used commands from the keyboard. Keyboard shortcuts save time and reduce unnecessary mouse motion as well as the frustration of returning your hands to the wrong position on the keyboard.

Kicker: Short phrase located above a headline. Introduces the headline. See *eyebrow.*

Knock out: White type reversed out of a photograph. Instead of printing the text in white, a "hole" is cut into the photograph, allowing the background color of the paper to appear through the photograph.

Layering: Contemporary page layout technique characterized by text that can be read in a non-linear fashion as the reader's interests dictate. Readers can read the primary layer, often a long article, and skip adjacent material set in a smaller type size, or read secondary articles as desired.

Leading: In typography, leading refers to vertical line spacing. Leading is as important as type size in determining the overall appearance and readability of a text element or column of type. See *auto leading*.

Legend: Color-coded key that explains the significance of each color in a chart.

Legibility: Measure of how easy it is for readers to identify the individual words of a headline or text phrase. See *readability*.

Ligature: Typographic term referring to single characters that replace two or more separate characters. Ligatures have been redrawn to overcome the problems that occur when certain letters appear next to each other. The most popular ligatures are replacements for fi, ffi, fl, and ffl. Many designer typefaces include ligatures.

Light: Special typeface design variation characterized by very thin strokes.

Line break: Command that allows you to break headlines at logical pauses without adding paragraph spacing. Line breaks also help you avoid extremely long lines followed by very short lines.

Lining figures: Numbers that come with a standard character set, which stand as tall as uppercase letters or the ascenders of letters such as *b, d,* and *t.* See *ascender* and *Old Style Figures*.

Linking: 1) Instead of importing (or *integrating*) a graphics file or scanned photograph into a document, many page layout programs only reference the original file. This reduces the file size of the document — an important consideration with documents containing many scanned images. 2) Many Windows-based word processing programs enable you to link a chart or illustration to the originating program. Double-clicking the image in the document loads the source program and enables you to edit the chart or illustration. In addition, if the source file is modified, the linked image is automatically updated.

Live area: The area of a page containing text or graphics, as contrasted to the physical dimensions of the page. See *trim size*.

Logo: A firm or association's name set in type in a distinctive way, often accompanied by graphic accents or symbols.

LPI: (lines-per-inch) A measure of the sharpness of a screened halftone. Photographs intended to be output on a laser printer and printed on coarse paper can range from 50 to 75 lines-per-inch. Acceptable lines-per-inch for photographs in publications to be output on a high-resolution imagesetter and printed on a quality, glossy paper can range up to 500 lines-per-inch. See *continuous tone*, *halftone,* and *screen*.

Margin: The space between the live area, or space occupied by text columns or visuals, and the physical edge of a page. Margins provide white space, which provides pleasing contrast with the text columns as well as a place for readers to place their thumbs while holding a page. See *live area* and *trim size*.

Mask: Tracing an object or portion of a photograph with an image manipulation program and applying a different creative effect to it, such as a blur, different colored ink, or texture. See *image manipulation program*.

Masthead: Publication design element containing address and phone numbers plus the names and positions of key staff members, such as the editor, assistant editor, proofreader, and so on. Often incorrectly used to refer to publication title. See *nameplate*.

Mirror: Capability of drawing programs that adds a second copy of a text or graphic object, facing a different direction.

Monospaced: Typeface designs characterized by letters of equal width, similar to the characters created by typewriters. In monospaced typeface designs, such as Courier or Letter Gothic, thick letters, such as *m*'s, are as thick as thin letters, such as *i*'s. See *proportionally spaced*.

Nameplate: Special typography and graphic accents used to create a unique publication title. The nameplate often includes a background, horizontal rules, a subtitle, and a tagline explaining the purpose of the publication. Not to be confused with the masthead. See *masthead*.

Oblique: Typographic term referring to sans serif typeface designs with letters that have been slanted rather than redrawn like a true italic. See *italic*.

Offset: Term defining the amount of space between text and an adjacent border or graphic. Also refers to the amount of space between text and adjacent borders within the cells of a table. See *cell*.

Old Style Figures: Alternate typeface designs accompanying the major serif typefaces that contain numbers scaled to the x-height of the typeface. Old Style Figures often descend below the baseline of the typeface. Old Style Figures don't attract as much unwanted attention as numbers that extend the full height of the typeface. See *lining figures*.

Optical alignment: Often, what your computer "sees" is not what your eye "sees." In page layout terms, often large characters containing overhanging elements, such as uppercase Y's and T's, have to be moved to the left when they appear at the start of a multi-line headline, in order to appear "right." This is because your eyes focus on the vertical stroke of the letter rather than the thinner horizontal element. Likewise, rounded letters often extend below the baseline or above the x-height of a typeface in order to appear properly aligned with adjacent characters.

Organization chart: Visual used to display hierarchy and responsibility.

Ornaments: Decorative typeface designs used to embellish headlines and subheads, separate text elements, or as icons in maps (for example, *campground, restrooms,* and *tollhouse*). See *icon*.

Orphan: Line of text or portion of a line of text left over from the bottom of a previous column or page, isolated at the top of a new column or page. See *widow*.

Palette: 1) A limited number of colors that project a unified image yet contain enough variety for both background colors as well as foreground colors. 2) In a program, a floating window that contains tools or options.

Perspective: Typographic effect of adding depth to titles and logos, making it appear that the text is growing as it approaches the reader.

Pica: Graphic designer's unit of measurement. There are approximately 6 picas to an inch and 12 points to a pica. See *point*.

Pictograph: Graphing technique using repeating picture elements (such as growing oil consumption illustrated by barrels of oil or honey bee production illustrated with bees) rather than solid or filled bars. See *infographic*.

PMS: Short for Pantone Matching System, a widely used color-coding system that allows designers to define colors by numbers.

Point: Typographic unit of measurement. There are 72 points to an inch. See *pica*.

PostScript: Device-independent page description language pioneered by Adobe. PostScript files can be output at 300 dots-per-inch on laser printers or 1,270 or 2,540 dots-per-inch at service bureau image setters. See *service bureau*.

Posterization: 1) Cleansing milk of harmful bacteria by filling laser toner cartridges with milk and unused toner and igniting. 2) Image manipulation technique that eliminates light and middle gray tones from scanned photographs, allowing only certain areas remain, creating impressionistic effects similar to line drawings. Posterized images can be preferable to boring, head-on photographs, especially when used for photographs that appear in each issue of a publication.

Process colors: Colors created by mixing the four basic ink colors (cyan, yellow, magenta, and black) on a page. Colors are first separated and then an individual layer of paper is output for the layers representing cyan, yellow, magenta, and black. See *spot colors*.

Proportion: The relationship between the height and width of an object. See *Golden Mean*.

Proportionally spaced: Most typeface designs are based on characters occupying different amounts of horizontal space. Wide letters, such as *m*'s, occupy more space than thin letters, such as *i*'s. This is in contrast to typewriter-based typeface designs, such as Courier, which are characterized by letters of equal width. See *monospaced*.

Pull quote: Short, significant phrase or sentence, often set in a different typeface and a large type size, that summarizes materials in adjacent columns of text. Pull quotes reinforce important ideas and provide an opportunity for readers skimming through a publication to become interested enough to start reading the adjacent article.

Radial screen: Background fill feature found in illustration and presentation programs that allows one color in the center of a circle to extend outward and smoothly blend into a second color, or black or white. See *gradient fill*.

Rag: The difference in length between short and long lines in text set flush-left/ragged-right. The rag should be sufficient to indicate that the text is not justified but not so noticeable that short lines follow long lines. The line endings should not form irregular shapes along the right margin.

Raised cap: Oversize initial cap that extends above the paragraph it introduces, creating visual interest by adding white space. See *drop cap* and *initial cap*.

Readability: Measure of how easily readers can comfortably comprehend extended text passages. See *legibility*.

Receding colors: Colors to the left of the color wheel (blues and greens) best used for backgrounds. See *advancing colors*.

Registration marks: Help your print shop carefully align each layer (or page) on the printing press so that consistent margins are maintained on each page. Most page layout programs let you add registration marks.

Removable storage media: Hard disks designed to be removed from one computer and either stored or used in another. Unlike information stored on tape backups, information stored on removable storage media can be accessed. See *service bureau* and *CD-ROMs*.

Resolution: When referring to output devices, resolution is a measure of the sharpness with which pages are created. Office inkjet and laser printers usually create 300 dot-per-inch images. The film-based imagesetters at service bureaus typically create images at 1,270 or 2,540 (or even more) dots-per-inch. Increased resolution creates sharper images and smoother graduated background fills.

Reverse: Placing white text against a black or dark-colored background. See *screens*.

Rivers: Visual distraction in page layouts typically caused by spaces inside consecutive lines of text that line up with each other. Often found in narrow columns of justified text where two spaces follow each period.

Roman: Regular, non-italic, or non-bold typeface designs.

Rotate: Setting type or a graphic at angles.

Rules: Graphic accents created with a program's line-drawing tool. Rules can be used as borders, between columns, to emphasize text, or indicate the end of one text element and the beginning of a new unit.

Run-in: Short phrase, usually set in bold-face, bold italic, or italic, used to draw attention to and introduce a paragraph. Basically, run-ins can be considered third or fourth level subheads placed within the text paragraph instead of above or next to the paragraph. See *subhead* and *sidehead*.

Saccadic eye movement: The left-to-right eye movements that readers use to scan groups of words. Readers don't focus on single words; they focus on word groups.

Sans serif: Category of typeface design lacking the small finishing strokes that provide letter-to-letter transitions. Sans serif typefaces often have more impact at large size because of their design simplicity. See *serif*.

Saturation: Measure of the strength of a color; colors printed at full strength, or 100%, strength, compared to colors printed at tints such as 10%, 20%, or 50% strength.

Scale: Increasing or reducing the size of a text or graphic element while retaining the proportion (height-to-width ratio) of the original.

Scalloped columns: Page layout technique characterized by columns of different length. Instead of beginning a new paragraph at the bottom of a column, when there is only space for a few lines, the entire paragraph is moved to the top of the next column (or page). This technique saves production time and adds visual interest by creating irregular amounts of white space at the bottoms of each column.

Scan: Convert photographs or 35mm slides into digital files. Scanning makes it easy to precisely crop and resize photographs and is a necessary first-step toward other photo-manipulation techniques, such as lightening dark areas or darkening light areas.

Scholar's margins: Narrow space along the left and right edges of a book, originally provided to allow scholars to comment on the material in the adjacent columns.

Screen: 1) To convert a continuous-tone halftone into a series of dots that can be reproduced as a halftone. The quality of the screen, which is influenced by the resolution of the printer and the quality of the paper the document will be printed on, is measured in lines-per-inch. See _continuous tone_, _halftone_, and _LPI_. 2) A gray, or tinted, background. Screens are often used behind short text elements, such as a publication's table of contents or masthead. Most software enables you to specify screens in 10% increments: a 10% screen indicates light gray, and a 90% screen is almost full-strength black. See _tint_.

Script: Typeface designs that mimic hand-writing. Often used in product packaging or short, decorative projects, such as invitations or diplomas.

Separation: Dividing colors into the four colors that can be used to recreate every other color. These colors are cyan, magenta, yellow, and black. This technique is used to print color documents.

Serif: Typographic term referring to the wedge-shaped or tear-shaped strokes at the ends of letters. Serifs enhance readability by guiding the reader's eyes from one letter to the next. Serifs also contribute to the unique shape of the letters. See _sans serif_.

Service bureau: Commercial firm with trained staffs that output files prepared on your computer by using expensive, high-resolution imagesetters. By making such services available as needed and charging on a per-page or per-hour basis, service bureaus eliminate the need for desktop publishers to purchase high-resolution output devices and color printers costing tens of thousands of dollars.

Shadow: Three-dimensional effect that makes it look like a text or graphic object is standing vertically and illuminated from the top or side, creating a background below and behind it.

Sidebar: Short text element, typically three to six paragraphs long, adjacent to a longer text article. Sidebars provide visual interest and let you devote space to a single aspect of the longer, adjacent article without interrupting the overall flow of the article.

Sidehead: Text (or subhead) placed adjacent to the text column rather than within the column. Used to attract a reader's attention to a new topic. See _run-in_ and _subhead_.

Silhouette: Removing the background of a photograph to create an irregularly shaped photograph containing just the main subject of the picture.

Sink: Reducing column height to add white space to the top of each page. Sinks unify a publication, providing page-to-page continuity. Also called _drops_.

Solarization: Creative effective added by using an image manipulation program. Allows you to convert all or part of a scanned image into a negative, preserving shapes but providing different colors and textures. See *posterization, masks,* and *filter.*

Spot color: Two or more colors used to add visual interest to a document. Each color is mixed in advance and applied in one pass. See *process colors.*

Spread: View of a publication showing both left and right pages together as readers will encounter them.

Standing heads: Short phrases that organize and introduce departments and topics that appear in every issue of a newsletter, such as "Message from the President," "New Faces," or "In the News."

Stipple: Paper that contains a noticeable pattern, often textured and made from recycled paper.

Stress: Difference in stroke thickness between the horizontal, or thick parts of a letter and the thin, often vertical, strokes of a letter. See *contrast.*

Style: Typographic option indicating which variation of a typeface will be used: Roman (or upright), boldface (heavy), italic (redrawn and slanted) or bold italic.

Styles: Time-saving feature that allows you to save the typographic formatting choices contained in a file as a template or style sheet. When working with a document using the template or style sheet, you can assign the various options to a text block by simply applying a style. You can also save graphic options (stroke width and color, fill pattern, and colors) as styles.

Subhead: Typographic device used to divide long articles into manageable, bite-sized chunks. See *run-in, sidehead,* and *chunking.*

Swash: Ornate characters intended to add visual interest to titles and logos. Swash characters usually contain an oversize element, such as an uppercase Q with a tail that extends to the right under the next character (or characters).

Swipe file: File folder containing samples of printed ads, brochures, newsletters, and other print communications. Reviewing the contents of a swipe file when you start a new project helps get your creative juices flowing and helps you avoid obvious mistakes.

Symbols: Typographic characters used to replace spelled-out words, such as © for copyright.

Symmetry: Design term used to describe individual pages or two-page spreads characterized by left-right balance.

Tabs: Keyboard command that moves text a pre-determined amount of space.

Table: Design technique that organizes complicated information in row-and-column format to allow easy comparisons. See *cell.*

Template: Read-only file containing the formatting information necessary to create a finished document. See *styles.*

Tension: Design technique based on creating unequal left-right balance. Often, a large vertical photograph at the left of a page is balanced on the right by a short text phrase.

Texture: The smoothness (or *weave*) of a column of text. The goal of fine typography is to create columns without distracting holes, (often created by excessive word spacing in lines of justified type containing a few long words or by inserting two spaces after a period at the end of a sentence) or areas of blackness created by words set in boldface.

Text wrap: Reducing the left or right margins of a text column to accommodate an irregularly shaped photograph or pull quote placed next to the column or extending from an adjacent column.

Thumbnail: Reduced-scale version of a document. Thumbnails let you experiment with alternate locations for headlines, photographs, and text columns. Many page layout programs enable you to print thumbnails, with up to 16 pages shown on a single 8¹/₂ by 11-inch sheet of paper. Many word processing programs enable you to preview up to eight pages at reduced size on the screen of your computer. Thumbnails can give you a better idea of the page-by-page development of your publication.

Tick marks: Small marks added to the x-axis and y-axis of charts and graphs to indicate minor intervals, as contrasted to the gridlines (or horizontal and vertical lines) used for major intervals.

Timeline: Type of visual that describes sequence and helps readers understand events in their historical perspective by placing events in a left-to-right or top-to-bottom sequence. The relationship between seemingly unrelated events becomes clear when readers can see when they occurred in relation to other events.

Tint: Graphic elements printed with less than 100% ink coverage. See *screens*.

Tombstone headlines: Two or more parallel headlines in adjacent columns, placed in a way that encourages readers to jump the column gutter, reading the separate headlines as one long headline.

Tracking: Increasing or decreasing letter spacing uniformly throughout a headline or column of text. In most cases, letter spacing is too generous. Slightly reducing letter spacing often improves the appearance of the text.

Trim size: The physical measurements of a page, as contrasted to the live area, or area between the margins, of a page. See *bleed*, *live area*, and *margins*.

True Small Caps: Uppercase letters that have been redrawn to equal the x-height of a typeface. The use of True Small Caps to emphasize book titles is preferable to using scaled small caps, which are created by most software programs. This is because the width of the stroke comprising the True Small Caps equals the stroke weight of adjacent letters, instead of appearing lighter (strokes of letters become thinner as type size is reduced).

TrueType: Typeface format promoted by Apple and Microsoft. TrueType fonts often print faster than competing typeface formats on laser printers. See *Type 1*.

Type 1: Adobe's universally accepted typeface format. Type 1 is characterized by the largest selection of typefaces and the easiest acceptance by service bureaus. See *TrueType*.

Typeset punctuation: True punctuation marks, such as open and closed quotation marks and em and en dashes, in contrast to "typewriter" punctuation created by using inch marks and double hyphens.

Visualization: The very exciting (and often rare) creative act of "seeing," or conceiving, how you want a finished project to look when finished and printed.

Watermark: Background text or graphic element that appears on each page, behind the primary text or graphic elements. Watermarks are very light and can be placed anywhere on the page.

Weight: Many typeface designs are available with strokes of different thicknesses. These range from Light to Heavy. This permits you to add visual interest to your publication and "voice" your text without choosing a different typeface, which might distract from your message.

White space: Page layout term referring to areas of rest and quiet on a page, free from text, visuals, or graphic accents. White space provides the contrast necessary to frame text and visuals.

Widow: A short line, a third (or less) than the width of a column. Widows are especially annoying when they contain just a single word or — even worse — a portion of a word (left over from a hyphenated word on a previous line). Widows are especially noticeable when they occur at the bottom of a column or end of a page.

Wizards: Microsoft's term for macros that make typeface and page layout choices for you based on your responses to on-screen questions.

X-height: Typographic term referring to the height of lowercase vowels *a, e, i, o,* and *u.* The x-height of a typeface plays a major role in its apparent size. Typefaces with a high x-height look significantly larger than typefaces with a low x-height, even when both are the same size.

Zoom: Choosing a different screen magnification to reveal less of a page at large size or more of a page at small size. Zooming enables you to position text and graphic elements with great precision at high magnifications and then "zoom out" to get an overall view of the page.

Appendix B
Some Great Resources

● ●

*F*ollowing is a list of resources that I have found particularly helpful.

Adobe Systems, Inc.
P.O. Box 7900
Mountain View, CA 94039
1-800-833-6687

Adobe's PostScript page description
language forms the basis of desktop
publishing. They currently offer the largest
selection of fonts in the Type 1 format.

Bitstream, Inc.
215 First Street
Cambridge, MA 02142
1-800-522-3668

The Bitstream Typeface Library is an
unlocked CD-ROM containing over 500
typeface designs and numberous variations.

ColorUp
Pantone, Inc.
590 Commerce Boulevard
Carlstadt, NJ 07072-3098

ColorUp is an interactive software program
that teaches you about color. You'll learn
about color harmony, color printing techniques, and the psychology of color, as well
as see how (and why) certain combinations
of color work with each other or against
each other.

Color for Impact
By Jan V. White
Westport, CT
203-226-3298

Available directly from the author. Glorious
$8^1/_2$ by 11-inch volume by one of the leading
authorities in the field.

FontHaus, Inc.
1375 Kings Highway
Fairfield, CT 06430
1-800-942-9110

In addition to selling fonts from all publishers, FontHaus publishes *x-height,* a quarterly
review of typography that contains news
about the newest typefaces as well as
reviews of books about type.

Galapagos Design Group
215 First Street
Cambridge, MA 02142
617-661-2041

Typical of the new breed of small, entrepre-
neurial typeface foundries introducing new
designs to the market.

Monotype Typography, Inc.
150 South Whacker Drive, Suite 2630
Chicago, IL 60606
1-800-666-6897

The Monotype FontFonts CD-ROM contains over 3,000 fonts from the leading typeface libraries (including Adobe), including numerous samples of clip art and initial caps.

Paper Direct
100 Plaza Drive, 2nd Floor
Secaucus, NJ 07074
1-800-APAPERS

Paper Direct is one of the largest suppliers of colored paper suitable for use in inkjet or laser printers. Ask for a copy of their 150-page catalog, which contains an offer to buy a comprehensive Paper Selector Kit containing hundreds of sample papers ready to laser print or photocopy.

Precision Type
47 Mall Drive
Comack, NY 11725
1-800-248-3668

The *Precision Type Reference Guide* lists every digital typeface available from every typeface vendor. The book is copiously cross-referenced and illustrated.

URW
4 Manchester Street
Nashua, NH 03060
1-800-229-8791

In addition to the first type-filled unlocked CD-ROMs, URW'S Kernus kerning program can improve the appearance of any Type 1 or TrueType font.

NEWSLETTERS FOR DUMMIES®

by Roger C. Parker

IDG Books Worldwide, Inc.
An International Data Group Company

Foster City, CA ♦ Chicago, IL ♦ Indianapolis, IN ♦ New York, NY

Table of Contents

Part I

Planning a Successful Newsletter

INSIDER TRADING

THE JOURNAL OF ETHICAL INVESTING

VOL. 16, # 986
MARCH 14, 1995

Are ethics as important as everyone says?

Dolor sit amet, consectetuer adipiscing elit, sed diam nonummy nibh euismod tincidunt ut laoreet dolore magna aliquam erat volutpat.

Ut wisi enim ad minim veniam, quis nostrud exerci tation ullamcorper suscipit lobortis nisl ut aliquip ex ea commodo consequat. Duis autem vel eum iriure dolor in hendrerit in vulputate velit esse molestie consequat, vel illum dolore eu feugiat nulla facilisis at vero eros et accumsan et iusto odio dignissim qui blandit praesent luptatum zzril delenit augue duis dolore te feugait nulla facilisi.

Lorem ipsum dolor sit amet, consectetuer adipiscing elit, sed diam nonummy nibh euismod tincidunt ut laoreet dolore magna aliquam erat volutpat.

Lorem ipsum dolor sit amet, consectetuer adipiscing elit, sed diam nonummy nibh euismod tincidunt ut laoreet dolore magna aliquam erat volutpat. Duis autem vel eum iriure dolor in hendrerit in vulputate velit esse molestie consequat, vel illum dolore eu feugiat nulla facilisis at vero eros et accumsan et iusto odio dignissim qui blandit praesent luptatum zzril delenit augue duis dolore te feugait nulla facilisi.

Lorem ipsum dolor sit amet, consectetuer adipiscing elit, sed diam nonummy nibh euismod tincidunt ut laoreet dolore magna aliquam erat volutpat. Ut wisi enim ad minim veniam, quis nostrud exerci tation ullamcorper suscipit lobortis nisl ut aliquip ex ea commodo consequat.

Lorem ipsum dolor sit amet, consectetuer euismod tincidunt ut laoreet dolore magna aliquam erat volutpat.

Freedom without recourse offers great investment opportunities!

Keeping in touch while out of touch

Dolor sit amet, consectetuer adipiscing elit, sed diam nonummy nibh euismod tincidunt ut laoreet dolore magna aliquam erat volutpat.

Ut wisi enim ad minim veniam, quis nostrud exerci tation ullamcorper suscipit lobortis nisl ut aliquip ex ea commodo consequat. Duis autem vel eum iriure dolor in hendrerit in vulputate velit esse molestie consequat, vel illum dolore eu feugiat nulla facilisis at vero eros et accumsan et iusto odio dignissim qui blandit praesent luptatum zzril delenit augue duis dolore te feugait nulla facilisi.

Wizywig ad petulam et valor und system crash. Lorem ipsum dolor sit amet, consectetuer adipiscing elit, sed diam nonummy nibh euismod tincidunt ut laoreet dolore magna aliquam erat volutpat.

Lorem ipsum dolor sit amet, consectetuer adipiscing elit, sed diam nonummy nibh euismod tincidunt ut laoreet dolore magna

Continued on page 3

IT Insider Trading

Published infrequently by the RCP et al New Horizon Institute of Freedom and Ethical Responsibility, PO Box 697, Dover, NH 03820. $999/year

*p*art of the challenge in creating a newsletter is the need to constantly balance change with consistency. You have to balance flexibility with recognizability. Each issue of your newsletter must accommodate a different mix of text and graphics and must look different enough to announce that it is a new issue. For your newsletter program to succeed in the long run, each issue also must maintain a familiar, or *family,* appearance.

Newsletters are also typically produced under last-minute conditions with limited budget and printing resources. Newsletters rank far below advertisements, annual reports, and brochures when budgets are prepared, but they are likely to be distributed to a very critical and knowledgeable audience.

To make matters worse, newsletters often must undergo an approval cycle involving everyone from the Chairman of the Board to the latest hiree. Little wonder that so many newsletter editors end up conducting one-way white water rafting expeditions in Montana!

Chapter 1

Starting on the Right Foot

● ●

*T*he first step in creating a successful newsletter is to answer some fundamental questions. The more planning you do at this stage, the easier it will be to design an appropriate format and prepare the contents for each issue.

Why Do a Newsletter?

Start by defining the goal of your newsletter as specifically as possible. The two most common goals are to establish credibility and maintain awareness. You can't buy the respect of prospective customers, but you can *prove it* by showing that you know your subject well enough to write about it. A newsletter is an excellent credibility builder, allowing you to prove your expertise in an educational way, avoiding the "claims" of advertising.

Market awareness is the second most popular reason to do a newsletter. Just as market leaders such as Coca Cola and McDonald's spend millions of dollars each year maintaining visibility on television, you can buy "mindshare" among your target market by sending them a newsletter.

What Will Be in Each Issue?

What are you going to include in your newsletter? Are you going to devote each issue to a single topic, or will your newsletter "tease" readers with several shorter features? How many visuals will be included? How important are the visuals? Will there be many illustrations, photographs, or charts?

The content of your newsletter should determine the column layout. A newsletter containing an assortment of long and short articles plus several photographs of different sizes requires a more complex column layout than a newsletter featuring one or two long, analytical stories and few visuals. What items are likely to be repeated from issue to issue? Does each issue have to contain features, such as a calendar of upcoming events, a list of personnel changes, information about new product introductions, or a barometer of stock performance? Do you have to accommodate ads in your newsletter?

Who Will Read the Newsletter?

Next consider the needs of your market. What are their concerns? What types of information do they need? How likely are they to be interested in what you have to say? How easy must it be for readers to locate information? Are they likely to read each issue cover to cover, or must you struggle to attract and maintain their interest? What are their quality expectations? Are they looking for evidence of frugality or elegance? How motivated are they? Are they casual readers or devout enthusiasts?

What is the image you want to project? How do you want readers to think of you and the firm or association your newsletter represents — safe and conservative, forward-thinking and avant-garde, formal or friendly?

If there are any other newsletters competing for your reader's attention, hang them on your wall and constantly refer to them. Make your newsletter look as different as possible. Also make it accommodate your firm's corporate identity by using as many of the same typefaces, type sizes, column arrangements, page borders, and logo placement used elsewhere in your firm's correspondence, advertisements, brochures, documentation, and other print communications.

How Often Will the Newsletter Appear?

How often will your newsletter appear? Will it appear weekly, monthly, bi-monthly, or quarterly?

Consistency is more important than excellence. Sorry, but that's the way it goes. It is far more important to always be on time than to appear "irregularly." Although your primary purpose may be to build awareness, people quickly forget. Each day between newsletters increases the chance that your market will forget you when it comes to buy.

A monthly two-sided newsletter printed on a single piece of 8 1/2 by 11-inch paper will do more for most businesses than a bi-monthly four-page newsletter or a quarterly eight-page newsletter.

Remember that not everyone is ready to act at the same time! By being constantly present in your prospect's mailbox, your name will be the first one remembered when your prospect is ready to buy. If six weeks or two months has elapsed since your last newsletter, there is a good chance that your name will have been forgotten — or that a competitor's mailing may have arrived in the meantime.

What Are My Time and Budget Limitations?

The best time to recognize time and budget restraints is before you begin working. How many hours per week do you have available to work on your newsletter? How much money do you have to work with?

These questions cannot be answered in isolation. They should be analyzed in the context of your expected income, the profitability of the product or service you're offering and the context of your target market.

Time and budget constraints should play a role in determining the size of your newsletter, its frequency, your use of color, and the paper your newsletter is printed on.

What Will I Name the Newsletter?

One of the most important decisions you have to make when publishing a newsletter is choosing the right name.

Choose a name that identifies the market you want your newsletter to appeal to or identifies the contents or the approach of your newsletter. Here are some suggestions:

- ✔ **Avoid naming a newsletter after yourself.** You represent one of only three people who are interested in your words. (The others are your mother and your spouse.) Everyone else is more interested in *What's in it for me?* Newsletters with the name of the individual or firm in them are more likely to appear as propaganda and advertising than news.

- ✔ **Avoid empty words such as *The* and *Newsletter*.** If readers want *The* in front of the name, they'll supply it when they read your name.

- ✔ **Use as few words as possible.** Fewer words translates into more white space around the title and/or a larger, more noticeable type size.

- ✔ **If possible, choose words of similar length.** This makes it easier to contrast words with each other.

 The best way to develop a name for your newsletter is to write down a dozen or so different phrases that describe your newsletter's function. Say the name out loud and rephrase it using fewer and fewer, shorter and shorter words. It will probably take several hours until you come up with a short, memorable restatement of your newsletter's purpose.

Simplify and add typographic contrast to nameplates

Before

After

Simplify and add visual interest to the newsletter's title, or nameplate. The Before version (left) lacks impact because all the words are set in the same weight. Foreground/background contrast is reduced by the shaded background. Interest is added to the After version by setting "Desktop Publishing" in a different typeface than "Design" and by replacing the word "and" with an oversized, shaded ampersand. The nameplate is simplified by eliminating the unnecessary word *newsletter* and by moving the issue number and date information to the table of contents box.

Chapter 2

Choosing the Right Format

Formatting decisions should be considered long-term decisions. They should last for years to come. When you change horses midstream, you can confuse your reader and lose the momentum established by previous issues. You need to make two types of formatting decisions: physical (size, length, paper, and color) and design.

What Size Is Best?

Avoid non-standard sizes. Don't be seduced by the lure of tabloid (or 11-by-17 formats). Newsletters with $8^{1}/_{2}$ by 11-inch pages offer many advantages.

- **Economy.** Most inkjet and laser printers can easily prepare $8^{1}/_{2}$ by 11-inch artwork. In addition, most print shops are comfortable working with this size. By avoiding non-standard sizes, you can choose from a wider variety of printers and enjoy a wider selection of in-stock paper.

- **Readability.** Newsletters printed on $8^{1}/_{2}$ by 11-inch pages are easy to read. They are easy to hold at a convenient distance from the eyes and make it easy to focus on a single story.

- **Distribution and storage.** An $8^{1}/_{2}$ by 11-inch newsletter easily fits in a standard file folder and is cheaper to mail.

How Many Pages in Each Issue?

Remember that in most cases, the primary purpose of your newsletter is to create credibility and maintain visibility and awareness. This requires consistency, and consistency is based on affordability and practicality. A four-page newsletter is not twice as hard to produce as a two-page newsletter — it's eight times as hard. An eight-page newsletter is even harder. Each time you make your job harder, you're likely to fall behind schedule or abandon the program.

You're better off editing your contents to the bone and including just enough information to "tease" your reader into contacting you or visiting your place of business than attempting too much and failing.

If your goal is to communicate professionalism, you'll do this better by publishing a well-written two-page newsletter that arrives like clockwork on the tenth of every month instead of a four- or eight-page newsletter that arrives at unpredictable intervals.

In most cases, limit your page count to multiples of four. Six-page newsletters present a challenge. You can insert a single sheet in the middle (which often falls out in the mail or lands on the reader's lap when read) or you can use a six-panel, wide format. The six-panel format costs more to produce because not every printer can accommodate it and not all papers are available that wide.

In addition, the six-panel format presents its own unique set of design challenges. Instead of seeing a two-page spread when they open your newsletter, your readers encounter three parallel pages. This format makes it difficult for readers to concentrate on a single story. The six-panel format also makes it harder to design pages that work well with each other.

What Type of Paper and Color Works Best?

Paper and color should be considered at the same time. This is where a good swipe file comes in handy. Hopefully, you've been collecting newsletters and have a good selection. Another good starting point is to contact a paper mill, such as S.D. Warren, and request paper samples. Most paper mills can send you a variety of samples.

In many cases, you may want to investigate alternatives to standard "white." Pure white paper not only looks "everyday," but it is often harder to read because of glare. Investigate off-white colors such as creams, ivories, and light grays.

Recognizing your own limitations is one the keys to success in desktop publishing. Just because you are going to produce your own newsletter doesn't mean you can't hire a designer to consult with you on paper choice and colors. Allow them to make informed decisions at an early stage, and carry on from there on your own.

Adopt a consistent headline style

Before

After

The Before example (left) lacks unity because each centered, uppercase headline is set in a different typeface and type style. Most of the headlines are underlined, which makes them hard to read. In addition, there is no clear headline hierarchy; the headline at upper left is the same size as the headline in the center column (which appears awkwardly large). In the After example (right) all headlines are set in Helvetica Condensed Black set flush-left. The primary headline is larger than the two secondary headlines. The table of contents headlines is smaller, still. All headlines are set flush-left for unity. Note that the Condensed Heavy sans serif typeface saves enough space to allow extra body copy to be added without crowding the page. Note also that the "New" in the "Edible Laser Toner" headline has been set slightly smaller and in italics for emphasis. (Once you set up a consistent structure, you can easily add emphasis by modifying it.)

Line and word spacing has also been refined. Default, or "auto" leading has been replaced by tighter line spacing. The open look of No Tracking has been replaced by the tighter, more visually pleasing look of Normal Tracking.

Chapter 3

Creating Repeating Elements

● ●

*1*n addition to headlines and body copy, certain text elements are repeated in
every issue. Because these elements often appear at large size, they greatly
influence the image your newsletter projects. Repeating text elements include
the following:

✔ **Nameplate:** The nameplate is the title of your newsletter, usually designed
as a separate graphic elements that can be copied and resized as a unit,
perhaps reproduced at small size along the top of inside pages.

✔ **Table of contents:** Unless you give them a good reason, many readers
won't encounter stories on the inside pages of your newsletters. The table
of contents is your opportunity to "advertise" and reinforce stories located
on the inside pages of your newsletter.

✔ **Masthead:** The masthead of your newsletter is your opportunity to
publicly thank those who have assisted you in preparing your newsletter.
You can include the name and purpose of the association or business
sending the newsletter as well as miscellaneous information, such as
telephone, fax, and e-mail, and Internet addresses where readers can
contact the editors and send subscription requests or change of address
information.

✔ **Department heads:** Department heads organize the contents of your
newsletter and help readers quickly locate desired categories of information. Department heads can also visually unify your newsletter by mimick-
ing the nameplate's design and typography. Typical categories include
"President's Message," "Newcomers," and "Milestones."

✔ **Headers, footers, and borders:** Headers and footers refer to text and
graphic accents that appear on every page. Graphic accents include
borders, which can be four sized boxes around each page or borders
added to the headers and footers.

Figure 3-1 shows a sample newsletter containing each of these elements.

Nameplate

 IT **INSIDER TRADING**

THE JOURNAL OF ETHICAL INVESTING

Folio

VOL. 16, # 986
MARCH 14, 1995

Are ethics as important as everyone says?

Dolor sit amet, consectetuer adipiscing elit, sed diam nonummy nibh euismod tincidunt ut laoreet dolore magna aliquam erat volutpat.

Ut wisi enim ad minim veniam, quis nostrud exerci tation ullamcorper suscipit lobortis nisl ut aliquip ex ea commodo consequat. Duis autem vel eum iriure dolor in hendrerit in vulputate velit esse molestie consequat, vel illum dolore eu feugiat nulla facilisis at vero eros et accumsan et iusto odio dignissim qui blandit praesent luptatum zzril delenit augue duis dolore te feugait nulla facilisi.

Lorem ipsum dolor sit amet, consectetuer adipiscing elit, sed diam nonummy nibh euismod tincidunt ut laoreet dolore magna aliquam erat volutpat.

Lorem ipsum dolor sit amet, consectetuer adipiscing elit, sed diam nonummy nibh euismod tincidunt ut laoreet dolore magna aliquam erat volutpat. Duis autem vel eum iriure dolor in hendrerit in vulputate velit esse molestie consequat, vel illum dolore eu feugiat nulla facilisis at vero eros et accumsan et iusto odio dignissim qui blandit praesent luptatum zzril delenit augue duis dolore te feugait nulla facilisi.

Lorem ipsum dolor sit amet, consectetuer adipiscing elit, sed diam nonummy nibh euismod tincidunt ut laoreet dolore magna aliquam erat volutpat. Ut wisi enim ad minim veniam, quis nostrud exerci tation ullamcorper suscipit lobortis nisl ut aliquip ex ea commodo consequat.

Lorem ipsum dolor sit amet, consectetuer euismod tincidunt ut laoreet dolore magna aliquam erat volutpat.

Border

Freedom without recourse offers great investment opportunities!

Inside this issue

Keeping in touch while out of touch

Dolor sit amet, consectetuer adipiscing elit, sed diam nonummy nibh euismod tincidunt ut laoreet dolore magna aliquam erat volutpat.

Ut wisi enim ad minim veniam, quis nostrud exerci tation ullamcorper suscipit lobortis nisl ut aliquip ex ea commodo consequat. Duis autem vel eum iriure dolor in hendrerit in vulputate velit esse molestie consequat, vel illum dolore eu feugiat nulla facilisis at vero eros et accumsan et iusto odio dignissim qui blandit praesent luptatum zzril delenit augue duis dolore te feugait nulla facilisi.

Wizywig ad petulam et valor und system crash. Lorem ipsum dolor sit amet, consectetuer adipiscing elit, sed diam nonummy nibh euismod tincidunt ut laoreet dolore magna aliquam erat volutpat.

Lorem ipsum dolor sit amet, consectetuer adipiscing elit, sed diam nonummy nibh euismod tincidunt ut laoreet dolore magna Continued on page 3

IT **Insider Trading**

Published infrequently by the RCP et al New Horizon Institute of Freedom and Ethical Responsibility, PO Box 697, Dover, NH 03820. $999/year

Masthead

Table of Contents

Figure 3-1: Elements of a newsletter.

Nameplate

The nameplate, or title of your newsletter set in a unique typeface on the front page of your newsletter, is likely to be your newsletters single most noticeable repeating element. The nameplate will do more to create a distinct image for your newsletter than any other element.

If possible, nameplates should be created by using an illustration or drawing program and imported into your word processing or page layout program. This provides added flexibility for controlling letter spacing, manipulating type, and manipulating foreground/background contrast. Also, if the nameplate is created as an individual file, it can be easily imported and added to other print communications, such as letterheads, as well as placed on the inside pages of your newsletter.

Avoid cluttering your nameplate with association seals and your firm's logo. If these must be included on the first page of your newsletter, relocate them to the bottom left. Remember, the purpose of your nameplate is to "sell" the contents of your newsletter.

You don't have to create your nameplate by yourself. You can hire a freelancer to create an electronic file for your newsletter that you can add and place in your newsletter.

Table of Contents

One of the least expensive ways you can add interest to the front cover of your newsletter is to include an interesting table of contents. Consider the table of contents an advertisement designed to attract readers into the inside pages of your newsletter. Remember that the front covers of some of the most successful publications in the world consist of nothing but the table of contents!

As always, avoid doing anything out of habit. Ask yourself: "Do I need a table of contents?" A table of contents can be considered optional on two-page newsletters (those printed on the front and back of a single page), for example.

Although a table of contents often appears at the lower right or lower left of the front page, it doesn't have to appear there. The tables of contents can also appear at the top of the front page above the nameplate, or to the left or to the right of the nameplate. These locations are more likely to attract the reader's eyes and won't interrupt articles.

Ten ways to create a newsletter nameplate

1. **Emphasize the most important word.**

   In most cases, some words are more important than others. Emphasize the most important words by making them larger or heavier than lesser words. For example, et the important word in a Heavy typeface, and then set lesser words in Light version of the same typeface. You can also experiment with serif versus sans serif contrast as well as style contrast — try using italics for one of the words.

2. **Add borders.**

   Large words by themselves often appear to "float" on the page. Use one, or more, horizontal rules to frame the words and/or "anchor" the nameplate to the page. Be careful with four-sided boxes, however. Boxed nameplates often present a clichéd appearance.

3. **Add a background.**

   Reverse one or more words out of a black or colored background. But don't feel that *all* the words have to be reversed. Try reversing just the most important word, or the shortest (or the longest). Be creative. Also experiment with placing one or more words against shaded or colored backgrounds.

4. **Avoid long titles.**

   Because it is often easier to add impact if the words are short and large, break cumbersome long titles into a short title amplified by a longer subtitle. The subtitle can "translate" and amplify the meaning of the short title.

5. **Allow selected letters to touch or overlap.**

   You can create a distinct icon out of a series of individual letters by using a drawing program to modify letter spacing, allowing selected letters to touch or overlap each other. If you have access to a font editor, you might even want to add or remove serifs, or make other modifications to change "off-the-shelf" letters into distinctive visual elements.

6. **Bleed backgrounds and graphic accents.**

   Bleed the background behind your nameplate or one of the text or border elements to extend to the physical edge of the page. This makes your nameplate look larger than it is. It also avoids an inadvertent "white frame," which makes the nameplate appear smaller.

7. **Align the nameplate with one of the text columns.**

   Avoid centering the nameplate unless centering creates a deliberately-desired effect. Centering often creates nameplates that "float" on a page, instead of being anchored to the text or graphics that follow.

   Try left-aligning the nameplate with the underlying grid. This creates a pool of white space to the left of the nameplate, emphasizing the first letters in the name.

8. **Add equal spacing between the letters.**

   Many page layout and word processing programs offer a Force Justification option that can automatically equally space letters across a column or page. This makes it easy to create interesting visual contrast between a short, large word set on top of a long, small word.

9. **Use right alignment.**

   Experiment with right alignment, especially if the first line of the title is shorter than the second title. This rarely used technique can build white space to the left of the nameplate.

10. **Eliminate unnecessary words, symbols and graphic elements.**

    Don't use newsletter in the title. Readers will usually recognize that your newsletter is a newsletter and not confuse it with an advertisement, brochure, or bill from the phone company.

If your newsletter is designed to be a self-mailer, consider placing the table of contents on the back cover, adjacent to the mailing label. Your newsletter will likely appear in your reader's mailboxes mailing-label up, so readers will encounter the back-page table of contents before they would encounter it on the front page!

Masthead

Mastheads are another under-appreciated repeating element in newsletters. The masthead identifies the firm or association mailing the newsletter, its frequency of publication, as well as the names and positions of everyone associated with producing your newsletter. The masthead presents an ideal location for adding association seals and other "must be present somewhere" information that often clutters a newsletter nameplate.

Most mastheads are dull — if not downright ugly. This is because they are characterized by undesirable space between "positions" and "names" as well as a lack of typographic contrast. In many cases, the problem is compounded by placing the masthead in a tall and narrow box. Often, a better choice is to use a shorter, wider masthead.

Note that the masthead doesn't have to be on the front page of your newsletter, although many people place it there. Because its purpose is to honor the staff and let readers know how to contact them, it can be placed on the second page of your newsletter or the back page. Its location should remain consistent from issue to issue, however.

Borders, Headers, Footers, and Department Heads

Avoid adding a box around each page, unless you definitely want to create a conservative or classic image. Boxing pages creates barriers that can discourage readers from reading each page. Consider simpler horizontal and vertical borders which reinforce the text area of each page.

Headers and footers provide a convenient location for information such as page numbers as well as the issue number and date of each newsletter. Consider repeating the nameplate of your newsletter at small size in the header of each page. This unifies your newsletter and is an especially good idea if there is a chance readers may photocopy individual articles and distribute them to friends.

Ten alternatives to a boring table of contents

1. **Add typographic contrast to page numbers.**

   Instead of setting page numbers in the same typeface and type size as the articles, use oversize page numbers or a contrasting typeface. For example, if you are using serif type for the articles, use large sans serif page numbers.

2. **Place the table of contents at the top left.**

   Most people will read your page in a Z-shaped direction from upper left to lower right. By placing the table of contents at the upper left of the page — perhaps in the white space created by a right-aligned nameplate — you'll attract your reader's attention when they begin reading the page.

3. **Surround the table of contents with white space.**

   If you are using a three-column format, eliminate the first column of text and place the table of contents in the white space created.

4. **"Sell" article content.**

   Replace article titles with a short description of the contents and importance of the articles on the inside of your newsletter. Or place the article titles in bold and use a sentence below to describe the article.

5. **Eliminate empty or unnecessary words.**

   Unless you're doing a newsletter that will be archived in the Library of Congress, avoid listing articles that appear on the same page as the table of contents. Likewise, avoid repeating the word "page" in each entry.

6. **Include photographs.**

   If you're preparing a formal newsletter and the inside articles contain photographs, reproduce the photographs at small size on the front cover of your newsletter.

7. **Use right and left tabs to maintain consistent spacing.**

   To avoid trapped white space between titles and page numbers, use right-tabs to align the titles flush-right and set the page numbers flush-left. This locks the titles to the numbers, regardless of the length of the title or the number of digits in the number.

8. **Avoid unnecessary graphic accents.**

   Avoid the cliché of a table of contents placed in a screened box. The background screen is likely to make the article titles and page numbers harder to read instead of easier to read. Likewise, boxes tend to be over-used. Instead, surround the table of contents with white space and use a single pair of horizontal rules to define its top and bottom boundaries.

9. **Place page numbers before titles.**

   You can add visual interest to your table of contents by decimal-aligning page numbers before the titles. This locks the numbers to the titles, regardless of the length of the title and maintains consistent spacing regardless of the number of digits in the page number.

10. **Use a table to maintain constant spacing.**

    A borderless (or gridless) table provides an ideal structure for a good-looking table of contents. A table makes it easy to use a larger type size for the numbers than the article titles and maintains precise vertical alignment and horizontal spacing regardless of the number of lines in the title.

The typography used to organize your newsletter into various departments can reflect the typography used in your nameplate. This will further unify your newsletter. When creating your newsletter nameplate, consider creating separate files for the various categories of articles likely to be repeated in each issue, such as Upcoming Events, President's Message, Personnel Changes, In the News, and Readers Speak Out.

Six ways to create a good-looking masthead

1. Center each line.

Try centering titles and names on a single line, separated by a typographic symbol, perhaps an em dash or one of the symbols contained in the Microsoft Wingdings or Zapf Dingbats collection. Be sure to add a space before and after the symbol to separate the titles and names.

2. Use tabs to add a consistent amount of space between title and name.

Use flush-right tabs to align the last letters of each title and use left-tabs to align names. This separates titles from names by a consistent amount of white space.

3. Employ typeface contrast.

Visually emphasize the difference between title and name by using typeface contrast. Try using a sans serif typeface for titles and a serif typeface for names. Because the typeface contrast will be sufficient to separate title from names, you can safely eliminate the colon that is frequently used.

4. Employ weight contrast.

If you are using a sans serif typeface in your newsletter, you could use the Light weight of the type for the title and the Heavy version of the type for the name. This makes the names stand out — a sure-fire crowd pleaser!

5. Employ style contrast.

If you are using a single typeface, set the titles in italic and use Roman type for the names.

6. Eliminate boxed borders and screened backgrounds.

Typeface legibility will be enhanced if you eliminate boxed borders and screened backgrounds Then you can use a smaller type size and still present a lot of information in an easy-to-read format.

Unify subheads with headlines

Before

After

The subheads in the Before example (left) do not emerge with impact because they are set in the same typeface and type size as the adjacent body copy. They are also extremely hard to read because they are set in underlined bold italic. Their impact is diluted because they center-aligned over left-aligned text. As a result, each subhead begins a slightly different distance from the left (sometimes more—sometimes less) than the first line indent of the adjacent paragraphs. In the

After example (right), the subheads are are set in a contrasting typeface, Helvetica Black, which matches the headlines and are left-aligned to match left-aligned text.

Line spacing and word spacing have also been refined. Default, or "auto," leading has been replaced by tighter line spacing and No Tracking" has been replaced by Normal Tracking, which tightens letter spacing.

Part II

Choosing the Right
Page Layout and Typography

VOL. 16, #986
MARCH 14, 1995

THE JOURNAL OF ETHICAL INVESTING

Are ethics as important as everyone says?

Dolor sit amet, consectetuer adipiscing elit, sed diam nonummy nibh euismod tincidunt ut laoreet dolore magna aliquam erat volutpat.

Ut wisi enim ad minim veniam, quis nostrud exerci tation ullamcorper suscipit lobortis nisl ut aliquip ex ea commodo consequat. Duis autem vel eum iriure dolor in hendrerit in vulputate velit esse molestie consequat, vel illum dolore eu feugiat nulla facilisis at vero eros et accumsan et iusto odio dignissim qui blandit praesent luptatum zzril delenit augue duis dolore te feugait nulla facilisi.

Lorem ipsum dolor sit amet, consectetuer adipiscing elit, sed diam nonummy nibh euismod tincidunt ut laoreet dolore magna aliquam erat volutpat.

Freedom without recourse offers great investment opportunities!

Lorem ipsum dolor sit amet, consectetuer adipiscing elit, sed diam nonummy nibh euismod tincidunt ut laoreet dolore magna aliquam erat volutpat. Duis autem vel eum iriure dolor in hendrerit in vulputate velit esse molestie consequat, vel illum dolore eu feugiat nulla facilisis at vero eros et accumsan et iusto odio dignissim qui blandit praesent luptatum zzril delenit augue duis dolore te feugait nulla facilisi.

Lorem ipsum dolor sit amet, consectetuer adipiscing elit, sed diam nonummy nibh euismod tincidunt ut laoreet dolore magna aliquam erat volutpat. Ut wisi enim ad minim veniam, quis nostrud exerci tation ullamcorper suscipit lobortis nisl ut aliquip ex ea commodo consequat.

Lorem ipsum dolor sit amet, consectetuer euismod tincidunt ut laoreet dolore magna aliquam erat volutpat.

Keeping in touch while out of touch

Dolor sit amet, consectetuer adipiscing elit, sed diam nonummy nibh euismod tincidunt ut laoreet dolore magna aliquam erat volutpat.

Ut wisi enim ad minim veniam, quis nostrud exerci tation ullamcorper suscipit lobortis nisl ut aliquip ex ea commodo consequat. Duis autem vel eum iriure dolor in hendrerit in vulputate velit esse molestie consequat, vel illum dolore eu feugiat nulla facilisis at vero eros et accumsan et iusto odio dignissim qui blandit praesent luptatum zzril delenit augue duis dolore te feugait nulla facilisi.

Wizywig ad petulam et valor und system crash. Lorem ipsum dolor sit amet, consectetuer adipiscing elit, sed diam nonummy nibh euismod tincidunt ut laoreet dolore magna aliquam erat volutpat.

Lorem ipsum dolor sit amet, consectetuer adipiscing elit, sed diam nonummy nibh euismod tincidunt ut laoreet dolore magna

Continued on page 3

Insider Trading

Published infrequently by the RCP et al New Horizon Institute of Freedom and Ethical Responsibility, PO Box 697, Dover, NH 03820. $999/year

*A*fter you have determined the overall "look" of your newsletter, it's time to add text and visuals to your newsletter. Your first task is to determine the number and placement of columns. The size and placement of columns influences the ease with which text can be read as well as the amount of white space on each page.

Chapter 4

Building White Space into Every Page

•••

Gray pages are definite readership killers. Pages filled top to bottom, left to right with text are enough to discourage even the most determined reader. There are three places where you can build white space into your newsletter pages: margins, headers and footers and columns.

Adjusting Margins

Start by manipulating top, bottom, and side margins. Margins influence the distance between the physical edges of a page and adjacent text and visuals. You can add vertical white space to your pages by increasing the left and right-hand margins. You can add horizontal white space on each page by determining the placement of headers and footers on each page and the amount of space between headers and footers and adjacent text. You can open the tops of your pages by including a sufficient amount of white space between the top and bottom edges of the page and header and footer rules. You can add white space to your pages by increasing the distance between text columns and footer rules as well as the distance between footers and the bottom of the page.

Working with Column Grids

You can add white space to your pages by manipulating the number, size, and placement of columns.

A wide, single column of text extending the width of a page, for example, can communicate an informal, "late breaking news" image. This layout is extremely easy to produce when time is limited. It's an ideal choice for word-processed newsletters. If you choose this approach, include a deep left margin and increase the right margin. This adds white space which will contrast with the text on the page. Or add extra leading, or line spacing, to compensate for the long line length. Headlines and subheads can be "hung" to the left of the text margin, adding to their impact.

Another alternative is to use combine a narrow headline column with a wide text column. Headlines and subheads can be placed entirely within the narrow column on each page. Short text features, such as the table of contents, masthead, and pull quotes, can also be placed within the narrow column. You can also use the narrow column for articles of lesser importance than your primary stories placed in the wide columns.

The two-column format is one of the most common. It's easy to produce with just about any word processing or page layout program. The primary difficulty of two-column formats is their symmetry and the difficulties they present when adding photographs. Photographs in two-column newsletters are often placed in the center of the page, creating undesirable text wraps and boring left/right, top/bottom balance. For this reason, two-column formats are best reserved for text-intensive newsletters rather than newsletters containing a variety of large and small photographs.

Three-column formats and four-column formats can work well, especially if care is taken in selecting the right typeface and type size. The key to successfully employing three and four column formats is to avoid filling each column with text. Always do something different with one of the columns on each page or two-page spread. You can place a pull quote, masthead, calendar or—even better—a short text feature in an empty column or use it for a short text feature set in a contrasting typeface.

Avoid using more than four columns of text on a page because the columns will likely become too narrow for easy reading.

Combining Text Columns

Your design abilities will quickly grow in power when you become accustomed to combining columns. Combining columns involves setting up a page with an underlying grid consisting of five or seven columns and creating text frames that extend over two or more columns. (This technique works better with page layout programs than word processing programs.)

Pages based on five- or seven-column grids permit both consistency and flexibility. You can enjoy endless variety by changing the way you arrange the text on the column framework, but there will be an underlying page-to-page consistency that will unify the pages of individual newsletters as well as create issue-to-issue consistency. The most common way to employ a five-column grid is to combine a single narrow column of white space with two double-width columns of text. The seven column grid allows you to combine three double-columns of text with a single column of white space.

One of the major advantages of five- and seven-column formats is the added flexibility they offer for placing photographs. Small, square photographs can be placed entirely within the narrow column, while large, rectangular photographs can "grow" into the narrow, fifth column.

Choosing between Horizontal and Vertical Layouts

If your newsletter contains a variety of article lengths, you'll want to choose between horizontal or vertical article placement.

The tendency is to flow articles vertically. Although vertical placement may appear the most obvious, your readers might appreciate a horizontal placement. A series of short paragraphs arranged side-by-side appear easier to read than long columns of text, which is why newspapers stack articles the way they do.

Reduce paragraph spacing

Before

After

The Before example (left) is weakened by redundant paragraph spacing; both first-line indents and extra spacing between lines is used. Two hard returns are used between paragraphs, which creates distracting horizontal bands of white space. Worse, the first line indents are based on the page layout program's default half-inch indents, which is far too generous for the narrow columns used. In the After example (right), first-line indents have been omitted and paragraph spacing equal to one-and-one-half lines of type are used to indicate new paragraphs. The result is a more unified page, enough to allow a few extra of body copy to appear on the front page as well as more white space around the headlines.

Chapter 5
Making Informed Typeface and Type Size Decisions

· ·

The next important decisions you make concern the type you'll use for display text (headlines and subheads) and body copy text. Your two primary alternatives include making headlines as distinctly different from body copy as possible or you can choose different weights of the same typeface. Either alternative can work. The proper choice depends on the image you're trying to project as well as whether you possess the typeface resources necessary to choose contrasting weights.

The Joy of Opposites

One tried-and-proven technique is to contrast sans serif headlines and subheads with serif body copy. This is the "safe" approach that builds on the relative merits of each typeface category. It also works because headlines will appear so distinctly different from body copy. Sans serif type is noted for its *legibility*; readers will find it easy to locate and make out the individual letters of the headlines. Serif type is known for *readability*: the serifs form letter-to-letter transitions that help readers quickly decipher your message.

One of the best ways you can make the opposites approach work is to use the Condensed Heavy or Condensed Black versions of the sans serif typeface. Bold is usually not heavy enough to form a distinct contrast with body copy. Black or Heavy typefaces, (sans serif typefaces that have been redrawn with thicker strokes) attract more attention but take up more space. Condensed typeface designs offer the best alternative. Frutiger Condensed Black, for example, is distinctly heavier than Frutiger Bold and occupies far less space than Frutiger Black. By using a Condensed Heavy design, you can use a smaller type size than if you chose a Bold typeface without sacrificing the impact of the headlines.

You are unlikely to go wrong when combining serif and sans serif type as long as you limit yourself to a single sans serif typeface for headlines and a single serif typeface for body copy. Most serif typefaces will work with most sans serif typefaces, especially if you choose simple, straightforward typefaces, such as the various weights of Frutiger, Helvetica, and Univers. The only time you're likely to run into problems is if you mix two sans serif typefaces or two serif typefaces.

"All in the Family" Returns to Prime Time!

Great beauty often results when all text elements are based on a single typeface design. Pages become unified as if by magic. You can project either dignity and restraint or a stark, contemporary appearance, depending on whether a serif or sans serif typeface design is used.

Serif typefaces that are appropriate for newsletters based on a single typeface include Adobe Garamond, Minion, and Palatino. One of the reasons these typefaces are appropriate is that these designs include a variety of weights and alternative characters. you can purchase Semi Bold and Extra Bold alternatives to the Bold version. Extra Bold lets you "voice" your headlines with extra weight, and Semi Bold lets you add emphasis within text columns without "shouting" at your readers.

Single-typeface newsletters are not limited to serif typefaces. Several sans serif typefaces are equally at home when used at small text sizes as they are at large display sizes. Three sans serif typefaces available in a wide variety of Light and Heavy weights and Condensed widths include Frutiger, Gill Sans, and Optima.

Working as Efficiently as Possible

Save your work as a template after you have chosen an appropriate page layout, added a nameplate, and chosen appropriate typography for headlines, subheads, and body copy. Be sure to create styles for each element of page architecture. You'll probably create styles for the following text elements:

- ✔ Level One Headlines
- ✔ Level Two Headlines
- ✔ Level One Subheads
- ✔ Level Two Headlines

- ✔ Kicker (short phrase preceding a headline)
- ✔ Blurb (short phrase following a headline)
- ✔ Author by-line
- ✔ First Paragraph following headline or subhead (i.e. no first-line indent)
- ✔ Following Paragraphs
- ✔ Lists within articles
- ✔ Captions
- ✔ Photographers credit
- ✔ Table of Contents
- ✔ Folio information—issue number and date
- ✔ Masthead
- ✔ Sidebar
- ✔ Calendar listings

Adjust body copy type size and line spacing

Before

After

Desktop publishing design success is often a matter of subtle refinements. For example, the text in the Before example (left) set at 12-points, appears a bit too large. Line spacing is also a bit too generous. The result is a very "open" page. A half-point reduction in type size results in a more pleasing type size, one that doesn't appear so crowded. In addition, line spacing was increased to 14 points (from the default 13.8 points). This subtle change is enough to create a more open page as well as a little more white space, which can be used to surround the headlines, as the headline in the center column shows.

Chapter 6

Adding Reader Cues and Visuals

• •

*T*he final elements of page architecture needed to complete your newsletter design pages include momentum builders, such as subheads, pull quotes, and initial caps.

Subheads

Subheads are among the most important elements you'll add. Subheads should be significantly smaller than headlines but appear distinctly different from adjacent body copy. They can be set in a contrasting typeface (to match headlines) or in bold or italic. Subheads can be emphasized by horizontal rules extending over them, either the width of the column or the width of the subhead (either can be easily added by your software program).

Try to avoid articles rambling on without subheads. The easiest to read newsletters tend to be those with subheads breaking up articles every three or four paragraphs. Avoid six paragraphs in a row without a subhead.

Initial Caps

Insert initial caps if you want to break up a long text passage where a subhead would be inappropriate because a new topic has not been introduced. Raised caps are valuable as text-splitters because they add horizontal white space into the text column. Dropped caps are appropriate article introductions, because they do not create white space between the headline and the beginning of the article.

Pull Quotes

You can use pull quotes to extract short phrases that summarize adjacent text. In order to attract the reader's attention, pull quotes should be as short and noticeable as possible. Avoid distracting borders and backgrounds as these often interfere with legibility.

Eliminate unnecessary text wraps

Before

After

Although it might be fun to demonstrate your mastery of text wraps by placing an illustration between two columns, as at left, both columns suffer. Reduced column width usually translates into excessive hyphenation and, if you're working with justified text, awkward word spacing. If you're using flush-left/ragged-right text, as shown in the Before example (left), the reader is apt to be distracted by the contrast between the ragged line endings of the first column and the straight left margin of the right column. Eliminating the text wrap, as shown in the right-hand example, not only eliminates problems in the adjacent text columns but creates enough space to add four extra lines of text on the page.

Omitting the text wrap also speeds production by eliminating the need to re-position the illustration in order to avoid problems with the subhead appearing next to subheads.

Part III

Producing and Printing Your Newsletter

IT INSIDER TRADING

VOL. 16, # 986
MARCH 14, 1995

THE JOURNAL OF ETHICAL INVESTING

Are ethics as important as everyone says?

Freedom without recourse offers great investment opportunities!

Dolor sit amet, consectetuer adipiscing elit, sed diam nonummy nibh euismod tincidunt ut laoreet dolore magna aliquam erat volutpat.

Ut wisi enim ad minim veniam, quis nostrud exerci tation ullamcorper suscipit lobortis nisl ut aliquip ex ea commodo consequat. Duis autem vel eum iriure dolor in hendrerit in vulputate velit esse molestie consequat, vel illum dolore eu feugiat nulla facilisis at vero eros et accumsan et iusto odio dignissim qui blandit praesent luptatum zzril delenit augue duis dolore te feugait nulla facilisi.

Lorem ipsum dolor sit amet, consectetuer adipiscing elit, sed diam nonummy nibh euismod tincidunt ut laoreet dolore magna aliquam erat volutpat.

Lorem ipsum dolor sit amet, consectetuer adipiscing elit, sed diam nonummy nibh euismod tincidunt ut laoreet dolore magna aliquam erat volutpat. Duis autem vel eum iriure dolor in hendrerit in vulputate velit esse molestie consequat, vel illum dolore eu feugiat nulla facilisis at vero eros et accumsan et iusto odio dignissim qui blandit praesent luptatum zzril delenit augue duis dolore te feugait nulla facilisi.

Lorem ipsum dolor sit amet, consectetuer adipiscing elit, sed diam nonummy nibh euismod tincidunt ut laoreet dolore magna aliquam erat volutpat. Ut wisi enim ad minim veniam, quis nostrud exerci tation ullamcorper suscipit lobortis nisl ut aliquip ex ea commodo consequat.

Lorem ipsum dolor sit amet, consectetuer euismod tincidunt ut laoreet dolore magna aliquam erat volutpat.

Keeping in touch while out of touch

Dolor sit amet, consectetuer adipiscing elit, sed diam nonummy nibh euismod tincidunt ut laoreet dolore magna aliquam erat volutpat.

Ut wisi enim ad minim veniam, quis nostrud exerci tation ullamcorper suscipit lobortis nisl ut aliquip ex ea commodo consequat. Duis autem vel eum iriure dolor in hendrerit in vulputate velit esse molestie consequat, vel illum dolore eu feugiat nulla facilisis at vero eros et accumsan et iusto odio dignissim qui blandit praesent luptatum zzril delenit augue duis dolore te feugait nulla facilisi.

Wizywig ad petulam et valor und system crash. Lorem ipsum dolor sit amet, consectetuer adipiscing elit, sed diam nonummy nibh euismod tincidunt ut laoreet dolore magna aliquam erat volutpat.

Lorem ipsum dolor sit amet, consectetuer adipiscing elit, sed diam nonummy nibh euismod tincidunt ut laoreet dolore magna

Continued on page 3

IT Insider Trading

Published infrequently by the RCP et al New Horizon Institute of Freedom and Ethical Responsibility, PO Box 697, Dover, NH 03820. $999/year

The end is in sight! Now is the time for the fruits of your labors to come together into a good-looking newsletter, one that does full justice to you, your firm, or the association you work for.

Producing your newsletter involves three distinct steps: planning, production, and fine-tuning. Although these are treated separately in the section that follows, most will take place simultaneously.

Evaluation should be an on-going part of your newsletter program. You should constantly strive to improve your newsletter by seeking the feedback of your readers and co-workers. Although consistency is a virtue, the best newsletters go through a continual process of "quiet refinement," making each issue better than its predecessor.

Chapter 7

Planning Precedes Production

∙∙

*P*lanning involves determining the content of each newsletter. This involves determining which features to include in your newsletter and how much space to devote to each feature. Planning reduces frustration and helps you work more efficiently, creating the time necessary to fine-tune the details of newsletter typography. You can plan your newsletter in two ways:

- One of the easiest ways is to choose a theme for each issue. After you determine a theme, relate it to each of the of the departments included inside the your newsletter (choose articles for the various departments which support or contribute to the theme).

- Another approach is to make a list of all possible article topics and — one at a time — eliminate articles until the only ones that remain are your first-choice selections.

The more time you spend planning your newsletter, the less time you'll have to spend later on shoehorning text and visuals into place and the fewer hard feelings you'll create when you discover you don't have room to include everything that you or your co-workers have written.

Thumbnails

After you have determined the content of each issue, you have to determine how much space to devote to each feature. The best way to do this is to determine article length *before* the articles have been written. Create a reduced-size mock-up of your newsletter, called a *thumbnail*, as follows:

- If you are creating a four-page newsletter, fold an $8^1/_2$ by 11-inch sheet of paper into half and trim off the bottom of the page so that the four pages are proportional to the dimensions of an $8^1/_2$ by 11-inch page.

- If you are creating an eight-page newsletter, fold the paper once more and trim the top edge. This creates eight correctly proportioned pages. Staple the pages together along their left edge.

Create several "blank" newsletters and have a sharp pencil and soft eraser handy. Start by drawing in the borders and page numbers on each page, and lightly indicate the location of columns and vertical downrules between columns. Then draw the nameplate and table of contents on the front page, the masthead on page 2 and the mailing label area on the back page. If certain departments always appear on the same place in each issue, draw them in at this point.

Indicate the approximate location and length of the articles and photographs you want to include in the issue. Don't worry about being too accurate at this point: work quickly and avoid self-censoring. Use parallel squiggly lines to indicate text, boxes with x's through them to indicate photographs and just write in headlines as clearly as you can at approximately the size they'll appear.

Don't be afraid if your initial attempts don't allow you to fit in everything you want to include in each issue — that's the whole point of a thumbnail. The goal is to make as many decisions as possible at the pencil and paper stage rather than after articles have been written, photographs taken and headlines and body copy text placed.

Copyfitting

One of the most important ways you can become a more efficient newsletter editor is to write to length and have contributors write to length. Rather than *reactively* laying out your newsletter on the basis of what's already been written, take a proactive role and assign articles and photographs on the basis of available space. Instead of saying "I want a long article on last week's Planning Board meeting," say: "I need a 600 word article on last week's Planning Board meeting."

Copyfittting is a skill you will quickly acquire on the basis of experience. Copyfitting can be as simple or as sophisticated as appropriate. The easiest approach is to count the number of words per column inch set in the typeface, type size, and line spacing used in your newsletter. Then determine how many words will fit in a column of type that extending half the length of the page. (This takes paragraph spacing into account.)

After you have these figures, you have a rough way of relating your thumbnail layouts to word-processed copy. This saves a lot of time producing your newsletter because you won't have to spend so much time editing or padding previously written copy.

Eliminate unnecessary graphic accents

Before

After

The Before example (left) is cluttered with rules (lines) and boxes. As shown in the After example (right), eliminating most of the rules and boxes opens the page and provides unity and selective emphasis.

The boxed border around the illustration in the left column was replaced with a pair of horizontal rules, allowing the illustration to be larger.

The boxed border around the page was also replaced with horizontal rules. The nameplate, which is becomes surrounded by white space, gains impact. Notice that the thickness of the horizontal rule at the top of the page is similar to the thickness of the type in the nameplate. This unifies the rule with the nameplate while separating the nameplate from the remainder of the page.

To further simplify the page, the boxed border around the table of contents and the unnecessary vertical downrules were also eliminated.

Chapter 8

Producing Your Newsletter

• •

*T*he production phase involves assigning articles and photographs on the basis of available space. Avoid verbal communications whenever possible. Prepare an Assignment Sheet for each article — even if it's one you're writing that clearly spells out desired article length, submission deadline and individuals to contact or resources to check.

Assign your articles as early as possible so that writers can write them as far ahead of deadlines as possible. This makes it possible to circulate approval copies of articles in word-processed, rather than formatted, form.

The more time you save at the manuscript stage, the more time you'll have for fine-tuning your newsletter.

Author Guidelines

If others routinely contribute to your newsletter, prepare a written set of Author Guidelines. These should specify the way manuscripts are to be provided to you. Here are some of the things to include in your Author Guidelines:

- Try to get everyone to submit their manuscript using the same word processor. If you can't get them to commit to the same word processor, have them save it in a common format — most word processors can save in a variety of their competitor's formats, as well as unformatted text.

- Describe how you want authors to indicate headlines and subheads.

- Try to get everyone to format their manuscripts using the same typeface and line spacing, with page numbers in the same location on each page. This makes it easier to edit and evaluate hard copy.

Your Author Guidelines should also remind your writers of the following:

- ✔ Do not add two spaces after periods.
- ✔ Avoid hitting the Return key twice at the end of each paragraph.
- ✔ Never use spaces to indent the first lines of paragraphs.
- ✔ Do not indent the first lines of paragraphs. (Your page layout software should handle formatting options like these.)

You probably will also want to indicate how you want your writers to indicate em dashes and en dashes, discretionary hyphens, and non-breaking spaces. (Chances are, you'll be adding these yourself.)

Tagging Copy

If you are in a high-efficiency environment, one of best ways to increase production efficiency is to investigate how your software program allows you to tag copy.

Tagging involves inserting non-printing codes into the manuscript which automatically apply the appropriate style when the manuscript is placed in your page layout program. Although many styles (or formatting characteristics) successfully carry over from word processor to page layout program, it will be harder to distribute up-to-date copies of your styles than to ask authors to add tagging symbols, such as [SUB2] before paragraphs intended to be formatted as subheads or [PAR1] before the first paragraphs following headlines or subheads.

You'll be surprised how much time tagging will save you, once you have saved styles for each element of page architecture and instructed all of your authors on applying the tags to their word-processed copy.

Avoiding Article Jumps

Avoid article jumps. Article jumps occur when more than one article begins on the front page and are continued on the inside pages of your newsletter. For example, an article might begin on page 1 and continue on page 3. Jumps are bad for the following reasons:

▶ You're apt to lose readers each time you include a jump.

▶ Readers who "jump" to inside pages are less apt to return to the first page to continue reading other articles on it.

▶ Readers are less likely to return to the pages separating the article to see what's on them.

Always strive to make it your reader's job as easy as possible. Design your newsletters so that readers can read your articles in a continuous, uninterrupted sequence from beginning to end.

Organize the table of contents

Before

After

The table of contents in the Before example (left) lacks color and organization plus cries out for simplicity. The only visual contrast is the bold serif typeface indicating the page number.

In the After example (right), table of contents projects a more interesting, organized image. Page numbers come first, right-aligned against a right tab. Article titles are set flush-left. The word "page" has been eliminated because it can be assumed that the table of contents does not refer to minutes, hours, days, or years. Page numbers are set in Helvetica Black to form a strong contrast with the adjacent serif typeface. To emphasize the contrast, the page numbers are set one-half a point larger than the article titles. This is enough to give them extra emphasis without destroying the unity of the page.

Chapter 9
Fine-Tuning Your Newsletter

• •

*T*here is a thin line between editing and design. Often, words have to be edited or transposed at the page layout stage in order to create attractive, easy-to-read pages. All of this takes time, which is why you should strive to plan ahead and work as efficiently as possible, so you'll have time for these last-minute revisions and refinements.

Rewriting Headlines

Often, one of the most noticeable ways you can improve a newsletter is to rewrite headlines so that they are as short as possible, lines are of equal length, and line-breaks occur at natural pauses (where you would pause when speaking).

No matter how well-written your headlines, it's impossible to know how they will look until they are formatted using your publication's headline style (set in the desired headline typeface, type size, style, weight, width, and case). With flush-left headlines, one line will often appear noticeably longer than the others. With centered headlines, the longer line may appear on the bottom of the stack, or the lines of a multi-line headline might create a strange shape.

Rewriting is the best way to cure these problems. Few headlines can stand up to rigorous editing. Empty words can almost always be identified, and long words can usually be replaced with short words.

Widows, Orphans, and Line Breaks

Widows (portions of words or phrases less than one-third of the column width appearing by themselves at the bottom of a column or page), orphans (isolated syllables of less than one-third of a line isolated at the top of a column or page) project a less-than-professional approach to page layout and typesetting. Likewise, occasionally several short-lines in a row appear in flush-left/ragged-right text following several long-lines. Or the line endings may create strange shapes.

Trial-and-error editing is one of the best ways to cure these problems. Try the following techniques:

- Transposing a word earlier in the paragraph often causes the line endings to reflow, eliminating distracting problems.

- Adding a discretionary hyphen earlier in the paragraph forces a word break which eliminates awkward line endings.

- Inserting a non-breaking hyphen can keep a hyphenated word from being split across two lines.

- With care, you can adjust the tracking of a single line early in the paragraph. This is often enough to smooth out line endings later in the paragraph. Use this technique with care, however, because a single line with tight tracking can often appear smaller than adjacent lines.

- You can "hang" punctuation earlier in the paragraph, (push a comma, semicolon, colon, or period to the right). Because spaces before a word are automatically omitted at the start of a line, this might create enough space to eliminate a word break later in the paragraph.

In most cases, simply transposing a few words early in the paragraph will troublesome problems later in the paragraph.

When There's Too Much Copy . . .

In an ideal world, this would never happen…but it does. Sometimes there's simply too much copy to be accommodated and further editing is neither feasible nor permitted. The key to solving problems of too much copy is to make your adjustments global — have them occur throughout your publication so that you do not inadvertently draw attention to just one story by making it appear "different." Options include the following:

- Reducing the type size of all of the stories in the issue by one-quarter point

- Uniformly reducing the space above and below headlines and subheads, modifying your headline and subhead style's Space Before and Space After specifications

- Reducing headline type size one-half point

- Slightly reducing space above headers and below footers, or the space between headers/footers and adjacent text

- Eliminating one or more photographs, reducing the size of large photographs, and/or reducing space around photographs

- ✔ Replacing captions under photographs with captions placed in the margin next to photographs
- ✔ Eliminating pull quotes
- ✔ Reducing the size of the mailing coupon
- ✔ Slightly reduce paragraph spacing

All of the preceding, of course, are less-than-desirable alternatives. When you use any of the preceding techniques, you take a chance on destroying the careful design of your newsletter. All these changes are noticeable. The best way to eliminate the problems is to use thumbnails to plan your newsletter and assign maximum length for articles.

When There's Not Enough Copy...

The exact opposite techniques can be used when there is not enough copy to fill available space. In addition doing the opposite of the preceding techniques, (adding slight amounts of space above and space after headlines and subheads, and so on) you can try the following:

- ✔ Use uneven, or scalloped, column endings instead of completely filling each column with text
- ✔ Add short features like a "Where are they now?" or "10 Years Ago"
- ✔ Add white space above or below the table of contents, use longer titles in the table of contents, or add more space between the lists in the table of contents
- ✔ Add small head-shot photographs of the authors of your lead editorials or key articles

Again, the key is to disguise the extra space by adding it uniformly throughout your newsletter.

Soliciting Reader Feedback

Even the best newsletters can be improved. When possible, seek the advice of your readers.

One inexpensive way to do this is to insert a one-page survey along with a self-addressed/stamped envelope in random newsletters you send out. Ask readers question such as the following:

✔ What do they like most about your newsletter and what they would like to see improved?

✔ Which parts of the newsletter do they read first?

✔ Which features do they consider hard to read?

✔ Do they have any suggestions regarding your newsletter's nameplate, headlines or body copy?

✔ Can they recommend any other newsletters they enjoy reading?

Even if you only sent out 50 surveys a month and only get back 10 responses, you'll notice that certain trends will quickly emerge. These will help you pinpoint areas requiring fine-tuning and improvement.

After you establish an image for your newsletter, changes should be incremental and barely noticeable. If you have done your work right during the initial planning and formatting stages, a complete redesign is rarely necessary.

Index

(continued)

• F •

(continued)

• G •

(continued)

(continued)

• *Q* •

• *R* •

(continued)

• *U* •

• *V* •

Notes

Notes

Notes

Notes

Notes

Notes

Notes

Notes

Notes

Notes

Discover Dummies Online!

The Dummies Web Site is your fun and friendly online resource for the latest information about ...For Dummies® books and your favorite topics. The Web site is the place to communicate with us, exchange ideas with other ...For Dummies readers, chat with authors, and have fun!

Ten Fun and Useful Things You Can Do at www.dummies.com.

1. Win free ...For Dummies books and more!
2. Register your book and be entered in a prize drawing.
3. Meet your favorite authors through the IDG Books Author Chat Series.
4. Exchange helpful information with other ...For Dummies readers.
5. Discover other great ...For Dummies books you must have!
6. Purchase Dummieswear™ exclusively from our Web site.
7. Buy ...For Dummies books online.
8. Talk to us. Make comments, ask questions, get answers!
9. Download free software.
10. Find additional useful resources from authors.

Link directly to these ten fun and useful things at
http://www.dummies.com/10useful

For other technology titles from IDG Books Worldwide, go to
www.idgbooks.com

Not on the Web yet? It's easy to get started with Dummies 101®: The Internet For Windows®95 or The Internet For Dummies®, 5th Edition, at local retailers everywhere.

Find other ...For Dummies books on these topics:
Business • Career • Databases • Food & Beverage • Games • Gardening • Graphics • Hardware
Health & Fitness • Internet and the World Wide Web • Networking • Office Suites
Operating Systems • Personal Finance • Pets • Programming • Recreation • Sports
Spreadsheets • Teacher Resources • Test Prep • Word Processing

IDG BOOKS WORLDWIDE
BOOK REGISTRATION

Register This Book and Win!

We want to hear from you!

Visit **http://my2cents.dummies.com** to register this book and tell us how you liked it!

- Get entered in our monthly prize giveaway.
- Give us feedback about this book — tell us what you like best, what you like least, or maybe what you'd like to ask the author and us to change!
- Let us know any other ...*For Dummies*® topics that interest you.

Your feedback helps us determine what books to publish, tells us what coverage to add as we revise our books, and lets us know whether we're meeting your needs as a ...*For Dummies* reader. You're our most valuable resource, and what you have to say is important to us!

Not on the Web yet? It's easy to get started with *Dummies 101*®: *The Internet For Windows*® *95* or *The Internet For Dummies*,® 5th Edition, at local retailers everywhere.

Or let us know what you think by sending us a letter at the following address:

...*For Dummies* Book Registration
Dummies Press
7260 Shadeland Station, Suite 100
Indianapolis, IN 46256-3945
Fax 317-596-5498

BUSINESS AND GENERAL REFERENCE BOOK SERIES FROM IDG

COMPUTER BOOK SERIES FROM IDG